THE HOUSE ADVANTAGE

THE
HOUSE
ADVANTAGE

PLAYING THE ODDS TO WIN
BIG IN BUSINESS

JEFFREY MA

FOREWORD BY BEN MEZRICH

palgrave
macmillan

Basketball charts that appear in Chapter 5, "Expected Points vs. Time Remaining" and "Difference in Expected Points vs. Time Remaining" are reproduced courtesy of Gabriel Desjardins, behindthenet.ca.

"Basic Strategy Chart," which appears in the Appendix, is reproduced courtesy of Mike Aponte—www.MikeAponte.com.

First published in 2010 by
PALGRAVE MACMILLAN®
in the United States—a division of St. Martin's Press LLC,
175 Fifth Avenue, New York, NY 10010.

Where this book is distributed in the UK, Europe and the rest of the world, this is by Palgrave Macmillan, a division of Macmillan Publishers Limited, registered in England, company number 785998, of Houndmills, Basingstoke, Hampshire RG21 6XS.

Palgrave Macmillan is the global academic imprint of the above companies and has companies and representatives throughout the world.

Palgrave® and Macmillan® are registered trademarks in the United States, the United Kingdom, Europe and other countries.

ISBN 978–0–230–62272–2

Library of Congress Cataloging-in-Publication Data

Ma, Jeffrey.
    The house advantage : playing the odds to win big in business / by
Jeffrey Ma ; foreword by Ben Mezrich.
        p. cm.
    Includes bibliographical references and index.
    ISBN 978–0–230–62272–2
      1. Commercial statistics. 2. Gambling—Statistical methods.
    3. Success in business. I. Title.

HF1017.M275 2010
658.4′033—dc22   2010013625

A catalogue record of the book is available from the British Library.

Design by Newgen Imaging Systems (P) Ltd., Chennai, India.

First edition: July 2010

10 9 8 7 6 5 4 3 2 1

Printed in the United States of America.

For my parents

CONTENTS

ACKNOWLEDGMENTS

THAT I COULD write a book seemed absurd to me. In fact, if you had told me a year and a half ago that I would be on the last legs of a real business book, I would have told you, "Well, anyone can write a book then." The reality is that it was only with the help of those listed below that this book could happen. A huge thanks goes out to all of you.

I give credit to my Dad for first suggesting it. He has always believed that I could do anything and empowered me to do so, and in this case his seemingly absurd suggestion planted a seed in my head.

I give credit and thanks next to Peter Jacobs from CAA who was the first person in the business to suggest that it was a next natural progression for me. I've been on the speaking circuit for the last five years, and much of the material and ideas that appear in this book came out of that work. Peter was the first to suggest that those 60-minute part-standup, part-motivational, part–business lesson speeches could be turned into a real book.

As I got into the process of developing the proposal and selling the book, two literary agents gave me important insight. Michael Harriot, who was the first agent to take the time to go through my proposal, gave me valuable feedback that I didn't want to hear. But boy, was he right.

Michael Broussard, who eventually became my agent, opened doors all over the publishing world for me and helped me dream big. Maybe one day he'll introduce me to Chelsea Handler.

During the research process there were many in the sports world that gave me their valuable time and stories. Daryl Morey spent time with me in San Francisco over lunch at the Ritz-Carlton. Paraag Marathe, a close friend, ignored his normal reluctance for any press and allowed me to use stories that I've accumulated over many years of conversations with him.

Dr. Bob opened his home and his storied career to give me insight into what makes a professional handicapper tick.

The original PROTRADE consultant team has branched out into bigger and better things, but their spirit, if not their help, was a big part of this book. Roland Beech, whose unique perspective never disappoints, provided insight from the NBA road. Ben Alamar developed much of the work that allowed our relationship with the Trail Blazers. Aaron Schatz, a true pioneer in football analytics, served as a tremendous inspiration. Mark Kamal has always been a trusted resource and was the man behind many of PROTRADE's good ideas. And Gabe Desjardins, always a solid partner, when I need something screen scraped or when I need to understand what a three-line pass is.

Thanks go out to John Huizinga and Sandy Weil for tolerating my assault on their hot-hand theory, and thanks to John Hollinger for proclaiming himself a "hot-hand" atheist. Thanks to KP and the rest of the Blazer staff for allowing a guy with a slow release and a negative vertical to be a part of their basketball world.

Thanks to Tim McGhee, Doc Eliot, Tom Woo, Dr. Mike Orkin, and Dennis Yu for sharing their industry-specific expertise.

Thanks to David Jeske for giving me insight and encouragement. Having someone as smart as you read and enjoy the book was certainly encouraging.

To all of my friends at SAS and their partners, Mario Iannicello, Nick Curcuru, Craig Duncan, Stu Bradley, Todd McClain, and Ken

Bland, your support, resources, and success in analytics is the reason that a book like this can even get published.

To my personal editors, Catilin Blythe and Brian Timpone, the time you gave this project amazed me, and your help to turn an engineer's words into readable prose was immeasurable.

To Dr. Michael Blum and my close friend Omar Amr, MD, my medical consultants, your expertise helped turn my theories about EBM into a real point of view.

To my baseball buddies, Craig Breslow and DP, your differences are immeasurable but your similarities were the fodder for a fascinating unique story in data-driven decision making.

To my blackjack buddies, Andy Bloch and Mike Aponte. Andy was the only one who could really help me with my analysis of poker versus blackjack, and Mike is the most trusted source on all things probability in blackjack.

And while I'm on the subject of blackjack, I must thank the man that started all of this, Ed Thorp. My phone interview with him was one of the most meaningful parts of this process. Not only was he quick to respond, but his insights were unique and valuable. Thanks for starting this for all of us.

To my resident economist, Phil Maymin, I have to thank you for your responsiveness, your candor, and most of all your encouragement. Having someone like you tell me that my book was interesting alleviated many fears.

To my resident decision theorist, Russell Andersson. The time you spent looking over chapters, providing feedback and ideas, was truly a Godsend. The book would not be the same without you.

To Nate Silver, who, despite being in the process of writing his own book, spent time with me and shared tales about how he has become the most famous prognosticator in the world.

To Ted Bretter, thanks for helping me relive the O'Connor days.

To Ed Vilandrie, who I met playing water polo over 20 years ago, your success amazes and inspires. Thanks for the contribution of your most valuable resource—time.

There are three books that provided inspiration for much of this work: Peter Bernstein's *Against the Gods*, Roger Lowenstein's *When Genius Failed*, and William Poundstone's *Fortune's Formula*. I hope this book can live up to the tremendous standard that you three have already set for writing in this area.

I always say that two books fundamentally changed my life: *Bringing Down the House*, for obvious reasons, and *Moneyball*, for creating a new way of thinking. Michael Lewis has become a friend and somewhat of a mentor in my journey as a writer, and I thank him for the lunches at Saul's over the years.

Very special thanks to Ben Mezrich, who gave me a platform and presented my story in such a way that the masses wanted to read it. There aren't many writers who could have done that.

To Brian Mead and his crew, who lived with me literally through most of this process, without your distractions I would have gone crazy and thrown my laptop out the window.

To my business partner, Mike Kerns and his original partner, Jeff Moorad, thanks for getting me into sports and giving me the opportunity to make a name for myself outside of the casinos.

To Kevin Compton, a true inspiration professionally and personally, I always say if you bought a McDonald's and asked me to go work there I would. Thanks for your words of encouragement along the way.

Thanks to two good friends, Steve McClelland, for his infectious laugh and comedic moments at the blackjack table, and Niel Robertson, a tremendous resource, personally and professionally. You are two people I know I can always count on.

To my editor, Airié Stuart, who took time out of her other job as a publisher to edit my book. That you believed in me enough to buy the book and take it on as your project made me believe that this could really happen.

To the Helfrich and Belden families, you have always made me feel welcome and have somehow always made me feel interesting. Thank you.

To my family, Dad, Mom, Yvette, Vivian, you're responsible for who I am, and any success that I have achieved comes from the strong foundation that you gave me.

And finally to Katherine, to say you have the patience of a saint would be both cliché and an understatement. The love and support you have showed me throughout this process was both empowering and amazing. You are truly the most special person I have ever met.

FOREWORD

I THINK IT was the hundred-dollar bills that really caught my attention.

Ten minutes past one. A dive bar squatting in MIT's long shadows extending across the icy Charles. A place called Crossroads that reeked of cheap beer and over-spiced chicken wings. A dump, really, one that I'd visited maybe three or four times in my ten years of living in Boston; but this particular night, I hadn't wandered into Crossroads by accident. I was there to meet an MIT kid named Jeff Ma.

I was there to hear a story.

I'd been introduced to Jeff once before, at a mutual friend's party. But I'd only spoken to him briefly; I knew he and his friends had done something interesting, but I certainly didn't know the extent of it. Though I'd already written six pop thrillers to moderate success, I was still searching for that one story that was going to change my life. To be honest, when I first walked into Crossroads that icy November night, I didn't think this MIT kid could really be the key to the story I was looking for.

And then I saw the hundred-dollar bills. Jeff had just leaned up against the bar, nearly laying waste to a metropolis of Knickerbocker longnecks and half-finished pitchers of Miller Lite, when he opened his wallet to pay for the next round. I couldn't help but notice the huge wad of Benjamins inside.

The thing is, in Boston you never see hundred-dollar bills. In New York or L.A., hundred-dollar bills are no big deal. You see bankers throwing them around strip clubs and restaurants, Hollywood players using them as cocktail napkins. And in Vegas, well, they come right out of the ATMs. But in Boston, you never see hundred-dollar bills. And this kid, this MIT math whiz who lived right down the street from me, had a wallet teeming with them.

I was immediately curious. As a writer, I had trained myself to seek out inconsistencies, and an MIT kid buying drinks at Crossroads with a wad of hundred-dollar bills was hard to ignore. I decided to dig a little deeper. A few days later, Jeff invited me to his house in Boston's tony South End, where the inconsistencies only grew in scope. Stacked above his laundry were more hundred-dollar bills, in dozens of banded wads, ten thousand dollars each.

The next thing I knew, I was on my way to Las Vegas. Jeff was on the plane with me, along with five of his friends from MIT. When we hit Vegas, a limo was waiting for us—but the driver kept calling Jeff "Mr. Lewis." We were brought to a lavish suite at a mega-casino on the strip, the kind of room that has a glass shower in the living room and floor-to-ceiling windows instead of walls. Once inside, Jeff and his friends began to pull money out from under their clothes—maybe a million dollars, in more banded stacks of hundreds.

The rest, as they say, is history. Jeff and his friends were the current incarnation of the MIT blackjack team, and they had been hitting Vegas for years, earning about six million dollars with an ingenious mathematical system. Blackjack was beatable, and—as I wrote in my book about Jeff's escapades—they beat the hell out of it. More than that, they turned blackjack into a highly profitable business.

Before meeting Jeff and his friends, I wasn't a very good blackjack player. I was one of those gamblers who would drop ten grand at a table playing hunches, using my emotions to guide my decisions. Even worse, before meeting Jeff Ma, I wasn't good with money in general. To say that I was naive about business would be a gross understatement; by the age of 29, I had blown through almost two million dollars in book, TV, and movie contracts and had nothing to show for it but massive debt and an IRS agent who knew me by name.

There's a great line in Hemingway's *The Sun Also Rises*, an answer that a character named Mike Campbell gives when asked how, exactly, he went bankrupt. Four little words that resonate so perfectly: "Gradually, and then suddenly."

Although I've never officially been bankrupt, I certainly know the feeling. Meeting Jeff, and the journey that came of that meeting for both of us, changed all that. Not simply because this was the story that I'd been searching for most of my adult life, but also because the ride that I would take to write Jeff's tale taught me things about business and money that I could never learn anywhere else.

It is no coincidence that after *Bringing Down the House* I went on to write more books about young geniuses chasing fortunes in a variety of different worlds—from the wild, exotic locales of Tokyo and Dubai, to the vicious cubicles of Silicon Valley. The thrill of what Jeff and his friends had done in Vegas pushed me to find more people who had broken the rules and built businesses out of adrenaline, who lived in the gray areas of risk and reward and took chances that most of us could never imagine. Jeff taught me unique ways to look at money and business and the sort of success that could only come from those gray areas and those broken rules.

Jeff's secrets, carved from the system that he and his friends had perfected and used to such success against the casinos of Vegas, had inspired me, as I'm sure they will now inspire you.

Ben Mezrich
Boston, MA

THE HOUSE ADVANTAGE

1

THE RELIGION OF STATISTICS

WE ALL HAVE a defining moment in our lives—a moment that is a leap from hesitation to action, a single decision that sets us on a completely new course. My moment came at a blackjack table in Caesars Palace casino in Las Vegas.

I was 22 years old and a professional card counter. I had recently graduated from the Massachusetts Institute of Technology (MIT) with a bachelor of science in mechanical engineering, but I was using almost none of that formal education in my daily life. Instead, I was using math and statistics to beat the game of blackjack. I had perfected some straightforward formulas and simple equations that told me how much money to bet on each hand, and if I followed these equations correctly, I won.

The night of my defining moment, I walked up to the table and was passed information by my MIT teammate via a secret code. My teammate had been keeping track of the cards that had been played at the table and by saying the code word aloud was transferring that knowledge to me.

Using this information and the equations, I knew I should bet two hands of $10,000 each. I sat down and put ten yellow $1,000 chips in each betting circle, looking up at the dealer to signify that I was ready.

The dealer seemed none too concerned with my large bets. She dealt me an 11 on one hand and a pair of 9s on the other, and then dealt herself a 6 up. Blackjack is a game of pure math, and to that end the decision of whether to hit (take one more card), stand (take no more cards), double (double my bet and receive only one more card), or surrender (give up on the hand, losing half of my bet) left no room for improvisation. My decision was based on something elementary to all card counters called "basic strategy."

Basic strategy is a set of rules for optimal play in blackjack. Displayed in matrix format, it tells the player, based on his cards and the dealer's up card, exactly what action should be taken. It changes slightly based on the rules at the table, but as long as you are familiar with these rules and have them memorized, basic strategy reduces the casino edge to less than 1 percent. It was developed in 1957 by four army technicians who used approximations of mathematical algorithms and then ran calculations on a desktop calculator to determine probabilities of all possible combinations of hands.[1]

In my moment, the dealer had a 6 up; basic strategy told me I should double my first hand, the 11, putting another $10,000 down and receiving only one more card. I stacked ten more yellow chips and placed them next to the original ones, signifying my double down. The dealer dealt me a 7, giving me a total of 18 on my first hand. Typically, 18 is a losing hand. But, when the dealer has a 6 up (as she did then), an 18 still stands a reasonable chance to win.

The next hand was a pair of 9s. I split—putting another $10,000 down, I would be able to play each 9 separately. On the first 9, I received a 2, making the total sum of that hand 11. At this point, the dealer gave me the option to "double down" again and, following the rules of basic strategy, I did so. I reached into my pocket for ten more of my rapidly dwindling yellow chips and stacked them prettily in line next to the four stacks of chips already on the table.

And then, a whirlwind. The dealer gave me a 5 on that 11 to make a total of 16 and then moved on to my final 9. She dealt me a 10 on this 9 to give me a total of 19 on that hand. I now had $50,000 on the table and had a 19, a 16, and an 18 against the dealer's 6 up. Even for a practiced card counter like me, this was a stressful situation.

In blackjack the goal is simple: Aim for 21 without going over. In a casino, you play only against the dealer. The others at your table—their games, their stories, their skill or luck or genius—do not matter. My only nemesis that night, then, was the dealer and the house that stood behind her. She flipped her hole card (the card that lay face down throughout play) and revealed a 5. This simple flip gave her a very dangerous starting total of 11. Because her total was less than 17, she was forced by rule to take cards until she reached 17 or greater. That night, she needed only one card. Sure enough she dealt herself a 10, for an unbeatable total of 21. I lost every last hand and all $50,000.

A woman behind me shrieked, "My lord! That is my entire mortgage!" I stared hard at the table. I was a trained card counter using math to beat blackjack, and I had learned not to react. I made a new calculation with the information from the cards that had been played on the previous hand and deduced that my bet should now be three hands of $10,000. A devoted believer in our model and method, I put down my three stacks of ten yellow chips without hesitation. On the first hand I received a 9 (a 5 and 4), a 19 on the second, and a soft 15 (an ace and a 4) on the third. The dealer had a 5 up. Because my next move was dictated by math and there was really no "choice" for me, I doubled on the 9, putting another $10,000 down and received a king for a relatively strong 19. I stood on the next hand, the 19, and then doubled on the soft 15, receiving a 4. I had a total of 19 on that hand.

I stacked a total of $50,000 worth of chips onto the table. Out $50,000 from the last round, this was my chance to either win back all the money or wind up down $100,000. I'd only been playing for about five minutes. I felt sick to my stomach and wondered how I, with my very conservative upbringing, had come to this point. But this was blackjack, I reminded myself. There is barely time for cogent calculation and planning, let alone time for nostalgic reflection.

There were only two out of thirteen cards that would beat me out-right, a 5 or a 6. Furthermore, the information gleaned from my card counting would lead me to believe that there weren't many of those cards left in the deck. The dealer paused for a second and then flipped her next card, revealing a 6—one of those two evil cards. Again, she had a total of 21.

I lost all three hands and, with them, another $50,000.

As part of the MIT Blackjack team—a group of MIT students who had learned and perfected the science of card counting—I used math and statistics to beat the casinos legally. We were some of the most successful card counters in the world, and we believed in what we were doing because it *always* worked. Yet here I was, faced with a serious test of my faith.

It may sound dramatic, but for us, belief in the power of analytics and statistics was not unlike believing in God. Truly religious people of all denominations and creeds may be tested along the way, but they always believe. My faith, as it were, in the religion of statistics was being mightily tested in that moment.

I trudged upstairs to my room at Caesars and collapsed on the floor, staring up at the ceiling and reviewing the events of the past ten min-utes. Where had I gone wrong? I replayed the hands and the decisions again and again in my mind. They were all consistent with the basic strategy, and yet I had lost. How could this be? Maybe the math wasn't right. Maybe it didn't work after all.

Doubt crept into my head as I continued to be haunted by the possi-bility of this unprecedented moment of loss. In my year as a card coun-ter, I had surely lost before but never to this extent—comparatively, this loss was catastrophic.

I believe we are all faced with these moments of doubt. How we choose to deal with them is telling. In my case, I had nothing left to lean on but my faith in math and statistics. I knew it worked. It wasn't as if the fundamentals of blackjack had suddenly changed in the middle of those hands. The method that we developed was surely still sound regardless of what had happened at that table.

I pulled some spreadsheets and a calculator from my suitcase and ran through the numbers. I soon realized that on the first of those hands I had roughly a 5 percent advantage over the casino and, on the second, roughly a 6 percent advantage. Both were huge advantages for the game of blackjack, but neither represented the proverbial "sure thing."

To boil it down further, in the first hand I had only a 52.5 percent chance of winning. The casino would still win 47.5 percent of the time. Obviously, at different points of the hand I thought my odds of winning were significantly higher in light of the cards I saw on the table, but when I put my money into the betting circle, my advantage was still only 5 percent and 6 percent.

Doing the math helped me put the night's events into perspective. I had to choose between two alternatives: to quit or to continue playing. I told myself that to give up here would be to give up on everything that I had worked for in all the nights spent dealing cards to myself and practicing with my teammates. I couldn't quit. It was not a viable alternative.

So I made the decision to go back down to the casino and begin to play. I played for the entire weekend, winning back the $100,000 I had lost and then some. I won a total of $70,000 net. If I had won those first two hands I would have won over $250,000 for the weekend. But my faith in our system got me out of my $100,000 hole and then some.

I had become a true believer in the religion of statistics.

In 2001, I approached Ben Mezrich, an author, about an idea for his next book. I told him about my group of friends and how we used math and statistics to beat the casinos—for millions of dollars. We traveled on weekends from Boston to Las Vegas and were members of an elite team of blackjack players. Most of us were current students or recent graduates from MIT, one of the premier universities in the world. But while our classmates had knowledge as their reward, we had cash and chips—lots of cash and chips.

Ben was reluctant. Back in 2001, there was no poker on television and fewer casinos worldwide, and when people thought about counting cards, they had visions of Dustin Hoffman from *Rain Man*. They certainly didn't think of it as a riveting James Bond–like tale of whiz kids taking down the evil casinos. A book about card counters from MIT sounded more like a cure for insomnia than a *New York Times* bestseller.

But after seeing a full-blown demonstration of our "talents" in Vegas, Ben was on board, and the book *Bringing Down the House* was born. It represents "my story," or at least Ben's version of it. Because I wasn't sure how people would react to a book about gambling, I asked Ben to change my name. "Kevin Lewis" and "Ben Campbell" (as the main character was named in the movie version, *21*) became my alter egos, and my story was immortalized in what became a *New York Times* bestselling novel and a blockbuster movie. In both, my experiences were the centerpiece of entertaining and dramatic twists on our travails, but the piece that was not dealt with fully was the innovation, ingenuity, and business acumen required to beat the casinos, information I believed could be valuable to a wide array of business scenarios.

I took these lessons with me into my post-blackjack life, looking for opportunities to apply them outside of the casinos. There were some obvious choices. Of course, finance called me early on in my professional career, but it only held my interest for a short time. The industry I eventually turned to was sports. A tremendous passion point for me since childhood, sports represented the opportunity to continue my journey using math and statistics to create competitive advantage.

I started a company called PROTRADE with some incredibly smart people from the sports industry, and we were able to get an investment from Kevin Compton, one of the most successful venture capitalists in Silicon Valley (he's also the owner of the San Jose Sharks, a team in the National Hockey League), and Jeff Moorad, who at the time was one of the top sports agents (he is currently the owner of the San

Diego Padres). With my business partner, Mike Kerns, our goal was to revolutionize sports via technology and analytics. We began working with professional sports teams like the San Francisco 49ers and the Portland Trail Blazers. We helped them use statistics to make better decisions both on and off the field. Also, we worked with traditional media giants like ESPN and *Sports Illustrated* to enhance their content offering with advanced statistics. I launched a career speaking to corporations about how to apply the lessons of blackjack and sports to their industries. The notoriety I had gained had given me a platform from which to preach the religion of statistics to all who would listen. And as I tried to spread the message, I came across other like-minded followers who taught me important commandments necessary to gain the House Advantage.

If I'm known as the Bishop of the Blackjack Diocese, my friend Bob Stoll takes pastoral care of sports gambling. Over the last ten years, he has fostered the same belief system around betting on football and basketball that I had for blackjack.

With the rise of Internet gambling sites and the increased popularity of Las Vegas as a tourist destination, sports betting has become a big business. Forbes.com estimates that $82.5 billion to $382.5 billion is wagered on sporting events in the United States each year.[2] Sports betting shares one very important similarity with blackjack: It is a game that its players may beat using analytics and statistics.

A player simply needs to create a model that helps him pick winners at a rate higher than the casino/sports book commission. In the most standard and popular bet, the point spread, the casino takes a 10 percent commission. For example, in the most recent Super Bowl pitting the Colts against the Saints, the Colts were favored by five points. This means that if you bet on the Colts on the point spread, you would be betting on them to win by more than five points. If you bet $100 and the Colts won by more than five points, you will win $100. If you bet $100 and the Colts won by fewer than five points or outright lost the game, you will actually lose $110. So, the ability to pick winners against the spread at greater than a 50 percent clip is not good enough. You actually have to be able to average close to 53 percent.

How hard is it to do this? Ask the hordes of sports bettors who have bankrupted themselves over the years trying or the false disciples who sell their picks and boast about their records only to flame out when their information yields more losers than winners. One such tout once explained to me that he doesn't like to show the records of his so-called experts since that would only "discourage sales" as most of their records centered around 50 percent. In general, there are very few people who can consistently beat the casinos and even fewer who actually talk about what they do. Bob Stoll is one of those few.

Bob Stoll, or Dr. Bob, as he is known to the world, studied statistics at the University of California, Berkeley, and got his first taste of sports gambling during his sophomore year. He was already an avid Oakland Raiders fan and became more interested when a friend started a contest at a local bowling alley to pick each NFL game against the spread. The contest cost $2 to enter, and Dr. Bob decided that by using some simple statistics, he might have an edge on the competition.

As there weren't many real personal computers in the early 1980s, he did his calculations by hand, creating a simple equation that would help him use meaningful data from previous games to predict the points scored by each team in each game. He went 12–2 that first week picking NFL games against the spread and won $102 for his work. When he recounts these winnings, he smiles as if recalling one of the proudest moments of his life. He has since won millions of dollars wagering on sporting events, but for someone like Stoll, it isn't so much the money that drives him—it's the challenge of figuring out the system and beating it.

As Stoll continued the pursuit of his statistics degree, he saw parallels between what he was learning in the lecture hall and his newfound sports gambling hobby. During one specific class, he thought there might be a direct application to use the Fourier series[3] to forecast team performance over time.

He had noticed some similarities in the performance of NFL teams over time with the patterns he was studying in the Fourier series, and he hypothesized that this type of analysis could be used to help predict the performance of sports teams. After discussing it with his professor, he was introduced to a colleague named Dr. Mike Orkin. Orkin had developed a piece of software called a Point Spread Analyzer. It allowed a bettor to search through large data sets of past games and query how teams had performed in the past when faced with different situations. Stoll and Orkin shared ideas about how teams' performances changed from week to week, and technical analysis in sports gambling was born.

Stoll began writing articles for a well-known gambling publication called *The Gold Sheet* on this concept of technical analysis in sports gambling. For a long time people had known that teams behaved in strange ways throughout the course of a season—like let-downs after a big win or suddenly playing well and bouncing back after a big loss—but until Stoll's work, no one had really found a way to predict it reliably. This publicity helped launch Dr. Bob's career as someone who provided advice to gamblers, and his business grew with the rise of the Internet and e-mail. Eventually, Sam Walker, writing for the *Wall Street Journal*, proclaimed him "The Man Who Shook Up Vegas."[4]

Reading about Dr. Bob, one might think of him as a maniacal genius locked away in a basement with huge mainframe computers and servers storing terabytes of data. But as I sat with him on a Sunday evening in his townhouse in the Haight-Ashbury district of San Francisco, it didn't occur to me that he is the most brilliant mathematical mind I've ever met. But he could be the most confident.

Every pore of Bob's being exudes this confidence. It's not a distasteful arrogance or even an annoying cockiness; rather, it is a reassuring confidence. I remember an earlier encounter with Bob when we were working on an Internet project together. He came by my office on a Monday afternoon, and I asked him about his weekend. He proceeded to tell me about the flag football game he had lost over the weekend. "See, the problem was I'm the best wide receiver in the league and nobody can cover me. But our regular quarterback wasn't there. Since I'm also a great quarterback, I ended up having to play quarterback. Not having me out there as a wide receiver really hurt us." For some, to say this would be arrogant, but Bob was simply stating a fact: In his mind, he is the best at what he does regardless of what it is.

So as I sat across from him and marveled at his confidence, I asked him a very simple question: "Have you ever contemplated quitting?" I wondered about his faith in the religion of math and his confidence in using it consistently to win in the difficult world of sports gambling. I thought about my own moment of crisis on the floor of my room in Caesars Palace.

Just as quickly as I asked the question, Dr. Bob answered.

"Nope," he said.

Here was a guy who had gone through prolonged streaks of losing, but he claimed never to have lost faith or considered quitting. Dr. Bob is certainly the most confident mathematician I have ever met. His greatest trait is this überego. It's what gets him through losing streaks that might make others quit. It's what gives him such tremendous faith in the religion of statistics.

And the proof is in his results. Not the short-term results. Not two weeks of results or two months of results or even a season of results. The proof is in a career that has yielded on average a 56 percent record against the spread—a record good enough to give him a business with thousands of subscribers, a beautiful house in one of the world's most expensive cities, and more than a million dollars in annual revenue. Dr. Bob's confidence comes from a faith that these career numbers are the only thing that matter and are the true measure of his abilities.

I'm not sure whether I have ever had this type of confidence in myself, but I certainly did have similar confidence and faith in our card-counting system. That's what got me through my $100,000 loss and what kept me going back to Vegas. My test of faith was one of the most valuable lessons I learned during my time as a card counter, and as I entered the working world I looked for a job that could give me similar confidence in my abilities.

My version of the post-college rebellion was to forego medical school for a job in finance, and my first job was at an options trading firm in Chicago called O'Connor and Associates. O'Connor was dubbed "a powerful but virtually anonymous firm that helped create the modern options business."[5] When options were first created, many people didn't understand how to trade them, which led to great arbitrage opportunities, and O'Connor was one of the first firms to take advantage of these opportunities. But, as the options market matured, so did O'Connor. In the early 1990s, it was part of a new wave of firms in which the brightest quantitative minds from places like MIT were whisked away from engineering jobs offering mediocre pay by the promise of making swift millions. I was supposed to be one such mind.

It didn't matter to O'Connor that I had never taken a finance or business class at MIT. In fact, I had never even taken an economics class. I learned later that this was by design as O'Connor did not hire MBAs and preferred to work with a clean slate. One of my colleagues, Ted Bretter, recalls that O'Connor would not have been interested in hiring him if he'd had previous training at another firm. "I was told they wouldn't want to waste the time on someone that they would have to reteach all the incorrect things another firm had taught them." They were certainly confident of their place in the finance ecosystem.

So with no formal education in finance, every interview I had with the firm centered on a small line at the bottom of my resume. In the "Other Interests" section I had listed "Card Counting."

I was incredibly nervous for my first interview because I didn't know much about options or about finance in general. I had read a book on options so that I would at least understand the basic vocabulary, but I really had no idea what they would actually ask me. I entered the beautiful suite the firm had rented at the Hyatt Hotel in Cambridge, Massachusetts, with extremely low expectations.

The interview began with basic questions but moved very quickly to more intense ones.

"Suppose we are playing a game where I roll a six-sided die and pay you in dollars whatever the result of the roll is. In other words, if I roll and it's a one, I pay you $1. If it's a six, I pay you $6. How much, per roll, would you pay *me* to play this game?"

My nervousness subsided instantly. This wasn't finance, it was just statistics. This was easy.

"Well, the expected value (the average of the roll of the dice) on each roll is actually three and a half. So I guess I'd pay $3," I answered. This was enough to impress the interviewer and get me through to the next round where an in-depth discussion of card counting landed me the job.

My plan was to work in finance and continue my journey into the religion of statistics. Blackjack had been a good introduction, but now I would take my faith to the next level, making millions of dollars in a more acceptable and legitimate profession. I mean, your parents can't very well tell people at a cocktail party that you went to MIT and you're a professional gambler.

But something funny happened along the way.

In 1994, O'Connor enrolled all of their new recruits in an intensive training program that taught us everything we needed to know about derivatives and derivative theory. And, yes, after eight weeks, I knew enough about finance to be dangerous.

After training, I was thrown directly onto the floor of the Chicago Board of Options Exchange (CBOE), where I worked as a clerk. Clerking was an apprenticeship position at O'Connor, and it was usually a twelve- to eighteen-month term. Upon its conclusion I would become a trader. As I gained more experience clerking, my responsibility would increase. There were many clerks at O'Connor who managed trading positions before they became actual traders.

Traders were the breadwinners for O'Connor. They utilized statistical models to find options that were priced too expensively and sold those. They looked for options priced too cheaply and bought those. The mantra was simple and classic: Buy low, sell high. Of course, O'Connor did much more complicated things to make money, but this was the gist of what I worked on in my first year. Even in this simple world there was an important question. How did O'Connor know which options were cheap and which were expensive?

An option is a financial instrument that gives the owner the right, but not the obligation, to buy or sell an underlying asset at some point in the future. You can have an option on anything—a stock, a bond, a house. The price of the option is the premium you are willing to pay for the right to lock in a price on the underlying asset; it's almost like an insurance premium. Let's say you are in the market for a house but won't have the money to buy for another year. You've found the perfect house and the $1 million price is agreeable, but you simply don't have the money right *now*. Additionally, you have a feeling that prices are going to rise in the next year. You agree to pay the seller $5,000 for the right to buy the house sometime in the next year. The value of that option depends on many things, but the main factor is how much the market is going to change in the next year. This is called the "volatility" of the market.

In this housing scenario, you are only unhappy if the price of the house stays the same, that is, there is zero volatility. If housing prices go up and the house is actually worth $1.1 million, you are happy that you have the right to buy it for $1 million. You've saved yourself $95,000. If housing prices go down and value of the house drops to $900,000, you are certainly happy that you didn't buy the house initially; now you can decide not to exercise your option and instead buy the house for $900,000, again saving yourself $95,000. The value of this option is driven by the volatility of the market since high volatility implies there is a higher probability of the option finishing in the money.

At O'Connor and Associates, I worked in the equities department and traded options on stocks. We had complex quantitative models using historical data to predict the future volatility of each stock that we traded. It was these models that we utilized to price options, helping us decide what to buy and what to sell. It was similar to blackjack in that there were numbers that told you when to bet more (buy) and when to bet less (sell). This parallel made me comfortable enough to become a believer in our methods, at least for a while.

During my first year of work at O'Connor, I was still involved with the blackjack team. During the week, I was gambling on the CBOE and on the weekends I was gambling in casinos. It was only natural that I began comparing the two. It occurred to me that our advantage in the casinos was much stronger than it was on the trading floor. The card-counting system was based on hard math that wouldn't change unless the rules of blackjack changed. Every bet we made had a theoretical edge that would be realized over time. There was very little risk as long as we had enough money to withstand the impact of variance. There was very little "gambling" to what we were doing in the casino. The trading system was another story. When I really broke it down, it simply fell short of the certainty of blackjack. During my time at O'Connor, two particular events convinced me of these shortcomings.

O'Connor was full of colorful characters and was a mix of highly educated graduates like myself and guys who had more street smarts than formal education; I clerked for a man who fell into the latter category.

Each trader covered a group of equities broken down geographically by where they were traded on the floor. Telmex (Telephonos de Mexico), the Mexican phone company, was one of the stocks in my trader's portfolio. He stood in the Telmex pit with the other traders, identifying bargains to buy and overpriced options to sell. Every day he watched as the theoretical money he had made with his trades became realized gains as the actual volatility came more into line with our theoretical models and the options he bought appreciated, while the options he sold became less valuable.

Our models worked and the firm made money. Until one day they didn't.

In 1994, there was an economic crisis in Mexico centered on the devaluation of its currency, the Mexican peso, which was historically pegged to the U.S. dollar. President Ernesto Zedillo announced that he would be increasing the historical fixed rate band and, in reaction, the government essentially let the peso float. Without the support of the U.S. dollar, the peso crashed.

The Mexican economic crisis had an incredible impact on the volatility of Telmex, and the options on Telmex blew up, becoming very expensive. Our volatility models told us that these prices were too expensive, and we sold as many options as we could. For the entire week, I spent each day running back and forth from the pit to our booth, entering trades, helping my trader run calculations, and making sure that he had the support he needed.

When I went home at night, I would reflect upon the day's events. I was concerned that a fundamental change had occurred in the environment around the underlying asset. How could our models, which were based on history, account for something that had never happened before? The devaluing of the peso was a monumental event and had no parallel, and yet we made trades with tremendous faith in our numbers. It was generally accepted as a good method, but it just didn't seem right to me. It was as if the dealer had changed the rules of blackjack midgame.

Soon after, I was working with this same trader in the Chrysler pit. Chrysler was a heavily traded stock at the time with rumors swirling that it was about to be sold. People wanted options on Chrysler stock and hoped to strike it rich when the company was purchased. Billionaire Kirk Kerkorian, the automaker's largest shareholder, attempted a hostile takeover, and the stock price immediately went haywire. Because of the high volume of trading and the increased volatility, we made hundreds of trades each day. But again I wondered, how did our historical models take into account a once-in-a-lifetime occurrence like a takeover?

It wasn't that I didn't think the people at O'Connor were smart. To the contrary, I thought they were some of the smartest people I'd ever met. And for the most part they were incredibly successful. But the incredible faith that I had in our blackjack system made me feel that the gamble of working in finance was riskier than any I'd ever taken in a casino.

It all came to a head one day as I sat in our booth on the trading floor. As a clerk, whenever you were sitting, you were supposed to be looking over positions, scrutinizing chances to make money. Instead, I stared into space, daydreaming about the next trip to Vegas. My boss, whose job it was to train all the clerks, got in my face and shouted, "What's your delta in Chrysler?"

He was asking me for an update on our position in Chrysler. I should have been so on top of it that it would be on the tip of my tongue, but instead I mumbled something unintelligible. It wasn't that I didn't know the delta, which I did, but more that I was tired of his training techniques.

He lashed into me. "Why can't you look at this floor," he started pointing at the entire trading floor, "the same way you look at the casino? I know you look at a casino and see dollar signs and you challenge yourself to find every way to bleed every damn last dollar out of that casino. You need to look at the trading floor the same way. You need to be way more aggressive."

As he walked away, I fiddled with the computer in front of me to give the impression that I was working, while I actually thought about his questions. Why couldn't I look at this job the same way I looked at blackjack?

For a few months, I worked harder than ever and did and said all the right things. I received glowing reviews from my boss, but I was still not a believer. Eventually, I resigned my position, moving back to Boston to look for a new job while focusing even more energy on blackjack.

On the day I resigned, my boss was surprised and said something I will never forget. Smiling slightly, he said, "For someone at the stage you are at, to make this kind of decision, you must really have conviction in your choice." I was leaving a firm that would itself flourish, later to be bought by Swiss Bank Corporation. But blackjack had me believing in an extremely high standard of analytics—a standard that was not met during my time at O'Connor.

This high standard comes from blackjack's absolute adherence to the rules of mathematics, and the juxtaposition with my brief stint in finance helped me gain some perspective on the fundamental principles necessary to gain the House Advantage. These principles are our commandments and will continue to surface throughout this book. But more than anything they serve as the backdrop for how to succeed using an analytical approach.

The first commandment is the importance of understanding variance. When I learned to get comfortable with variance, I embraced it. Even when the odds are with you, whether it be in blackjack or in business, it is not uncommon to walk away a loser. Imagine that I offered to play a game with you in which I would flip a fair quarter; every time it landed on heads, I would give you $1.02, and every time it landed on tails, you would give me $1.00. Understanding math, it's a game you would undoubtedly want to play. But if after ten consecutive flips of tails you had lost $10, you might be tempted to quit. However, quitting at that point would be a monumental mistake. Instead, you should run to the bank, get out a thousand dollars, and sit there with me until I was bankrupted. You lost ten flips by simply being on the negative side of variance.

Variance is a very difficult concept for people to become comfortable with. In 2007, Dr. Bob had a run where he went 5–32 (5 wins and 32 losses) and received hate mail from his clients. "I told them, 'Don't worry. These things are going to happen from time to time. Don't stop betting. My methods still work and I fully expect to be 56 percent, my career record, going forward.' "

"The problem," he said, "is that people just don't understand variance. Just because I had lost 32 out of 35 games, it didn't suddenly mean my methods didn't work."

"It's like if you became manager of the St. Louis Cardinals and the first week that you were there, Albert Pujols (widely regarded as the best player in baseball) went 5 for 37. Would you decide to bench Pujols? No. Of course not. You'd keep him in the lineup and expect him to perform as he had his entire career, not as he had for the last week," Dr. Bob explained.

Yet Bob's clients began canceling their subscriptions and deciding not to follow him. "This was the worst thing they could have done," he explained. "I was confident that going forward I would continue to win at around a 56 percent clip. Like I always had."

And win he did, to the tune of 38–7 over the next three weeks. Those who stuck with Dr. Bob reaped the benefits of their faith. Those who quit were victims of variance and their atheism regarding statistics.

Learning to cope with variance is an important lesson regardless of whether you bet on blackjack or on sports or never plan to set foot in a casino. As Dr. Bob said, "I'm trained to ignore short-term fluctuations. In my life I'm very even keeled in everything I do. A lot of business people would be wise to learn this lesson and not to react to short term results, which might just be the product of variance."

The second commandment of our statistical religion is the importance of a long-term perspective and the commitment to invest in it. Dr. Bob's bad run over 37 games destroyed both the confidence and bankroll of his non-believing clients. He had a terrible success rate of 14 percent in those 37 games, but his record in nearly 20 years and over 10,000 games was a solid 56 percent. Maintaining the mental perspective to withstand these types of streaks is just as important as maintaining the proper financial resources. While some of Bob's clients were simply wiped out emotionally and decided to stop following Bob, others might have remained confident in Bob but, owing to poor money management, no longer had the resources to continue betting. This was a costly mistake.

Because most successful analytical strategies are only going to give you a small advantage, it is important to maintain a long-term perspective. And you are going to need a lot of trials and a lot of patience to realize that advantage and turn a real profit. To go back to our quarter-flipping game, your advantage each time the quarter was flipped was only $.01 (you have a 50 percent chance of losing $1 and a 50 percent chance of winning $1.02). So if we played 100 times, you would only be expected to win $1. In order to make any real profit, you would need to play thousands, maybe even millions, of times. And if you did have the patience and the bankroll to play one million times, you would expect to make yourself $10,000. Not bad for flipping a coin.

The same type of patience applies to businesses looking to employ analytics. Recently I was talking with my friend Niel Robertson about the importance of our long-term perspective in blackjack; not surprisingly, he said he sees the exact same phenomenon in his new business, Trada.

Trada helps businesses place and optimize ads on search engines like Google and Yahoo. When you type a search into Google, say "blackjack tables," you'll see both the normal results from Google and a number of sponsored links above and to the right of the regular search results. These sponsored links appear next to your search results because the advertisers you see have told Google they would like to show their ads next to the search results when someone types in "blackjack tables." The challenge is that advertisers also have to tell Google to show their ads when someone searches on "poker tables," "gaming tables," "betting tables," "casino furniture," "casino games," "company casino game night," and any possible other combination of words relevant to their products.

Niel started Trada because this matching process was very complex for most small- and medium-sized businesses. Very few of them had access to expert knowledge on how to set up and run their advertising campaigns. Trada created a system in which, rather than matching one expert to a business that wants to run a search campaign, they get hundreds of experts to work on every business in their marketplace and pay everyone based on individual performance. Trada is part of an emerging field called crowdsourcing that focuses on the idea that groups of people can often produce vastly better results than a single expert working on a problem alone.

My conversation with Niel centered on the challenge of working with small businesses that have an emotional attachment to each and every dollar spent and may not completely understand variance. The comforting thing is that search-engine marketing tends to produce about the same expected outcome for all parties, albeit over a lot of clicks. The industry standard is that 1–2 percent of people who click on an ad will end up buying the product offered. While there are exceptions to this rule (some websites convert customers much better—some convert worse), Trada's across-the-board data prove over and over again that 1–2 percent is a very safe rule of thumb. For Niel, the problem was small businesses that were extremely spending-conscious.

If businesses paid for 100 clicks (on Google advertisers pay every time a searcher clicks on their ad), they expected to see a sale 1–2 percent of the time because of the averages that Trada had quoted them. Sometimes they had "a winning streak," closing customer after customer in 50–60 clicks a piece. But sometimes they had to wait for 100, 200, or even 300 clicks to get a sale. These dry spells leave a lot of businesses scratching their heads and biting their nails while the clicks (and costs) continue and they don't see any profits for a while. Trada constantly counsels businesses to wait it out. And inevitably the sales do come. Again and again, at steady state (after thousands of clicks) the 1–2 percent conversion rate emerges.

You can have a bad streak in advertising, just as you can in blackjack.

Long runs of bad luck in Vegas constantly tested our nerves and our belief in statistics. It's very hard to lay down $1,000 chip after $1,000 chip (much like Niel's customers laying down dollar after dollar for each click), only to have it swept from the table. We had to maintain a long-term perspective, and, more important, we had to have a big enough bankroll to ride out the inevitable downward swings. Niel told me something very similar about how he sets expectations concerning the necessary bank account customers will need to do search-engine marketing.

"They [Trada's advertisers] must sign up for three months' worth of advertising spend. We've learned to require this to protect our customers from getting too emotionally worked up by the inevitable dry spells that their, and frankly everyone's, campaigns go on from time to time. In the end the numbers always return to the expected average. Every time," Niel explained.

So the lesson in business, as in blackjack, is that you need to have a long-term perspective and the corresponding financial commitment to make analytics pay off. And, like Dr. Bob, you must remain positive and confident that it will pay off.

Finally, you need to truly be confident in your strategy or model. I realized later that this was the essential piece missing for me in my trading days. The Mexican financial crisis and Chrysler's attempted takeover made me doubt how stable our strategies really were. But I was confident that our card counting strategies would work until the end of time or at least until someone changed the rules of blackjack.

Herein lies another unique principle of blackjack—the rules of the game never change and therefore neither does the math that governs it. This distinction will come into play later in the book as we explore the difficulty many have had in applying analytics where human behavior can change the rules of the game.

Most strategies will not stay stable over time because the world and people in general are in constant change. And this is the tremendous challenge when implementing analytics in the real world, whether it is in business, finance, or sports. You must have the agility to reevaluate your strategy when things change. If you are dealing with a dynamic situation, you must constantly check and test your strategy. That is the only way you will be able to maintain the confidence to succeed.

Blackjack gave me the ultimate baptism into the religion of statistics, as football did for Dr. Bob and marketing efficiency did for Niel. Its unique properties gave me faith in the power of numbers and an understanding of the fundamental principles needed to apply analytics to win in business.

2

WHY THE PAST MATTERS

History teaches everything including the future.

—Alphonse de Lamartine

AS MY BLACKJACK career progressed, I looked to apply statistical analysis to other areas. But in order to do so, I had to understand the core principles of card counting. Why did it work? And what could it teach in a broader sense about decision making?

One of the most common misconceptions about card counting is that you must be a genius to do it. People assume I have a photographic memory, that I'm some sort of savant with numbers, or that we did some kind of voodoo magic on the cards to make winning certain.

None of that is true. To be fair, I graduated from MIT with a degree in mechanical engineering, so I'm good with numbers. But those credentials are not necessary to gain success as a card counter. You simply need to study the math behind card counting and then practice diligently. It takes hard work and commitment, but the inherent nature of blackjack makes it beatable—not some voodoo magic.

Blackjack can be beaten because it has a memory. Cards played in the past will have an impact on cards played in the future. In an academic sense, this property of memory is called conditional probability. Conditional probability is defined as the chance of something happening given the occurrence of another event. An example in this case might be the chance that an ace appears after an ace has been dealt. If we know that there are 52 cards in a deck and there are four aces in a deck, we know that at the start of a deck there is a 4 in 52 chance (7.7 percent) of seeing an ace as the first card. If an ace is dealt as the first card, then the probability has changed to 3 in 51 (5.9 percent). More simply, seeing an ace has changed the probability of seeing another ace.

Blackjack can be contrasted to other, more random, casino games, such as roulette. Roulette is played with a wheel that typically has 38 slots, numbered 1 through 36 as well as 0 and 00. Each non-zero number is colored black or red, and the two zero numbers are green. The roulette dealer spins the wheel and drops in a small ball that rotates around for several seconds until landing randomly in one of the slots. Players can bet on each spin of the wheel and can bet whether the ball will land on red or black, on odd or even, and on an exact number.

There is usually a brightly lit scoreboard above the roulette wheel that shows the results of the last 20 spins. Players believe they can gain some insight by studying the board. Imagine you are in a casino, looking at that big board and see that in the last 10 spins, the ball has landed on red each time. The natural inclination might be to think that in the next spin, the ball is sure to finally land on black.

I've witnessed this type of faulty logic many times. Toward the end of my blackjack career, I traveled to Vegas with civilian friends (that is, friends who were not members of my team) who were eager for a glimpse into the high-roller world. On one of these weekends, I went to Vegas with my friend Brian, an avid gambler. At the time I was still allowed to play blackjack at the Hard Rock Hotel and Casino (which is, unfortunately, no longer the case). Under my tutelage, Brian won about

$2,000. As it was approaching 11 p.m. on a Friday night, we decided to meet up with friends who were headed to a club.

As we stood up from the table and headed to the cage to cash out our chips, something caught Brian's eye. Before I could say anything he ran to the roulette table, placing one of his newly acquired $1,000 chips on the table and called out "$1,000 on black." As I came up behind Brian, I saw what had caught his eye. On that roulette scoreboard was a sea of red numbers. Looking closer, I saw that the last eight numbers called at that table had been red.

Because Brian's money was already on the table, reasoning with him was useless. The dealer spun the wheel and we watched as Brian's $1,000 hung in the balance. After what seemed like an eternity, the ball came to rest.

"Red, 12," called the dealer.

Brian had lost his $1,000 but was still up $1,000 for the night from his blackjack winnings—not the end of the world. I grabbed his arm and started to pull him away from the table, but he was now a man on a mission.

"$1,000 on black," he called again to the dealer, putting another $1,000 chip on the table.

"Dude, what are you doing?" I asked him.

"Come on, man. Don't you see what's going on here? Been nine reds in a row here. No way this isn't black," he explained.

"Brian, you're being stupid. That's absolutely not true. Those last nine spins don't mean anything," I said. He ignored me and stared at the wheel as the dealer initiated the next spin.

I sat back and watched helplessly, hoping against hope that black would come up and we could get out of this fiasco unscathed. I could then sit down with Brian and gently explain his folly. Unfortunately, we would not be so lucky.

"Red, 7," called the dealer.

Brian had lost all the money I'd helped him win at the blackjack table. There was still no stopping him. He reached into his pocket and pulled out another yellow chip, placed it on the table, and called out yet one last time, "$1,000 on black."

I pleaded with him, "Dude, I'm telling you. You are being an idiot. Let's get out of here."

He turned to me and said, "Listen, Jeff. I know you know statistics and blackjack and all that math stuff. But roulette is different. This is gambling and I *know* gambling." Brian repeated the process three more times. He lost $1,000 each time as red came up a seemingly remarkable 13 times in a row.

But how remarkable was it, really? If you consider that there are 38 slots on the wheel and 18 of them are red, you realize there is an 18 in 38 (47.4 percent) chance of red coming up. The chance of it coming up 13 times in a row is actually about 1 in 16,544. So yes, this result was remarkable. But the problem was that the Brian was never betting against red coming up 13 times in a row. He was betting on black coming up on one individual roll and the odds of that were still only 47.4 percent.

Brian's behavior is something known as the "gambler's fallacy." It is defined as the belief that if anomalies from expected outcomes occur in repeated independent trials of some random process, then these anomalies are likely to be evened out by opposite occurrences in the future. To break down the definition, the "anomalies from expected behavior" were the eight consecutive reds that came up before we arrived at the table. The "independent trials" were the result of each spin of the roulette wheel. "Independent" is a key word because in Brian's mind, each spin was not independent and therefore was not random. Brian's behavior fell right in line with this definition.

When Brian walked up to that table, the previous eight spins told him nothing about this ninth spin because each spin was truly independent. There was no change in the probability of black based on the previous result of red. There was no conditional probability. When calculating the odds of black coming up, I don't need to know anything about the previous ten spins. Clearly, roulette is a game with no memory and is not beatable over time in the way that blackjack is.

The same can be said of craps. In craps, a shooter rolls two dice and all the players, including the shooter, bet on the outcome of the roll. There are many different bets that players can make, but one of the most popular is the Yo 11, a one-time bet that the shooter will roll an 11. If won, the Yo 11 pays the player 15 times what was wagered. This seems like a great return until you realize that the actual pay-off should be 17 to 1. The difference in these payoffs means the house has an 11 percent advantage over the player. Compare this to the small 1.41 percent edge the casino has on the most basic craps bet, and the Yo 11 seems like a pretty poor bet. Even so, the Yo 11 remains one of the most popular bets on the craps table.

Although card counting is not illegal, casinos, as private property, have the right to refuse service to anyone they wish regardless of reason (we will cover the legal reasoning behind this later in the book). Most casinos have invoked that right with me, and in most locations, I am no longer allowed to play blackjack. Since I can't play blackjack, I spend most of my casino time these days playing craps with my friends. I play with full knowledge that over the long haul I will lose money, but it's a fun game with some of the best odds in the casino. As mentioned earlier, on the most basic bet, the house only has a 1.41 percent edge over the player, and the game is quite social—when you are winning there are very few games as fun as craps.

Observing people at the craps table is a fascinating psychological experiment. More than any game, craps breeds superstition, which makes players susceptible to biases like the gambler's fallacy. Allowing one of the players to roll the dice adds an element to the experience that players would like to think reduces randomness and introduces player skill. Players will hopelessly judge the shooter based on looks and their previous rolls, hoping to find a skilled player who can overcome the odds.

Standing at a craps table one day, I decided to count how many different times I heard someone make a comment that fell into the category of the gambler's fallacy. Settling in at one of my favorite tables at the Hard Rock, I laid out some $1 chips on the rail and planned to move them to the other side of the rail when I heard any kind of fallacious comment, basically using the chips to count, like with beads on an abacus.

It wasn't long before a middle-aged man in a striped shirt walked up to me and asked, "How's this table been?"

"Sorry, I just got here," I told him.

"Okay, well I guess I'll just start out small then," he said, dropping a $5 chip on the table. I moved one $1 chip across the rail, signifying my first observation of an erroneous judgment. It was clear that he was placing some importance on the history of this table. If I had told him the table had been "hot," he likely would have bet more. He was trying to learn something about the table by learning something about its history, when, really, its history meant nothing.

The stick man pushed the dice over to me, and before I even picked up the dice the middle-aged man turned to me and asked, "You a good shooter?"

I moved another $1 chip across the rail and smiled at him. "Hopefully, I will be this time." The idea that there are good shooters and bad shooters is fairly common at the craps table. However, unless you are a dice mechanic (someone who has spent hours practicing how to role the dice), every shooter is as good or as bad as the next.

I rolled the dice across the table and they came up a six and a one. "Winner, seven!" the stick man called.

"Good, get those out of your system," my new friend said to me.

I moved another $1 chip across the rail. The man was hoping that by rolling sevens now, it would be less likely that I would roll a seven later, when doing so would cause us to lose all of our bets. In the next 15 minutes, there were another three comments that caused me to move over another three $1 chips, and I proved my hypothesis. Most people at a craps table simply don't understand that every roll of the dice is random. The reality is that a past roll means nothing to a future roll.

But, as I've said, blackjack is different. If I had a deck of cards and took out all four aces, the chance of you dealing yourself blackjack (an ace and any ten card) would be zero. Since there are no aces, it would simply be impossible. Likewise, if you were in a casino at a single-deck blackjack game and were tracking aces as they came out, you would have a pretty good idea that when the fourth ace came out you should probably walk away from that table if you were hoping to get blackjack.

Because of this unique attribute, blackjack has always fascinated mathematicians. It wasn't until the work of a professor named Edward Thorp in the early 1960s that people realized how beatable the game was. Thorp received both a master's and doctorate from UCLA and was an expert in an obscure branch of mathematics called functional analysis.

Initially, Thorp had little interest in blackjack or gambling, and even after planning a family vacation to Las Vegas, he still had no plans to spend any time at the blackjack tables. He was focused instead on the ample buffets, swimming pools, and glitzy shows. But shortly before departing for Sin City, a colleague showed him an article from the *Journal of the American Statistical Association* that described the work of four army technicians. They had worked for three years to prove that with optimal strategy you can reduce the casino edge in blackjack to near zero—these were our friends from Chapter 1 working on the first version of basic strategy.[1]

Thorp's previous reluctance to gamble while in Vegas came from his knowledge of the large house edge in games like roulette and slot machines, but with his newfound knowledge of an optimal strategy in blackjack he decided to try his hand at the tables. Utilizing the strategy devised by the army technicians, which he kept on a card with him at the table, Thorp approached the table more like a scientist than a gambler.

Thorp stuck with the army techs' rigid guidelines, initially becoming an object of derision as the other players at the table laughed at his seemingly unorthodox decisions and reliance on a hand-written card. Splitting a pair of 8s against an ace, standing 12 against a 4, and doubling a soft 15 against a 4 were just some of the decisions that made Thorp look like a sucker. But as he continued to stick with this system, he eventually won the crowd over and outlasted all the others at his table. Thorp's initial foray into the world of blackjack ended in a $8.50 loss, but his time at the table had fueled a new interest. He hypothesized that this blackjack game may indeed be beatable.

As a member of the faculty at MIT, Thorp had resources not available to most in in the 1960s: namely, an IBM 704 computer. Thorp fed all data into the computer and in three hours had the answer for how to beat blackjack. He published his preliminary finding in a paper called "Fortune's Formula," and the legend of Edward Thorp and card counting was born.

Thorp went on to prove his theories in actual casinos, winning consistently enough to become persona non grata in casinos across Reno and Las Vegas. He changed the game of blackjack forever and went on to write a book called *Beat the Dealer* that is largely regarded as the bible of card counting and that was the inspiration for our MIT blackjack team.

So what did Thorp actually discover? What was his breakthrough?

Thorp's brilliance came from his hypothesis that each card might have a different impact on the player's odds of winning, and, via simulation, he could actually determine the exact impact of each of those cards. Using his IBM 704, he simulated hands of blackjack with certain cards missing from the deck. First, he simulated how the odds of the game changed when all four of the 2s in the deck were removed. Next, all the 3s and then all the 4s, finally working his way all the way up to the aces. This work illustrated that each card in the deck has a distinct impact on the odds of the game.

What he found was that 2, 3, 4, 5, and 6 were all bad cards for the player. Tens, face cards, and aces were all good for the player. Sevens,

8s, and 9s were close to neutral, meaning they neither helped nor hurt the player. Operating under the premise that the cards played tell you about what cards remain, players can predict the composition of the remaining cards by tracking the cards they have already seen. Equipped with an understanding of the impact of the cards that remain, a player knows what his odds of winning are going forward.

Of course, the next question is what to do with this knowledge, and, actually, the answer is pretty simple. All that card counters do is bet more when the odds are in their favor and bet less or stop playing when the odds aren't in their favor. Also, with knowledge of what cards are left, card counters can deviate from basic strategy at times. Both of these skills contribute to the advantage that card counters are able to gain over the casino, and both skills are only possible with a full knowledge of the cards' past.

Card counting is not magic—rather it is a simple illustration of the importance of using the past to predict the future. This fundamental lesson was something our blackjack team firmly believed in, and it helped establish our data-driven culture. We tracked everything. Starting in the casinos, each player kept a running journal of every detail of each table and situation in which they played. Carrying a small pad and pen at all times, we would periodically duck behind a slot machine or into a bathroom and record things like what time we started playing, how much money we had bet, how many different tables we had played, how much we won and lost, and how many other players had been at the table when we sat down.

After each weekend trip, we analyzed the data and used it to determine how to divvy up all the winnings. It told us what casinos at what time provided the most profitable playing conditions, helping us determine where and when to send our team to optimize revenue. We used the data to keep an ongoing prospectus of each casino. Players noted details about casino personnel. Information like "Caesars's night shift manager used to work at Mirage" or "graveyard pit manager near buffet is very suspicious" could be shared to help players avoid an unwanted encounter. Other observations about different dealers' tendencies could prove very useful. The bottom line was the more data that we recorded in the casinos, the better.

Establishing a data-driven culture is essential for any organization attempting to establish their own House Advantage. Companies must actively seek to capture and understand as much data about their business as possible. Niel Robertson's first company, Service Metrics, was one of the first companies to collect data to quantify the end user's experience on the web. They did this by focusing on how long it took to perform common website activities, such as buying a book, executing a stock trade, or bringing up a homepage. They set up a network of computers all over the world (literally traveling to places like Tokyo, Buenos Aires, and New York) and downloaded clients' web pages. They timed everything that happened and then sold the resulting data back to the website owners.

Though this may seem somewhat irrelevant today, in the late 1990s, when everyone was logging onto the Internet with 14.4 kbps phone modems, as opposed to the 14 mbps cable modems commonly used today, a big House Advantage was the speed of your website. If you were trying to buy a book on BarnesandNoble.com, for instance, and it was too slow, a user would jump over and buy it on Amazon.com instead.

The vestigial limbs of this speed race can still be seen in the minimalist designs of websites such as Google and Yahoo. They spent a huge amount of time stripping every single byte out of each page so that excess baggage didn't have to be shipped to the end user in Sydney or Moscow, thus slowing down access. The companies that knew their statistics and paid attention to their data (and those of their competitors—selling competitive data was about half Service Metrics' business) are mostly the ones that are still around today.

But simply collecting the data is not enough—having the ingenuity and innovation to actually use that data to make decisions is paramount. The Oakland Athletics and their general manager Billy

Beane were the first to truly embrace this concept in baseball, and it gave them an advantage over teams with more resources and dollars to spend on players. With their limited payroll, the A's were able to remain competitive among teams spending more than twice their budget, and they reached the playoffs four years in a row, 2000 to 2003.

In Michael Lewis's bestselling novel, *Moneyball,* Beane utters the unforgettable words, "We aren't selling jeans here." He was lamenting the old guard of baseball, scouts and managers, who evaluated a player's potential based on his physical attributes (a guy who would look good in an advertisement for jeans) rather than focusing on his past performance. Beane and his new guard had discovered that by looking at a player's past performance they could actually predict future success with far more accuracy than by simply watching games or evaluating a player's physical assets.

Moneyball caused a major chasm in the baseball world, with old guard spokesperson Joe Morgan likening it to "a bunch of geeks trying to play video games."[2] Morgan, a member of baseball's Hall of Fame and arguably its most well-known commentator, is a strong opponent of the use of statistics and computers to evaluate baseball players. Yet he has never read *Moneyball* and has missed its central point—the central point that made it one of the most important business books of the last decade. As Lewis puts it, *Moneyball* is "about using statistical analysis to shift the odds [of winning] a bit in one's favor, not to achieve perfect certainty, which is impossible."[3] Simply put, it teaches us that there is value to using the past to predict the future even in a game as unpredictable as baseball.

In order to use the past to predict the future, one must understand how to interpret and use data. In blackjack, Thorp did this by actually playing out the future in his computer simulations. However, simulation isn't always relevant or necessary. Beane and company looked for past statistics that translated well to future success—nothing too remarkable. Sometimes just looking at large amounts of past data will give you clues about the future. And large amounts of data are exactly what is available and easily manipulated in this new information age.

Industries like medicine are also looking at data to give them clues about illnesses like heart disease, cancer, and diabetes. Much of this work falls under the category of a relatively recent field called data mining. Data mining is the process of analyzing large amounts of data and looking for patterns that are statistically significant and therefore meaningful. The patterns can be used to make better decisions about the future. With the amount of information in the world growing at a record pace, the opportunities to find useful patterns in these data are likewise growing.

Specifically in the medical industry, data mining can help identify patterns using characteristics like age, sex, blood pressure, and blood sugar level to predict the likelihood of patients developing heart disease. With this added knowledge, doctors can make quicker, more informed decisions about treatment.

Data mining is becoming increasingly important in helping businesses understand their customers. Scouring databases of fan behavior and demographics, professional sports teams like the San Francisco 49ers are able to identify which of their season ticket holders are at the largest risk of not renewing. They can then have their sales people spend extra time with these customers, maximizing the chance of renewal and allocating their limited resources as optimally as possible.

Data mining is also used in the sports gambling world. Professor Mike Orkin's Point Spread Analyzer, mentioned in the previous chapter, allows gamblers to look through hordes of past NFL game data for patterns that give them an advantage over the bookies. The Analyzer looks for patterns, like how team A performs against the spread when they are more than a seven-point underdog, have a losing record, and are at home. Orkin's Point Spread Analyzer can evaluate this question with precision.

So how do home teams fare against the spread when they lost their last game, are at least 7.5-point underdogs, and their winning percentage is less than 10 percent for the season? Over the years from 1993 to 2006, Orkin's software tells us they are a remarkable 26–5 (84 percent) against the spread. Orkin's software picks this pattern out because it is statistically significant, which means there's less than a 5 percent chance that it occurred randomly.

But the problem with the increase in data and computing ability is that we are able to look at larger and larger data sets, meaning it's easier and easier to find patterns that a computer thinks are statistically significant. My simple roulette story illustrates a difficult aspect of data mining. Let's say that Brian had at his disposal an enormous database of the result of every roulette wheel at every casino around the world for a year. And he had his computer do some data mining where it looked for statistically significant patterns. For certain, his computer would find patterns of consecutive spins where red came up an unexpectedly large number of times and the computer deemed it to be non-random. But we know from the nature of the data that the result of each roulette spin is truly independent. There is no statistical significance to these patterns and therefore no predictive value. This is an example where simply trusting what the computer tells us is not enough.

Let's go back to Dr. Orkin and his football data to try and understand how to combat this problem. The math tells us that this home team pattern is not random, meaning it is indicative of something more than variance. And, taking a step beyond the data and looking at what the data represents, the performance of a bunch of human beings, we can say this is not simply like getting 26 reds and 5 blacks on every third Tuesday of the month at 7 p.m. at the roulette wheel. There may be more going on here.

Of course, the first thing I ask Orkin after hearing this crazy trend is, "So how would you have done since 2006 if you had bet on the home team every time this trend surfaced?" Surprisingly, he didn't know the answer. Orkin is not a professional sports bettor; rather, he is an academic who is intellectually curious and fascinated by the concept of data mining in sports. But the past is only valuable if it can help us predict the future, so answering this question is important.

This is dangerous ground for members of the religion of statistics. It is a declaration of this kind without some real-world explanation to back it that inspires quotations like this famous one: "There are three kinds of lies, damned lies and statistics." Originally a quotation from nineteenth-century British Prime Minister Benjamin Disraeli, Mark Twain popularized the aphorism in his book *Chapters From My Autobiography*. It highlights the issues that people often have with the way numbers are presented, but it also reminds us that declaring a trend of this type as significant and truly predictive without some type of qualitative support is a disservice to the statistics community.

So how do we come up with qualitative support for Orkin's trend sufficient enough to justify acting on it?

As soon as he presented it, my mind raced to come up with explanations. In order to come up with anything substantial, I needed to dive deeper into the data. I needed to understand what the data was saying. Since there are only 16 games in an NFL season, a team's winning percentage is seldom less than 10 percent unless they are winless for the season. So for the most part we are talking about winless teams hungry for their first victory of the season.

The second criteria, teams coming off a loss, eliminates those rare occasions where a team is winless after the tenth game of the season and then suddenly musters up the effort to win a game. A team in that situation would likely be due for a letdown the next week. So again this filter makes sense.

The fact that this trend applies only to home teams also seems logical. Imagine you are a winless team. You certainly would get more motivated in front of your home crowd, your fans.

Finally, the last filter where this trend only applies to teams that are at least 7.5-point underdogs likely says more about their opponents than it does the team itself. A team that is favored by more than 7.5 points is likely to take a winless team lightly, and it is highly conceivable that they would not be completely focused for this game. Also, 7.5 points is a key number as the favored team could still feel very much in control of a game when up by seven points, not needing to push the score higher.

So what to do with this bit of knowledge? How do we act upon this information? And even more important, can we build a winning strategy based on it? An important question comes out of our lessons from Chapter 1. Is this trend something that is stable over time? Could we bring down the house by betting on the home team in these situations?

Unfortunately, the answer is not as cut and dried as our blackjack strategy. Yet if you are someone who bets on sports, utilizing this type of data is an important part of improving your results. In other words, echoing Lewis's sentiment about *Moneyball,* use of these statistics will certainly improve your results—they will not make them perfect.

And that is the important lesson here: Incorporating past data into your decision-making process will improve your results. And those that espouse this mantra, regardless of industry, will have a competitive advantage in this new age of information.

Shifting gears away from sports into an industry that affects everyone on a day-to-day basis, let's look at the role analytics is playing in the retail industry. Retailers like Brooks Brothers and the Limited are utilizing data and analytics to gain competitive advantage.[4] For years, these types of retail stores have been collecting data about their sales. They are finally using the data to its full potential. Starting with Orkin-like data mining and then layering in other information, they are able to more accurately predict and optimize their businesses. A good example of this is solving the complex problem of providing the right apparel in the right assortment to their various stores. This is complex because one size and assortment does not fit all stores.

To give some background: Even 15 or 20 years ago, a chain or department store retailer with central planning would routinely send the same number of garments and sizes to each of its stores. In some cases, they wouldn't even make a distinction between categories. For example, each store in the chain would get an identical assortment of dress shirts (say, 25 small, 25 medium, 25 large, and 25 extra large for a total of 100 for each style of dress shirt: button down, spread and straight collar, and two fabric styles), and that same assortment of sizes would be given in golf shirts and in several colors (say, blue, red, green, and white). That is more than 500 shirts arriving at each store for immediate sale. What happened? Some stores sold out of one or two sizes and colors and were stuck with the rest to put on markdown. That is why when you were a kid you got stuck wearing that ugly green shirt that your mom bought on 75 percent clearance. Markdowns were out of control and ate away at the profit.

Stores evolved by necessity into employing simple analytics (aggregating and averaging of past data), and they used a top-down store-average approach. If last year on average they sold 10 small, 15 medium, 30 large, and 45 extra large of the dress shirt line, that is the exact combination they would purchase the next year. The results were marginally better: Instead of 122 small shirts on clearance at a particular store, there might be only 20. This was an improvement from a markdown standpoint, though some stores still sold out of certain sizes and popular colors and were not able to meet customer needs. Those late-arriving customers looking for a popular size or color left the store empty handed and dissatisfied. Naturally, this jeopardized brand loyalty.

So retailers took their use of the past to the next level. Enter high-end predictive analytics to identify each store's different selling patterns and tendencies, ensuring that the right assortment of garments is delivered to each store to meet the exact customer demand for that store. How is this done? It comes down to the data that these retailers have been collecting over decades in their systems—such as point of sale, inventory, and ordering coupled with marketing and pricing history. By mining these systems, as Mike Orkin mined his NFL database, the smart retailer can get a good view of how items move through the supply chain and through the store itself (from the full-price racks to the discount racks). In the above dress shirt example, the retailer looks at dress shirt sales over the years to start to understand what, when, and how they are sold. Combine that history with what else is purchased on the same receipt and the retailer gets a "market basket" analysis of what else sells with dress shirts (such as, for each shirt sold, two ties and one pair of slacks leaves the store). This alone provides great value to improving assortment and inventory, but still is just a small part of the picture.

The sophisticated retailers layer in other data from outside their systems to complete the picture. The layered information will carry demographics (age and gender), behavioral information (usage and loyalty), and psychographics (interests and lifestyles) for the population that surrounds the store. They will bring in economic and market trends (very important in today's economic climate), weather predictions, and local and world events that can affect sales. This view allows the retailer to become more accurate when predicting future sales trends.

The retailer uses all the information the analytical models feed it and creates store, product, and customer profiles. These profiles then are grouped, or "clustered," by the common variables that drive the item sales. So, in the shirt example, a retailer may find that out of 1,500 stores, it has a selection of 55 stores that appear to have sales characteristics in common with one another but different from the other store groupings.

Using the specific store data, the retailer knows that the store has a shirt profile that sells predominantly medium and large shirts over five colors and three fabric textures. Layering in the additional data, from its own customer base and from readily available third-party sources of demographic and psychographic information, the retailer finds out *why* this is happening, similarly to how we determined why the home team was covering so often in Orkin's scenario. Perhaps the stores are located in areas with a relatively high proportion of young, single males ages 21–35, who shop at the store two to three times per month and are interested in fitness and men's fashion (evidenced by a markedly large number of subscriptions to *Men's Fitness* and *GQ* in the area).

Knowing all this, the system can recommend to the store's buyer that the "standard" size assortment in those stores should be disproportionately medium and large, and that a particular store in this cluster should have an assortment of 15 small, 60 medium, 75 large, and 30 extra large, and those shirts should be fashion forward (latest styles), offered in four different colors (lavender, burgundy, black, and off white), and three types of fabrics (flat, sheen, and textured) in all three categories. A lower-volume store with a similar customer profile might get the same proportions but in a lesser quantity. But a store with a more conservative or older customer base might get a completely different assortment and might not receive a particular style of shirt at all.

Note that the analytics supplement but do not replace the skill of the buyer. Getting the right assortment of the wrong goods still means the store will underperform. But using analytics greatly increases the "win" when the buyer gets it right and reduces the loss when the buyer gets it wrong.

Why go through all this analysis to make sure that the right assortment is available in the stores? Recent research shows that reducing out-of-stocks and the number of garments that are put on clearance can boost store sales and profitability. In one case the increment gain for each store is $3,850 in sales and $2,150 in profit. This seems small for all the work done, but take this incremental lift across the entire chain. The results become $6,160,000 in sales and $3,440,000 in profit for only one garment category, a dress shirt![5] This is just for dress shirts; do not forget the ties and slacks that are generally sold with them. There are few hundred fashion categories in retail, from dress shirts to women's dresses. The numbers add up rapidly and so do the profits. Retailers that look to their history and use it to predict their future gain a competitive market advantage just as a card counter uses the past to gain a competitive advantage at the table.

As card counters, we learned how important data and past information are to predicting the future. It has direct parallels in business, where better, smarter decisions can be made across all levels of an organization. Whether you are a card counter trying to beat blackjack, a sports bettor trying to figure out whether to bet the home team, or a retailer trying to reduce markdowns, the answer can almost always be found in the data.

For card counters the data—the past—was all that mattered. Knowing the cards that had been played was key to overcoming the House Advantage. This fundamental lesson provided the foundation for our incredibly data-driven culture. Enhancing this data-driven culture is something I have preached throughout my professional life.

This is the fundamental takeaway from card counting. Data matters, and your organization should proceed with that mantra at its core. Look to incorporate data into all of your decisions. Challenge yourselves to use data in every scenario imaginable. By creating a culture where data is embraced you will find answers for questions you never thought to ask.

As you try to establish a House Advantage within your life or business, think about what historical data is available to you. Likely you have been capturing information that you are ignoring or not utilizing. The average blackjack player ignores cards that have been played, but Thorp's breakthrough made us understand how costly that ignorance was. Likewise, retailers vastly improved their margins when they stopped ignoring their past and looked deeply into the data to find the key decision points that engendered profitability.

If you don't have data readily available to you, create an infrastructure to start collecting data. This may seem like a daunting task, but it is the first step toward better decision making. Having more information is clearly better than having less, and the sooner you start collecting the data, the sooner you will be able to make better decisions. Two key questions to ask yourself are: What do I wish I knew to help me make a better decision? How might I get this information from trusted, unbiased sources?

As you contemplate the importance of data and its role in your life, think about who you'd rather be: the learned card counter sitting at the blackjack table with full knowledge that there are lots of tens and aces left in the deck, or the foolish roulette player hoping against hope that that next spin turns up black.

3

THINK LIKE A SCIENTIST

You're a doctor, Izzie. A scientist. Think like a scientist.

—Denny Duquette, *Grey's Anatomy*

ONE OF THE most common questions people ask me when looking for advice about how to win at blackjack is, "How do you deal with the other people at your table?"

"What do you mean?" I sometimes ask.

"You know, when someone's at your table screwing things up for you."

I like to play dumb in these situations to get them to help me illustrate their point. "What do you mean by 'screwing things up'?"

"Well, you know, when some schmuck hits on a 12 or something when he isn't supposed to and they take the dealer's bust card."

What they mean is that someone at the blackjack table doesn't act using basic strategy, which would never advise this move. This "schmuck" happens to get a 10, thereby busting and automatically losing his hand. Then, the dealer flips her hole card and reveals a 10 to make 16 and draws a 5 to make 21. In the mind of most people, this means the other person at the table screwed everyone else over by taking the dealer's 10. If the schmuck had done the right thing and decided not to hit, the dealer would have received the 10 and would have busted. And everyone at the table would have won.

But there's a problem with that logic. Imagine that those two cards were reversed and the same schmuck had instead received a 5 to give him a hand of 17. And, imagine the dealer in turn received a 10 instead of the 5 and busted. In this case, the player would have saved the table with his equally dumb decision.

The person asking me this question is exhibiting something called confirmation bias.

He only remembers the times when the schmuck and his decisions hurt him and forgets all about the times he benefited. When you look at the situation objectively, you realize the cards are randomly in the mix, and the chance of the schmuck doing something that hurts versus something that helps is equally random.

The same rules apply in business strategy. Around you, others will make decisions and their results will vary, but you still have to stay on course. In a bit of good fortune, when I moved to Chicago to work at O'Connor, the Grand Victoria Casino opened about 40 miles away in Elgin, Illinois. I was a regular there in those days, playing blackjack for countless hours almost every weekend. There's an old saying: The further you get from Vegas, the less knowledgeable the players become. In Elgin, at any rate, this old intuition felt spot on. Understandably, most people don't really know basic strategy. They might try to employ what seems like common sense or intuition or some other strategy, but the important point is it's just not basic strategy. There are some decisions you make when following basic strategy that are mathematically correct but are simply counterintuitive. Sometimes math tells you to do strange things to maximize your opportunities.

On one Saturday in Elgin, I was playing with three teammates who had flown in from Boston for a "business trip." Our business trips did not take place in conference rooms or convention centers but in casinos like the Grand Victoria. After a few hours of play, I was about even for the night but anxious to make some money so we could stop playing and head into Chicago for some cocktails. So, when I noticed my friend Tom signaling me to his table, I was anxious to start putting some big money down. As I walked up to the table, I heard Tom turn to the woman on his left and say, "I really like your *ring*."

I sidled up to the table and touched my nose, signaling to him that I understood his compliment was really for me. "Ring" was part of our code. What Tom really meant was the count at the table was 14. I looked at the number of cards in the discard rack and calculated that I should bet two hands of the table maximum of $2,000. As I placed my chips in the betting circles, a man to my left wearing a Cubs hat spoke up. "Hey man, we're on a good run. Do you mind waiting until she shuffles again?"

This was not an uncommon request as gamblers are an inherently superstitious set. Unfortunately, it was a request that, if complied with, would ruin our team's strategy. If I waited until the dealer shuffled, then I would be starting back at square one and would have lost my edge over the casino. The information Tom gathered for me would be useless. With the count at 14, I had more than a 2 percent advantage over the casino. I had to play right away.

"Sorry man. I got a good feeling about this hand; I'm going to jump in," I said and put my two stacks of $2,000 into each betting circle.

"Rich asshole," the Cubs fan muttered.

The dealer, unmoved by the new tension before her, dealt me an ace and a 10 as my first two cards. The next three cards dealt after my hand were a 5 to the Cubs fan, a 6 to my friend Tom, and a 10 to the woman with the ring.

Cubs fan was quick to react: "See, you took my ace and made us take her 6," he said, pointing to Tom's 6 as the dealer continued to dole out the second set of cards. Cubs fan was trying to revise history, argu-ing that if I hadn't sat down moments before, he would have received that first ace and the 6 that Tom received would have gone instead back to the dealer.

I didn't respond and hoped that ignoring him might make him shut up. But it turned out to be the cards that helped accomplish just that. I got a 7 on my ace and then a jack on my 10 while Cubs fan was dealt a 6 on top of his 5. As the deal continued, the dealer revealed a 6 as her up card and all was wonderful in the world.

Cubs fan now had a great starting hand of 11 against the best possible card the dealer could have—a 6. Yet, there was no admission or apology from him, and what I was about to do was going to ensure that he and I would not be breaking bread anytime too soon.

I put another stack of purple chips next to my ace and 7 and told the dealer I would be doubling. I think if Cubs fan had a gun he would have shot me right then. "What are you doing, man?" he practically squealed.

"I'm doubling," I answered in earnest, as if he didn't already know.

"Have you ever played this game before? You have 18 already," he reminded me.

He was referencing what he considered to be my basic strategy mistake. But, in reality, doubling down on soft 18 here was absolutely the right play and not something that I would ever think twice about doing.

"Don't be greedy man. Leave the 10 for me," he pleaded.

I looked up at the dealer, hoping she would deal the next card quickly. She did, and the 10 that Cubs fan was waiting for never showed up. Instead, an ace landed on my ace/7, giving me a solid total of 19. Cubs fan quieted as he realized that if I had not doubled my hand, he would have received the ace and would have had a very poor total of 12.

"Eleven?" the dealer called as she looked to Cubs fan for a signal. He moved another $25 chip next to his first $25 chip, signifying that he, too, wanted to double. The dealer flipped a king onto his eleven, giving him an unbeatable hand of 21.

"Thank god there was another 10 left in there," he said, still apparently disgusted.

Tom and the ring woman both stood their hands and the dealer flipped her whole card. She revealed a 5 to go with her 6, giving her the dangerous total of 11. "Jesus Chr-," Cubs fan started to say, again almost under his breath. But, before he could get the next part of the savior's name out of his mouth, the dealer flipped an ace to give herself a total of 12. Since she did not yet have 17, she had to deal herself another card. Adding to the drama, she pulled not a normal card but the yellow cut card that signified the end of the "shoe." (Technically, the shoe is the physical container that the six decks of cards are placed in and dealt from but more colloquially it means the entirety of the six decks. The end of the shoe describes the last few cards or hands of the six decks before the dealer shuffles and starts all over again.) Unfazed by the suspension, she coolly placed the yellow card to the side and dealt herself the next card. It was a 10, for a total of 22. She busted; elation swept over the table.

Cubs fan, by contrast, was now uncharacteristically silent as the dealer doled out my $6,000 and his $50. I rose from the table to leave, as I could see one of my other teammates signaling me from across the pit. I gathered my chips and started to walk away. About five strides from the table, I heard Cubs fan turn to Tom to commiserate. "What a jerk!" he complained.

Tom replied enthusiastically. "Yeah, total asshole. Next time he comes over, we'll just all drop out so he has to play alone. Last thing we need is that guy screwing up our table."

I smiled to myself, as Tom and I both knew he was setting up a very profitable future situation for us. If they all dropped out of the table when he called me back, I would have a unique opportunity to play through all the good cards by myself. Essentially, Tom and the others at the table would eat all the bad cards and then I would go in and play only the good ones. I was also smiling because Tom was just fueling Cubs fan's confirmation bias. Even though everyone at the table won on the hand that I jumped in, Cubs fan would surely never remember that part of the story. The thing he would remember, and the thing he would surely repeat to his buddies back home, would be the rich, greedy jerk who jumped into his table and took his ace.

Confirmation bias is by no means limited to the blackjack table. It is present anywhere there is an ill-conceived notion that needs equally ill-conceived proof. It's a quirk of human nature that we all have a natural tendency to notice data that supports our point and ignore data that conflicts with it. That's why it's so important to impose a truly holistic, analytical approach when trying to confirm a theory or hypothesis. It's a natural, human response when we see a set of data to concoct a narrative, a story that gives us an explanation. But, unfortunately, sometimes we cling with more force to the story than the actual data and unconsciously accept that which comports with what we have decided to believe and ignore that which conflicts.

For instance, the guy who was convinced that a schmuck's mistakes and misinformation always hurt good players at the blackjack table could give up his confirmation bias and try to take a thoughtful, analytical approach to finding out if his theory were true. His first step would be to collect meaningful data. He might carry a pencil and notebook with him to the table and each time he sat with a schmuck record exactly what happened. He might note down a "1" when the schmuck's decision helped and a "-1" when it hurt.

Of course, the data collection might need to be a bit more complicated or nuanced than this, but the long and short of it is, at the end of his data collection, he would have an objective history from which he could draw conclusions. In other words, he wouldn't only have his inescapably subjective version of history.

If everyone had this much discipline, then we'd have a world without confirmation bias and, likely, a world without other ridiculous things like unconfirmed conspiracy theories. Most conspiracy theories are indeed examples of confirmation bias; otherwise intelligent human beings ignore facts and concoct their own version of history to confirm a dramatic hypothesis, like 9/11 being an inside job by the Bush administration, or we never really landed on the Moon. Of course, there *are* many unanswered questions surrounding both events, but the main flaw in the analytical work of conspirators is an undivided focus on facts that support a theory and confirm a bias.

When the questioner ignores the times that a schmuck's wrong decision actually helps him, he makes the same mistake as conspiracy theorists. The conspiracy theorist cites as one of his supporting facts for the Bush conspiracy theory that there were next to no signs of plane wreckage near the Pentagon and no indication of what happened to the plane's wing. This is in direct conflict to what Allyn E. Kilsheimer, the first structural engineer to arrive at the Pentagon after Flight 77 crashed, reported. He remarked that he "saw the marks of the plane wing on the face of the building" and that he had picked up parts of the plane distinguished by airline markings. He further said that he held the tail section of the plane in his hand and even found the black box.[1]

The conspiracy theorist ignores these facts, of course, because they don't support his theory.

Although equating a superstitious gambler's behavior with that of a conspiracy theorist may seem like a stretch, it is an important illustration of the dangers of decisions based on an incomplete or faulty data set. If conspiracy buffs actually recorded and recognized all the data, the staunchness of their belief would likely dissipate as rapidly as the legitimacy of their ideas.

All fun with conspiracy theories aside, confirmation bias can have a truly destructive side when business leaders fall prey and let it influence their decisions. Enron CEO Jeff Skilling, the man at the center of one of the largest corporate scandals in history, was a clear victim of confirmation bias. During his trial, the testimony of two former Enron managers highlighted his arguably near-pathological refusal to gather all the facts.[2]

Paula H. Rieker, initially a high-level executive in corporate relations and later the corporate secretary, did not correct Skilling when he reported false information to analysts often because she was afraid of his reaction. "My prior interactions with him had just conditioned me that he didn't want to be corrected," she said during her testimony in Skilling's federal trial.[3]

Enron's managing director of research, Vince Kaminski, consistently voiced concern about the company's questionable financial practices. And while Kaminski said initially he had a strong relationship with Skilling, his interactions became less frequent as Kaminski "found out it wasn't very useful trying to argue with him."[4]

Their testimony demonstrates how Skilling appeared to want only data and input that affirmed his preconceived notions. Later in the trial, Skilling's own testimony exposed his error beyond any doubt. Skilling revealed that he "increasingly sought validation for what he believed" and did not listen to what he was told of the company's problems.

In June 2001, Skilling sought validation that Enron's involvement in California's newly deregulated electricity market was copasetic. Skilling told Enron lawyer Richard Sanders that they had to be "absolutely pure as the driven snow," emphasizing that desire by repeating, "So one more time. We're pure as the driven snow, right?"

Even after being told that some of Enron's trading strategies were found to have contributed to market manipulation, Skilling continued to seek assurance from Sanders. When Sanders replied that legal had ordered the termination of the aforementioned questionable trading strategies immediately upon discovery, Skilling once again felt comfort that Enron was beyond scrutiny. He stated again, "O.K. So we're as pure as the driven snow?"[5]

Skilling was so hell-bent on confirming his pristine image of Enron that he failed to listen to the facts that may obviously have indicated otherwise. Rather than seeing all the data and viewpoints, he only saw those that supported his confirmation bias. The result, of course, was one of the largest corporate scandals we have ever seen.

Probably because it's also a human tendency to look for bad apples when something terrible happens, rather than have to think that whole systems might be flawed, we all might collectively want to think of Skilling as a calculating monster. But there was a lot more going on: tempting incentives, pressure from every end to inflate stock prices, and a human desire to ignore difficult facts. In other words, a bad situation more than a bad character was really at fault. But this situation was made worse by Skilling's confirmation bias.

So, how can we avoid confirmation bias? In Skilling's case, he could have simply listened to the experts around him, whom he hired for their thoughtful, dissenting viewpoints. He might have heeded their warnings. Rather than refuse conflicting data, he could have embraced it.

Studies show people are twice as likely to seek out information that confirms their beliefs than they are to consider evidence that contradicts them.[6] So, avoiding confirmation bias is not simple, as it seems to be part of our very make-up, but it is essential to long-term business success.

Business experts espouse organizational structures that allow for free information flow between executives and those closer to the problems. The logic is simple: Allowing more members of an organization to have input in strategic decision making ensures decisions that incorporate more information rather than less.

In investing, where confirmation bias can cause you to hold on to a losing investment for far too long, experts suggest several tricks designed to give you a fresh perspective to truly analyze your investment choice. Michael Mauboussin, chief investment strategist at Legg Mason Capital Management, suggests that before you make an investment decision, consider the probability that this is a bad decision. Perhaps there's a 20 percent chance that you have made the wrong call. Then if the investment does go awry, you can find solace that this was the one in five times that the decision went against you and you can more easily admit that you may have made a mistake.[7]

Another suggested trick is a pre-commitment strategy. Before buying the stock in the first place, write down some factors or events that might happen that would cause you to change your mind on a trade.[8]

For example, you decided to buy stock in Apple but decide that if CEO Steve Jobs leaves day-to-day operation of the company or Microsoft starts making a competitor to the iPhone, you will sell your Apple stock. If either of these events occurs and the stock starts to tank, it will be easy for you to cut your losses since you've already committed to that decision.

All of these are simply psychological exercises designed to allow you to make an objective, data-driven decision. But you needn't resort to trickery; instead, discipline yourself to collect all the relevant data and use it to make an informed decision. My challenge to the questioner from the beginning of the chapter was to improve his data-collection process and actually document the consequence of every "bad" decision another player made at his table. With a more complete data set, it would be hard for him to continue to worry about the schmucks at his table.

Likewise, Jeff Skilling should have spent more time with his employees and documented their fears and concerns. Perhaps he could have categorized the new information in a way that would have made it easier for him to be objective. Something as simple as a fraud versus no-fraud vote among his employees may have been able to help him overcome his confirmation bias.

At a recent sports conference, Houston Rockets general manager Daryl Morey, who we'll discuss in more detail later in the book, talked about his organizational philosophy: "I want people that will challenge my point of view and aren't afraid to argue their point with me." Unlike Skilling, Morey welcomes dissent, and that helps him avoid confirmation bias.

All of this is easier said than done, and, again, my position is shaped by the perfect world of blackjack—a game where math can easily prove a confirmation bias to be nothing more than a hoax. Yet, the lesson of trying to see the whole story rather than just your particular version is as valuable in blackjack as it is in business.

In the previous chapter we discussed the importance of using data and history to make decisions, but our cautionary confirmation bias tales tell us that a limited view of the past is worse than a failure to take the past into account. Any type of history that fails to capture a whole picture spells a plethora of problems.

Another similar and dangerous bias is that of selection. The classic example of selection bias comes to us from World War II. American military personnel, when evaluating returning planes damaged during warfare, noticed that "some parts of planes were hit by enemy fire more often than other parts." Analyzing the pattern of bullet holes in the returning planes, they decided to have these areas reinforced to withstand enemy fire better.[9]

Seems logical enough, but there is a clear problem with their analysis. Because they only get to see the planes that survived, they are only looking at a portion of the planes that were hit. Even more problematic, the planes that they are not seeing are the more important sample to look at. Since the damage inflicted on those planes prevented them from returning back to the base, it is imperative to look at them to determine what areas on the plane are critical to reinforce.

Their mistake is a clear case of selection bias as they are drawing incorrect conclusions by only looking at a selection of the data. Business analysts make a similar mistake when they look only to successful companies or leaders to unearth supposed keys to success.[10] Freek Vermuelen, London Business School professor of strategic and international management, discusses the danger of selection bias, debunking the myth that "innovation projects require diverse, cross-functional teams." The myth exists because analysis shows that successful "path-breaking innovation projects" are "often staffed by such teams."

Some experts believe the opposite to be true; that diverse, cross-functional teams are responsible for some of the biggest failures in history. However, the teams that failed produced nothing, and examination of only successful innovations would exclude the diverse, cross-functional teams that failed. This analysis produces results that skew toward the big wins produced by the diverse, cross-functional teams while ignoring the big losses. The reality is that, "on average, the homogenous teams—although not responsible for the few really big inventions—might have done better; always producing a reliable, good set of results."[11]

This lesson of selection bias, sometimes referred to as survivor bias, is important as we look at what makes a successful leader. The macho CEO, think former General Electric CEO and chairman Jack Welch, who takes risks and uses intuition rather than careful analysis, is often lauded as we examine their various successes. "However, risk, by definition, leads some to succeed but it also leads quite a few of them to fail and slip into oblivion."[12] Again, we never hear about the ones who failed, instead only seeing those who flourished—the survivors. By random variance some of the risk-taking leaders will come out on top, and unfortunately our selection bias will prevent us from knowing if their attitude is what caused their success.

Likewise, if our military personnel had looked at all the planes, not just the ones that survived, they would have drawn significantly different conclusions about what areas to patch up. Like confirmation bias, selection bias is a great example of why it is not enough to simply look at data from the past—you have to look at *all* the data from the past. Choosing the correct sample for your data can be as important as the decision to use data in the first place.

How can you ensure that you are looking at the *right* data? The simplest answer is that you need to make sure you are looking at all of the data, not just a portion of it. In order for us to be successful as card counters, we needed to see every card that had been dealt. We couldn't walk up to a table after four rounds had already been dealt and start to count the cards. Likewise, we had an objective strategy that we followed to a tee and did not get swayed by subjective notions that may or may not have actually had any real predictive value. We knew that the data we captured—the cards we counted—would truly help us predict our chances of winning and losing.

So as we look to create some rules around collecting data that can help you avoid common mistakes, let's start with rules that would help avoid our aforementioned biases. To avoid confirmation bias, it is impor-tant to objectively look at all data, not just the data that supports your hypotheses. To avoid selection bias, you need to have a comprehensive data set—not a set that intentionally or unintentionally excludes a sub-set of the population. In both cases, the rule of thumb is to try to look at as much data as possible.

But this raises an interesting concern. Not all data is created equal. In fact some data—even when objective and holistic in nature—can have very little predictive value. And that really is the main characteris-tic we want from our data. It needs to help us predict the future.

A great example of objective, holistic data that has little predic-tive value comes to us from the world of professional sports. Imagine we give Cubs fan a new task—to tell us what makes a football team successful. Cubs fan, being a believer in the lessons of the House Advantage, understands that the first step to answering this ques-tion is to look to the past. He has some preconceived notions, having watched football for many years, but he now understands confirma-tion bias and knows that he has to look as objectively as possible at the data collecting. Furthermore, he understands that only looking at data from successful football teams would put him back into a morass of selection bias. So he decides to look at data from all teams regard-less of record.

What he finds is that there is a high correlation between rushing attempts and winning. From 1995 to 2008, teams that have a running back with more than 30 rushing attempts in a game have won 84 per-cent of the time while teams with a quarterback throwing the ball more than 40 times have won only 28 percent of the time. This is backed up by the correlation coefficients[13] of pass (-0.16) and rush (0.55) attempts to winning over this same time frame.[14]

So our data tells us that teams that attempt more running plays win more games. But is this finding useful? Can we make the state-ment that running on every play will give a team a better chance of winning? Of course not. In fact, Aaron Schatz, one of the pioneers in advanced analytics for football, challenged this assertion and asked if it was possible that the causation actually ran the other way. Maybe teams that were leading games were running because they were winning and not vice versa. Instead of looking at rushing in the entire game, Schatz looked only at rushing in the first half. He saw little to no correlation between those yards and winning. The correlation grew much stronger when he included second-half rushing.

This was enough to help him draw the conclusion that while rushing is correlated to winning, it is not causal. Running the ball more does not cause you to win games. It is simply a byproduct of the fact that you are ahead in the game and want to take time off the clock in a conservative way.

Understanding the difference between causation versus correlation is a crucially important lesson because it is an important key to understanding the predictive value of data.

If you isolate the two words, it is easy to understand the difference. Causal means that event *a* causes event *b*: For instance, smoking cigarettes causes cancer. The relationship between smoking and cancer is causal. It is also correlated, since people who smoke have a high incidence of cancer. Correlation simply means that there is a reciprocal relationship between the two variables.

But two things can be correlated and not causal. Many people who are alcoholics, for example, are also smokers. These two behaviors are frequently seen together and, therefore, are correlated. But, smoking does not necessarily cause alcoholism or vice versa.

So why does this matter to the religion of statistics?

For some, the difference between causal and correlated is an almost religious argument. It relates to the discussion in Chapter 2 about data mining. Over the last few decades, two camps have emerged in the analytical movement—the computer people and the statisticians. The computer people tend to focus on things like data mining and look for patterns that are correlated. The problem they encounter is that because data sets are increasingly large and can be quickly analyzed in a variety of ways through computing, patterns may emerge as a function of merely looking at a large data set, and these patterns may be misinterpreted as stemming from a fundamental cause, rather than from random chance. They do not necessarily worry about whether the relationships they discover are truly causal. The statisticians believe much more in the power of modeling and testing, independent of utilizing large sets of data.

Mike Orkin and his Point Spread Analyzer looked for variables in football games that were correlated. In our Chapter 2 story about winless home teams, we had many different factors driving a trend. These factors were correlated but were they actually causal? The average computer person might say it doesn't matter much, since there is a statistically significant correlation. But the statistics person would never simply accept this. He would want to find a way to test this theory with independent trials or with a model utilizing other data from the season.

What truly matters here is whether the pattern or correlation you observe has some predictive value. Ultimately, what we really care about is answering whether a relationship can help predict the future.

It's similar to a business segmenting customers based on demographics and psychographics. With the amount of data and complex computer software available, modern businesses are able to locate which characteristics are correlated with the best customers. But, what we cannot immediately tell is whether these relationships are causal or correlated. In some respects, I'm not sure if that's the important question. Take a professional football team like the 49ers trying to figure out who its most profitable fans are on game day. Scouring their database, the marketing guys find that their largest revenues come from fans who ride bicycles to work. As they look closer into the data, they realize that most fans who ride bicycles to work often don't own cars and therefore have no means to tailgate before and after games. These fans tend to show up earlier, leave later, and spend more money on concessions. Since they don't have to worry about driving home, they also spend more money on beer.

In this case, riding a bike to work does not cause the fan to be more profitable, but the fact that they ride a bicycle to work is predictive of their potential revenue. The actual variable that causes this high revenue is the lack of car, yet that is hidden in the data. This type of variable is called a confounding variable. Finding the confounding variable can help you in a range of business scenarios if it is predictable.

Sometimes you will have a causal relationship that is useless to you because the variable itself is too difficult to predict. Let's go back to our study on what determines winning and losing in the NFL. Even more than rushing attempts, turnover margin (correlation coefficient of 0.67)[15] is correlated strongly with winning. This is intuitive, of course, as anyone who has watched a football game understands that a turnover is bad.

And certainly we all understand that this relationship is causal as well as correlated—turning the ball over causes you to lose. While this all makes sense and no one would argue that turnovers cause winning—or, in this case, losing—the problem is, turnovers are a difficult thing to control. Every professional football player understands the importance of turnovers and certainly would do his best to prevent them regardless of what the statistics would advise. This rhetoric reinforces the importance of turnovers, but it is useless unless you can really control them.

So, what is useful about the turnover insight? If I could predict which team would turn over the ball more in any given game, I could predict the winner in a high percentage of football games. I would move to Vegas and bring down the house all over again. The problem, though, comes when I try to predict which team will be plus two in turnovers. Turning to our friend Dr. Bob again, we learn a key lesson. In an e-mail to me, he states that interceptions and fumbles are about 65 percent and 90 percent random, respectively. For fumbles this means that if a team has been +1 in fumbles so far this season, you would expect that they would be +0.1 in fumbles per game going forward. Bob states that turnovers are the strongest indicator to point spread success or failure but also the most random statistic to predict. Because of that inconsistency, turnovers present inefficiencies for the sports bettor to exploit. By understanding the random nature of turnovers, smart sports bettors can look for value by betting on teams that have had the worst of the turnovers and are going against teams that have been fortunate in the turnover department. In other words, if you find teams that have poor records due to lots of interceptions and fumbles, they are likely to be undervalued by the public. Similarly, teams that have good records due to very few turnovers are likely to be overvalued. Dr. Bob jokes that "if the public understood the random nature of turnovers, then I might be out of a job."

In a nutshell, turnovers have little predictive value. They are an example of a tremendously correlated and causal variable to winning that is almost impossible to predict and therefore is of very limited use from an analytics standpoint.

In understanding how to apply this lesson to business, it is useful to look at interest rates as the financial analogy to turnovers. Like turnovers, changes in interest rates have enormous impact on winning and losing in finance. If you could predict the direction in which interest rates were going to move, you could likewise predict the direction of stocks and bonds.

But the problem is that interest rates, like turnovers, are very difficult to accurately predict. And while they are an important part of any financial model, creating strategies that hinge on you knowing in which direction rates are going is a bit of financial roulette—it's simply too hard to predict.

In fact, many successful traders devise strategies that profit regardless of which way rates move, knowing that the game of predicting rates is simply too difficult to win. And that is the key. To win using analytics, you must focus on variables where the past really does help you predict the future. Unfortunately, turnovers and interest rates do not fit into that category.

In a sense, that is the true lesson of this chapter. A simple focus on the past is not enough to give you a competitive advantage using analytics. There are some important caveats to how you should use the experiences of the past to guide your future decisions.

We need to look objectively at the past; otherwise we leave ourselves vulnerable to inherent biases. The best way to achieve this is to borrow from science—specifically, the scientific method. Defined as the process used by scientists to investigate and discover, the scientific method's guidelines center on an objective approach to analyzing observable, empirical, and measurable evidence. This approach is especially useful when applying analytics to finance.

Renaissance Technologies, founded by Jim Simons, is the most successful hedge fund that you've likely never heard of. Since 1989, the company's Medallion Fund has averaged 35 percent annual returns after fees,[16] placing it in the lead spot among all hedge funds. Renaissance "utilizes computer technical models to exploit mispricings in financial markets."[17]

Simons comes from the world of academia, where his Ph.D. in mathematics earned him teaching jobs at both MIT and Harvard University. He left that world in 1978 to begin his career in finance, but he did not leave the important lessons of science behind him. Although not much is known about the fund, due to Simons's distaste for publicity, one clear fact is that Simons embraces the use of the scientific method in finance.

"We don't hire people from Wall Street," says Simons. "We hire people who have done good science."[18]

Simons further explains his hiring philosophy: "The advantage scientists bring into the game is less their mathematical or computational skills than their ability to think scientifically. They are less likely to accept an apparent winning strategy that might be a mere statistical fluke."[19]

"Think like a scientist" is a good slogan for you to remember as you try to gain the House Advantage in your business. Certainly a good scientist would not fall for confirmation bias or design experiments subject to selection bias. Their training and education would not allow it.

Also, as Simons references, scientists are taught to question their results. This healthy skepticism creates an environment where data that is truly predictive wins out over all other data. It's not uncommon for a scientist to test many different variables in an experiment before choosing the relevant ones based on their performance.

A scientist would not simply trust an experiment that said that rushing yards were correlated to winning; instead they would question the underlying meaning of that statement, thereby uncovering the flaw in the experiment's design.

Finally, a scientist is pressed to find practical applications for their work, and if those practical applications do not exist they would look for other areas to pursue. Our scientist would uncover the difficulty of predicting turnovers and interest rates and then would move on to other indicators that were easier to predict.

Using the past to predict the future is an elementary lesson of analytics, but it certainly is not an elementary process. In order to truly harness the power of the past, it helps to remember the lessons of the scientist focused on objective data, meaningful results, and practical applications. Simons sums it up well: "We don't start with models. We start with data. We don't have any preconceived notions."[20] Learning those lessons and remembering Simons's words will help you gain the House Advantage.

4

THE IMPORTANCE OF ASKING QUESTIONS

He who asks a question is a fool for five minutes; he who does not ask a question remains a fool forever.

—Chinese Proverb

HAVING ESTABLISHED THE power of data—and not just any old data, but the right data—we need to take the next step and understand what to do with it. Data itself is only an enabler, as important as it is. Data can tell you nothing unless you know the right questions to ask. Having clarity on the right types of questions to ask is known as having the correct frame, and this is central to the overall investigative process.

There are many different statistical methods that people like Mike Orkin, Ed Thorp, and Billy Beane employ to manipulate data. Orkin used data mining to find statistically significant patterns in NFL data to beat the bookies. Thorp used Monte Carlo simulations to determine an optimal strategy for blackjack and card counting. Billy Beane and his A's team used regression techniques on historic data to project the future. While this may sound complicated, in truth, it's marvelously simple.

icient in basic statistical techniques can do this kind of
act of running a regression or using data mining soft-
art. The hard part, and perhaps more important one,
to challenge convention and ask the right questions
about the data regardless of what you fear it will tell you.

For many years, gamblers accepted their fate: They would win some and lose some, and in the end they would often lose more than they won at the blackjack table. Ed Thorp changed all of that by asking simple questions like, How do the odds of blackjack change when there are no 2s left in the deck? How about when there are no 3s left? Then he repeated the question with 4s and 5s all the way up to aces. This was the key insight that unlocked the problem. His entire card-counting strategy was built off a few very simple but relevant questions.

Of course, Thorp's creative brilliance (combined with his enviable resources) allowed him to do what gamblers had not been able to do before—create a simulation of a deck with no 2s, a deck with no 3s, and so on. With advances in technology since the 1960s, that resource advantage has virtually vanished. But understanding the right questions to ask is still as important as ever.

Likewise, the Oakland A's and Billy Beane challenged the baseball world with their assertion that statistics and not scouts might be a more complete way to predict future performance. He asked the key question, What historical data will best tell me how successful a player will be in professional baseball? Beane further asked the question, Do college or high school players have a more predictable path to success in professional baseball? The answers to these questions were all in the data and helped Beane devise a strategy where they would look to draft college players based on statistics such as On-Base Percentage. Again, once the key issue or frame was identified, the process they went through in search of the answer was completely straightforward.

Michael Lewis, mentioned earlier as the author of *Moneyball*, has written many other pieces on statistical geniuses both in sports and finance. Over lunch, he shared with me some insight on the commonality of all his "genius" subjects. Lewis began with the perhaps expected litany of universal character traits: smart, analytical, geeky. His voice then grew markedly and defied my expectations by finishing emphatically with, "creative."

"They [all] have a way of looking at numbers in a truly *creative* way. They understand the right questions to ask to let numbers solve these problems," Lewis explained.[1]

At the start of any decision-making process, whether it is perceived as analytical or intuitive, is a question or set of questions asked by someone seeking truth. This is called the "decision frame," and it is the first step in the decision-making process. Getting clarity on the core issue being addressed is the key to making good decisions. And it often requires creativity and a fresh perspective. Obtaining the correct frame has three interwoven components. First, purpose—what you hope to accomplish. In the case of Beane, he sought a better method for predicting baseball success. Second, scope—what to include or exclude in arriving at the decision. Beane decided to include past performance statistics and exclude aesthetic qualities. He reduced the scope of his search to data on performance. Third, perspective—your point of view in approaching this decision and how others might approach it. In this instance, Beane's perspective was that he believed aesthetics were misleading, even irrelevant. Rather it was the past performance, measured by relevant statistics, and by looking at the statistics alone that one can calculate baseball worth and predict baseball success.

In that sense having the right decision frame is not unlike taking a picture with a zoom camera: What we want to take the picture of is the purpose, what is included in the shot is the scope, and what angle we take the picture from is the perspective. Beane was already halfway to success when his key insight led to a frame that defined his search for a statistical method, focused on individual results that would enable him to grade and evaluate baseball worth. With that in hand, he had the filter to start looking for potential solutions.

Even people we would never consider "stats people" are guilty of using this process. Take NFL legend Bill Parcells. Parcells is considered one of the most successful professional coaches of the modern era. In addition to his coaching prowess, Parcells is a very successful team executive and has helped turn around franchises like the New York Jets, the Dallas Cowboys, and the Miami Dolphins. However, no one will be writing a football version of *Moneyball* about Parcells's strategies. He simply is not known as a guy who makes data-driven decisions. In one of his many famous quotes, Parcells laments the process of drafting as "an inexact science." His public persona is one of a man who knows football intuitively, who would be able to motivate virtually anyone to do anything and at any time.

And yet, Parcells displays a subtle analytical side, using rules of thumb developed by years of unconscious data observation, showing that these strategies can influence how you make decisions even if numbers are not your forte. When interviewed during halftime at the Jets/Dolphins game on October, 12, 2009, Parcells listed his top four criteria for drafting quarterbacks:

1. He must be a college senior;
2. He must be a graduate;
3. He must be a three-year starter;
4. He must have at least 23 wins.

These are all logical demands as they represent key indicators of important traits of an ideal quarterback. The first criterion indicates the importance of age and maturity. A senior has had four years to mature and learn at the college level so he is inherently a more finished product and will therefore need less time to realize NFL success. Focusing only on those players who have graduated tends to narrow the field to the hard workers who didn't quit and and who are willing to study and learn. The third criterion ensures that you don't have a "flash in the pan," so to speak. Anyone can have success for a year, but the true talents are identified early. Also, with three years as a starter, you have a more significant body of work to examine. Finally, focusing on players whose teams are successful helps ensure that you have a player who understands how to win and has demonstrated success as a leader. This is the frame by which Parcels examines quarterbacks, and with this in hand it is much easier to begin the search.

I have no idea how Parcells established these four criteria, but I'm guessing it started with a large set of data and a fundamental question. The large set of data would include the careers—professional and college—of all the quarterbacks drafted during Parcells's time in football. The question was, what did the successful quarterbacks have in common?

How did Parcells decide on the number 23 for total wins as the cutoff for who he would or wouldn't draft? There certainly was data driving that decision, and somewhere in the statistics this number revealed itself as an important cutoff.

Unbeknownst to him, Parcells has actually created a statistical model. Whether designed by a computer or simply by Parcells's brain, it is still a statistical model. He looked at a data set and then made a determination of what variables correlated with successful quarterbacks in the NFL. He even made the data easier to interpret by creating Boolean data types (that is, variables that may be classified as either yes or no). And, whether Parcells admits it or not, he's clearly a believer in using data to inform decisions.

Certainly, there are more complicated models that might augment Parcells's simplistic one. For example, we might want to know which conference develops the most successful quarterbacks. Or, is there a particular college major linked with success? Exactly how many wins does a draft pick have? Would incorporating any of this information help improve the success of this model? Maybe. Maybe not. You can certainly see how Parcells's simplistic framework could be adapted into a much more complicated and involved model for predicting the success of quarterbacks in the NFL. Parcells may not have either the skill set or the desire to build out this more advanced framework, but in our next story, our protagonist will.

But first, an important caveat. The glorification of complex statistical methods is not really my intention here. Instead, I can't emphasize enough how important the simple art of asking a question really is. Sometimes—as in Parcells's case—the question arises purely out of curiosity. Sometimes it arises out of self-interest. Take the case of Nate Silver. Early in the 2008 Democratic presidential nomination, Silver was sitting in an airport in New Orleans watching and reading the coverage of the race between Hilary Clinton and Barack Obama. He quickly grew annoyed. The pundits touted Clinton as the current leader in the race based on her early lead in the polls. This did not sit well with Silver, who, as a Chicago native, was a big Obama supporter.

At the time, Silver was the managing partner of Baseball Prospectus, a group of statistical savants devoted to advanced analytics in baseball. Silver was also well known in analytic-driven sports circles as the creator of PECOTA (Player Empirical Comparison and Optimization Test Algorithm),[2] which is widely considered to be the most accurate system for predicting the performance of baseball players. Introduced in 2003, PECOTA makes predictions for every major leaguer's seasonal statistics. In the six years since its introduction, it has become something of a gold standard in the field. Its hallmark is bold predictions that turn out to be incredibly accurate. Coming off a 90–72 season in 2006, Silver and his PECOTA system predicted that the White Sox would suffer a reversal of fortune in 2007. PECOTA predicted the revered team would actually lose 90 games and win only 72. This seemingly absurd prediction caused a huge stir, and even White Sox general manager Kenny Williams weighed in: "That's good because usually they're [Baseball Prospectus] wrong about everything regarding our dealings. What can you do? We put the best team together we can, and we think we're going to end up somewhere in the mid-90s."

The White Sox finished *exactly* 72–90 that season.

Going into the 2008 season, the Tampa Bay Rays were coming off a third straight season of winning fewer than 70 games. In fact, in their ten-year history they never won more than 70 games in a season. Yet Silver and PECOTA predicted the Rays would win 88 games, surpassing the previous year's win total by 22. By all historical accounts it was a ridiculous prediction, but the Rays proved Silver and Co. wrong by blowing past their "conservative" prediction and actually winning 97 games. The Rays went all the way to the World Series that year.

So, Silver, with his penchant for accurate predictions, was the perfect person to answer the question of whether the polls meant anything at that point in the race before the New Hampshire primary and the Iowa caucus.

By looking at historical data, he was able to answer this question with a definitive no, and this simple question spawned more questions. How accurate are polls anyway? Which polls are the most accurate? What other factors might be used to accurately predict the nominee? How important is demographic information to political forecasting? Unlike Parcells, Silver had the skill set to build out this more complicated model. After the smoke cleared and Silver's number crunching was complete, he had a new model for predicting the outcome of political races.

Silver created an alter ego named Poblano and began writing on a website he founded called Fivethirtyeight.com. Poblano gained credibility as his new model proved to be more accurate than all the methods that caused Silver's initial frustration that night in New Orleans. His notoriety reached a tipping point on May 6, 2008, after the North Carolina and Indiana primaries, where Silver made some bold and contrarian predictions akin to those he made previously about baseball. While the traditional polls suggested the race in North Carolina was incredibly tight, Silver predicted that Obama would win by 13 or 14 points. When the Illinois senator won by exactly 14 points, Silver was legitimized.

I sat with Silver in a small Italian restaurant in midtown Manhattan, and he laughed at how much credit he received for that singular prediction. "You always recieve too much credit when you nail a prediction like that. Just like Tampa and Chicago, getting that close takes a bit of luck."

Yet all the attention was still being thrust upon an unidentified figure named Poblano. But soon after, Silver revealed his identity to his readership and began to focus more time on his political forecasting and analysis. His newfound lack of anonymity further solidified his reputation as a sage. Successfully predicting the winner of 49 of the 50 states (as well as the District of Columbia, no less) in the 2008 presidential election, Silver ensured that his legend would continue to grow. As an encore, Silver also correctly predicted the winners of every U.S. Senate race.

Over dinner, he admitted to me that the work that elevated him to this status was much less rigorous than what he did in his previous, obscure world of baseball statistics. "I'd say that PECOTA was at least two and a half times as intense as the work in politics."

But that simply doesn't matter. Since his public unmasking, Silver has risen to cult status and has been featured on political talk shows like *The Colbert Report* as well as mainstream publications like the *New York Times*. He was been called a web celebrity by Forbes.com and was named one of the world's "one hundred most influential people" by *Time Magazine*.

And it all started with a simple question—do the polls mean anything?

Silver answered his question with data available in the public domain—but sometimes finding the data isn't quite so simple. Sometimes the data simply isn't there, or, rather, isn't there yet. In cases like this, you have to take a step back and actually ask a few questions just to begin collecting the data. And that's exactly what one young NFL executive had to do.

During the late 1990s, a strange thing happened to the NFL pay scale. Somewhere, somehow, someone decided that the left offensive tackle was one of the most important positions on the field and, to that end, should be one of the highest-paid positions on the team after quarterback. The reason for this can be traced back to guys like Lawrence Taylor, who are freakish athletes, so strong and so fast that they can overcome nearly any obstacle on their way to the quarterback.[3] Taylor himself set a new standard for QB sacks during his career. These athletes created a need for an equally freakish athlete to protect the quarterback's blind side. You need to protect your highest-priced asset, don't you? So Herculean offensive left tackles who could move with the grace of an antelope quickly became hot commodities in great demand. And, high demand with limited supply also begets Herculean prices.

This posed an interesting dilemma for NFL executives, as they had no statistics illuminating just which athletes would make "top" offensive left tackles. Positions like quarterback, running back, or wide receiver inherently came with easily obtainable data. Quarterbacks have completion percentage, yards per attempt, and interceptions, while running backs have yards per carry, fumbles, and receptions. These positions are relatively easy to evaluate. By contrast, similar data for offensive left tackles was noticeably absent. Statistics like sacks or team rushing averages had too many covariances. When a quarterback is sacked, who really knows exactly why or how it happens? Maybe the quarterback holds the ball too long; maybe some of the other offensive linemen fail to protect him. Or, maybe the coverage is simply too good. There are too many extraneous factors to learn much from the statistic of sacks.

So where does this leave executives trying to identify what offensive left tackles to sign and for how much? At least in my story, it left them at the mercy of scouts, who used their eyes and intuition to decide which offensive left tackles were the best.

This did not sit well with our young NFL executive. Wishing to remain anonymous, he told me the story of how he asked a question and then tried to answer it by asking even more questions.

He first asked, How can I objectively measure the performance of offensive left tackles? He quickly realized he didn't have an answer, so he turned to the football people in his organization and asked them another question. Gathering scouts and coaches alike, this curious football executive asked a very simple question, "What are all the things that an NFL offensive left tackle can do on a play?"

They answered with yet another question. "It depends. Is it a running play or passing play?"

As the young executive listened to this answer, an idea came into his head. "Let's assume it's a run."

"Well, he can have a lot of different assignments. Is he pulling, trapping, wham blocking?" The seasoned football person asked.

"Let's assume he's pulling."

The young executive went through this exercise individually with *all* the football people, and, as he asked his set of questions, he created a decision tree that gave him 32 different permutations of what an offensive left tackle can do on any play, good or bad. More simply, he built a framework to judge offensive left tackles on a play-by-play basis. The driving idea was that if somehow you could watch every play with this framework in mind, you actually create new statistics to judge the performance of an offensive left tackle. In the end, you can actually create a quantitative system to value this mysterious, pricey position.

So, the young executive gathered a group of high school football coaches (who were all too happy, by the way, to say they worked for an NFL team) and sat them in front of game film of every offensive left tackle in the league. From that effort grew the first-ever legitimate statistic for evaluating offensive lineman.

In this example, our NFL executive knew that he couldn't answer his first, basic question, so he asked people who could. And from his questions came answers to something seemingly unsolvable. He was incredibly creative; in the end, his clever approach gave him an advantage over his competition. And, again, it all started with a simple question—what does an offensive left tackle really do?

Of course, you can't always ask a question directly. And, often, you don't want to. In cases like this, when you're afraid to ask your colleagues, or your supervisors, or your friends, you can always ask the numbers. That's exactly what we had to do when trust became a problem for my blackjack team.

People often ask me what I looked for when recruiting a new person for the blackjack team. They expect that I would want someone excellent at math or with a photographic memory. But the most important quality, for me, is trust. Imagine you are going to hand $100,000 in cash to someone and tell them: go fly to Vegas, win yourself some cash. You will certainly want to be sure that person is someone you can trust.

As a blackjack team, trust was paramount, and we had a tremendous amount invested in one another. At the end of a weekend, the only person who really knew exactly how much someone won or lost was the person holding the chips. If someone went out to Vegas and won $75,000, he could very easily tell the rest of us he actually only won $50,000 and then slyly pocket the rest. No one would be the wiser and, in all likelihood, the team would be so pleased with the $50,000 win that we wouldn't suspect a thing.

Operating on an understanding of trust was vital to team dynamics. However, there were inevitably incidents along the way that called trust into question. One such incident involved a new player I'll call Todd. Todd was brought in by one of the members in the group and rapidly rose through the blackjack ranks, quickly passing all of the tests along the way. Before long, Todd filled the shoes of a "big" player.

As a big player, Todd was responsible for handling large sums of money and placing the large bets. He essentially held the profit and loss for every session in which he played. While Todd's rise to big player was quick and seamless, his actual performance as a big player was just the opposite. He had a very rocky first few months as a big player and consistently came back from the casino with large losses. In practice, we vetted his skills by throwing harder and harder tests at him, but each time he passed with flying colors. Even so, following each trip, he touched down at Logan airport in Boston with less money than when he had taken off.

It was a conundrum, and no one on the team knew Todd all that well. The player who brought him in vouched for him and was convinced that he could be trusted. But some of us soon began to have doubts. If

we accused him of cheating, we risked ruining the trust dynamic forever. If we were going to question his integrity, we might as well just
kick him off the team because once trust was damaged it might never be
repaired. Kicking him off the team also was not something to be taken
lightly as we had already made a considerable investment. Training a
new big player would be costly and take a long time.

So, we decided to ask the numbers the question that was bothering
us: Can we trust Todd?

To get paid, players on the blackjack team were required to record
every situation in which they played. We used these written record-
ings to simulate how much each player should theoretically have won
and then gave the player a percentage of the theoretical bounty. Our
convenient "database" meant we could actually go back and simulate
every table that Todd had played and see what he should have won
(theoretically, absent any luck). By applying some pretty simple statistical methods to this data, we could see if Todd's results were within
reason.

When we ran the numbers, it turned out that Todd's negative results
were actually within two standard deviations of the theoretical result.
Figuring out the standard deviation allows you to measure variance
and determine the likelihood that a result is caused by simple luck or
whether it is statistically significant. So, the standard deviation could
in fact tell us whether Todd was just serially unlucky or whether he
was cheating. Roughly speaking, a two standard deviation finding told
us there was still a 5 percent chance that Todd just had a case of bad
luck. And that 5 percent was enough for us. We decided we needed
to trust Todd. And so we continued to let him play without any comments or caveats. Soon, Todd started to win. He eventually got back on
track and for the rest of his career won right around what his statistics
projected.

Asking the numbers if we could trust Todd, rather than the source
himself, saved us from incorrectly jeopardizing an important business relationship. Likewise, in the non-blackjack world, banks are

starting to make similar moves so they don't have to jeopardize their relationships.

Have you ever received a concerned phone call from your credit card company asking you to confirm your last five purchases? More often than not this triggers a frantic search through your wallet, yielding the credit card in question. Yet you still have to painstakingly confirm each transaction individually so the credit card company won't shut off your card.

And what about the times that you've made a big purchase or traveled somewhere exotic and tried to use your credit card to pay, only to have the proprietor tell you that you need to call your credit card company?

We tolerate this kind of "help" because we understand that it is for our own good and our own safety. But what if the calls started happening too frequently? Wouldn't that be the same as us accusing Todd of cheating? Would that make you decide to switch credit cards?

Preventing fraud is serious business, but it does come at the expense of customer service. If you ask someone too many times to confirm something that should be running smoothly, customers will eventually find a company that's more in control and doesn't need to do so much checking.

So how do banks know when they should actually ask if something is wrong? They ask the numbers first instead.

"Banks are leveraging advanced analytic approaches to protect their consumers. However, they need to maintain the appropriate balance between fraud protection, customer service ratings, and operational efficiency. The last thing that banks want to do is to make the analytics too stringent, which will result in more fraud flags on transactions or accounts than their investigators can triage or too many transactions that are rejected at point of sale, making it extremely inconvenient for consumers to make purchases or access funds," said Stu Bradley who runs fraud strategy for software company SAS.

SAS works with banks to implement four different analytical strategies in detecting credit card fraud. First, they impose some basic rules, flagging transactions that are over a certain amount, initiated in a foreign country, or are unusually frequent. This will catch most fraudulent transactions, but will also cause a lot of false positives and next-day calls questioning the large bar tab from the night before.

So using rules alone is not nearly enough. SAS next recommends use of "anomaly detection," where rules are applied in a more advanced analytical way. Based on your past behavior, is your current behavior suspicious? If you have a propensity to travel overseas, then your three transactions in Paris will not be considered an anomaly and will not be flagged. Do you use your credit card for a personal business? Then large transactions would be normal, and anomaly detection would help keep your credit card company from bothering you.

Another strategy, predictive modeling, allows banks to look beyond the data to understand what different transaction behavior *might* mean. Imagine a transaction sequence starting with a gas station transaction, shortly followed by a card-not-present transaction (such as an Internet purchase), and concluding with an out-of-country purchase. Predictive modeling would flag this card because advanced analytics would predict that this sequence is highly likely to be the result of skimming. Skimming is the theft of credit card information during an otherwise legitimate transaction, like a dishonest waiter writing your credit card information down when you are paying the bill.

Finally, social network analysis (SNA) is used to complete bank fraud detection. In SNA, analytics are used to find relationships in transactions and user behaviors that can help determine if one person or a group of related people are doing any of the shady behavior flagged by the first three methods. Predictive modeling can use a flagged, skimmed card and SNA to identify a similar suspected card because it is being used by the same person—even if their behavior is slightly different. Allowing banks to ask the data millions of questions can help them avoid asking their customers any.

It is important to instill a culture of asking questions into any organization bent on successful use of analytics. Questions help spur creativity with numbers and also create a level of simplicity that allows anyone, regardless of statistical acumen, to begin the process toward creating complex mathematical models. Our blackjack team had a culture where problems were solved with questions. Simply asking questions gave us the power to overcome any problem using statistical analysis.

This model works equally well in the business world. People asking the important questions combined with the right people conducting the complex statistical analyses makes for an unbeatable team. My friends at the boutique consulting company Altman Vilandrie are a great example of such a team.

Founded in 2002, Ed Vilandrie and Rory Altman have grown the firm to 50 employees and $25 million in revenue. Consulting primarily in the telecom space, Altman Vilandrie specializes in using statistical analysis to solve their clients' complex business problems, like how to best price their services and decide which products to offer to their customers. They have helped companies that are merging figure out the financial and strategic rationale of their merger as well as the synergies and integration costs. And they have helped investors looking to make investments in the telecom and media space by performing very thorough strategic and business due diligence on their prospective investments.

But as Vilandrie explained to me, they really specialize in asking and answering simple questions. On a recent visit to Boston, I sat with Vilandrie in his office on one of the highest floors of one of the tallest buildings in the city. From his office windows, we could see everything from the Charles River to Boston Harbor to the MIT campus.

Vilandrie and I have known each other for more than 20 years. In fact, I tried to recruit Vilandrie to play blackjack many moons ago. Ed had all the things we looked for in a new recruit. He was smart, analytical, and hard-working, and, most importantly, we knew we could trust him. He never really committed to blackjack, and it's clear now that his time was better spent discovering his own House Advantage in the consulting world.

When we met in his office, I hadn't seen Vilandrie in over a year. I asked him what issues were hot for his clients right now—what important questions were his customers trying to answer? He told me that due to the poor economy, he was performing a lot of work on customer "churn management strategies" for wireless companies. When people lose their jobs or feel crunched by bills, they look to cut costs in their personal lives; for some that means canceling their cell phone service. His clients in the wireless industry now had a very simple question: How can we do a better job retaining our customers?

If you decide to disconnect your phone, you're motivated by reasons that are both within and outside the company's control. The phone provider can control price, overall customer care, billing, network issues, and the like. Other reasons customers switch are unavoidable, such as when a customer moves to another country, a layoff leads to a lack of funds, the customer's company switches mobile plans, or death.

By effectively taking the billing records of millions of customers over the prior one to two years, Vilandrie explained how you can sequence customers who disconnect month to month. Then, you can link this data to other potential time series data that is available (usually, right under the client's fingertips). This information shows causation. For example, the timing of a network outage or other customer disturbance may be linked to higher churn. In other words, you can very effectively re-create for a client what actually caused the churn.

From this, Vilandrie builds predictive churn tools based on regressions that help clients isolate and fix these issues and lower their churn greatly in subsequent months. They steer clients away from spending funds needlessly in areas where they can't control churn and cross some measure of customer value with customer propensity to churn, so that the calling centers and other outbound retention efforts can focus on the lion's share of the value that is at highest risk of leaving the company.

Churn is just one example of the ways in which they answer these questions for their clients, but it's a very important example in any economy. All customer-driven businesses should be asking, how can I do a better job retaining my customers? The answer to that question is often easy to solve if you just look at the data.

Once again, a very simple question helps focus a complex mathematical model, and that complex mathematical model helps solve a very important business problem. Asking questions—the right questions—is an essential step to establishing the House Advantage in your business. Ed Thorp influenced an entire generation of gamblers by asking and answering some very simple questions, solving what seemed like an unsolvable problem. Ed Vilandrie has been able to build a $25 million business by asking and answering questions for businesses. The subject matter may be very different but the process is exactly the same; it is mastery of that process that will give you the upper hand.

5

THE IMPRACTICAL SEARCH FOR PERFECTION

Perfect numbers, like perfect men, are very rare.

—René Descartes

THERE ARE MANY questions that statistics can answer—some are easier than others. Using statistics to answer questions about human performance falls on the harder side of the scale. Phenomenons like hot streaks present a challenge for even the most skilled numbers guru.

During my seven years as a card counter, there were times when I would go on big winning streaks or hot streaks—exuding confidence and feeling as if I couldn't lose. I'm not talking about a few hands in a row when the deck was in my favor, as statistically this was supposed to happen; rather, I'm talking about winning far more money than I should have statistically. Of course, being an avid believer in statistics, I knew that these streaks were caused by variance and not some sudden increase in skill or divine intervention. Even so, that realization didn't stop me from feeling confident and invincible during my winning streaks.

My friend Wes used to talk about "willing himself to win," and my friend Mike would say, "You just need to know you'll win and you will." While these statements sound brazen, there's definitely something to be said for the value of confidence in blackjack as it helps build fortitude—the type of fortitude you need when dealing with prolonged losing streaks caused by variance in the wrong direction. It is the same type of fortitude that you need to do the right thing when it may not be the intuitive thing. These same principles can be applied to business.

The world of blackjack is a perfectly mathematical world in which a human's performance can be explained and predicted solely by math and statistics. People win when the odds are in their favor and lose when the odds aren't. There is no higher being or immeasurable force that dictates our results. But human performance outside of the realm of blackjack is not so easily explained. Specifically, in the world of sports and business, many have asked, "Is there such a thing as hot streaks?"

Just like our "hot" blackjack players, there are athletes who believe that when they are on successful streaks that exceed their statistical norm, they have a kind of "hot hand." Basketball players go on streaks of hitting six or seven shots in a row and believe they can't miss. Baseball players go through streaks where they get five or six consecutive hits and say the ball looks as big as a grapefruit. Even golfers have moments where they sink every putt and post scores far better than their average.

So, is this an example of a "hot hand" or simply an example of variance?

Many studies have tried to prove the existence of the "hot hand" in basketball (the most famous is a study by Thomas Gilovich, Robert Vallone, and Amos Tversky[1]) but all have come back with the same conclusion. There is no statistical proof that such a phenomenon exists.

Recently, what was largely considered to be the definitive study[2] of the hot hand theory was presented by Sandy Weil, a recognized NBA statistics expert, and John Huizinga, an economics professor at the University of Chicago. In the study, Weil and Huizinga attack the hot hand theory from many different angles. Studying high-volume shooters from the past five seasons, Weil and Huizinga find that the possession after making a basket, that same player is likely to shoot about 16 percent more often than usual. However, they actually make their shot 3.5 percent less than usual.[3] Their findings were statistically significant, and many in the stats community have taken this to mean that there is no such thing as a hot hand.

Over the last ten years, in the world of advanced statistics in basketball, there has been no more influential figure than John Hollinger. His work has been featured by ESPN, *Sports Illustrated*, and even the *Wall Street Journal*. He tells me in an e-mail that he is a "hot hand atheist" based in large part on Weil and Huizinga's study.

Like Hollinger, I preach the importance of understanding variance and not looking for predictive powers where they don't exist. But as someone who plays sports and has interacted with many professional athletes, I know it's not that simple.

Five years ago, I became particularly interested in this hot hand theory as I prepared for a meeting with Harvard professor Carl Morris. Morris, currently a member of the Harvard University statistics department, was an avid sports fan and had significant interest in the intersection between sports and statistics. He was immortalized in *Moneyball* for some of his early research in baseball. The work referenced[4] centered on a matrix he developed using Markov models, a mathematical process where present states are used to predict future states. The matrix gave the expected number of runs that would be scored in an inning based on the current situation. With no one on base and no outs, an average team could be expected to score .54 runs in that inning. But with bases loaded and no outs, a team could be expected to score 2.4 runs. This matrix is useful for baseball strategy and is one of the main reasons that believers in advanced statistics believe that a sacrifice bunt early in a game with a man on first and no outs is not a good play because it actually decreases the amount of runs a team is expected to score from .91 to .70. The expected run value matrix is a great example of a practical use of statistics in sports.

Morris's work was not the first that had been done on this subject, but his was the most publicized at the time, and it was this notoriety that led me to Morris's office in the summer of 2005. I was excited by the idea of speaking to someone with Morris's legitimate academic credentials, and I entered his office in the Harvard mathematics building with great anticipation.

Morris definitely fit the bill of the stereotypical college mathematics professor. He has gray hair and glasses, and he speaks quietly yet deliberately. We traded stories about the things that we were both working on and then started to talk about sports.

As we dove deeper, it became clear to me that Morris wasn't just a statistics professor, he was also a huge sports fan. He loved the game of tennis and was an official statistician for the local professional tennis team. And he also played the games. Looking around his office you could see pictures of him playing tennis and other evidence that he loved playing sports. So I eventually led the conversation toward some of the more esoteric questions about using statistics in sports, questions you could only understand if you avidly played sports.

Here I was sitting with a thought leader in the world of statistics, an academic and a leader in one of the preeminent academic institutions in the world. This was my chance to get the definitive word on the hot hand theory from that camp.

"So what do you think of the hot hand theory?" I asked a bit sheepishly.

Morris looked at me and paused. He started slowly. "I am familiar with all of the work that has been done on this. There is no mathematical proof of the existence of the hot hand," he declared. "But anyone that has played sports, and I have played sports, knows that it exists."

So there it was. If anyone in the world was in a position to continue to sing the statistics community party line of "no such thing as a hot hand," it was Morris. Yet he was admitting to me that he actually did believe in it regardless of whether he could statistically prove it.

And speaking with many of my friends who enjoy the unique combination of working for professional teams while being statistically literate, the answer is similar. Paraag Marathe, vice president of football operations for the 49ers, remarked, "Being around athletes and coaches as much as I am, you definitely feel like there's something to it [the hot hand theory]."

Roland Beech, who started 82games.com, one of the first websites devoted solely to advanced NBA statistics, and who now works for the Dallas Mavericks, echoed Marathe's sentiment. "I know that coaches and players definitely believe in it, and I have to say that I believe that there's something there also."

I find this to be a very healthy and enlightened point of view, and I expected a similar reaction from Houston Rockets' general manager Daryl Morey when I asked him the same question. Morey, like Beech and Marathe, does not get to sit in the ivory tower of a college economics department. He has to talk with coaches who all played basketball at a high level. He has to talk to players who certainly believe that when they've made three shots in a row they better be getting the next three shots. I certainly would expect Morey to also have a pragmatic attitude toward the subject.

But Morey's tune is a bit different. "At its highest level I don't care about it," said Morey in response to my "what do you think of the hot hand theory?" question.

He continued, "I know I can't predict so I don't put much thought into it. I suppose I'm intellectually curious about it, but since it doesn't affect any decisions, I don't waste a lot of time on it."

I pressed him further on the subject. "I know people feel like they get in the zone and I think there's something there," he said and trailed off a bit. It was clear that Morey wasn't sure exactly how to answer the question simply because he didn't think there was much use in talking about the abstract.

Instead he shifted the conversation to a more tangible example. Taking a trip back to his first couple of months in Houston, Morey recalls a game where he noticed that in the fourth quarter, then–head coach Jeff Van Gundy departed from the normal player rotation and instead played point guard Rafer Alston for longer stretches.

After the game, Morey asked him a simple question, "Why?"

Van Gundy, a very intelligent and analytical mind, explained that because Alston (a very solid point guard but a notoriously poor shooter) was hitting his shots early, he believed he had a better chance to hit his shots late.

Morey neither disputed nor agreed with his assertion but knew there was a simple way to test for it. Looking at past game data, Morey was easily able to determine if there was any correlation between Alston's success in the first quarter or first half with his ultimate performance for the game. He looked hard and found none, seeing no correlation between any of Rafer's shots with his future success. He concluded that what Alston did in his first few shots or even the first half had no predictive value for what he was going to do that game.

"I told Coach Van Gundy, and to his credit he believed it and never did it again."

So in that specific instance, Morey cared about one specific case of the hot hand because he knew he could simply test it as it pertained to an individual player and could use that analysis to guide the decisions his coach was making. But in general he really doesn't care about it because he knows it doesn't have any practical value to him.

The main issue with the hot hand is that it is very difficult to prove statistically and certainly illustrates some great examples of cognitive biases. Remember confirmation bias from Chapter 3? Confirmation bias can certainly be used to explain belief in the hot hand. Players who make a shot will only remember the times that they made their following shot and will forget all the times when they missed that next shot. So as we espoused in Chapter 3, the best way to escape confirmation bias is to think like a scientist, and a scientist like Morey would try to test this assumption, not simply accept it.

But because of all the other factors that go into athletic performance, it is very difficult to isolate the streaks that may have been caused by a hot hand. Statisticians call this noisy data, and isolating streaks caused by hot hands seems as noisy as it gets—100 decibel noisy. This takes us back to our roulette wheel and our coin-flipping game. In both cases, we had streaks caused by variance that had zero underlying significance. Eleven reds in a row meant nothing more than 11 heads in a row of a coin flip. It was random, it was variance, and it's what a probability distribution looks like.

I do believe that most streaks in player performance are caused by this same type of variance, but it's hard to believe that the hot hand does not exist at some level. This brings us to an important lesson of statistics. Simply because it cannot be proven statistically does not imply a negative result. In other words, just because the academics cannot prove something doesn't mean it doesn't exist.

It's like saying since you cannot prove definitively that Jesus Christ was the son of God, that he wasn't actually the son of God. The reality is you haven't proven that he wasn't the son of God, you've only proved that you can't prove he was the son of God. Of course, this is the nature of the beast as it is very difficult to prove that something doesn't exist. It is much easier to prove that it does.

So instead of attacking this very real phenomenon from a statistical vantage point, let's instead attempt to explain it from a psychological point of view and try to understand its roots from a scientific level, again thinking like a scientist.

At the core of the hot hand theory is a belief that when a shooter makes a shot, he is more likely to make the next shot simply because he made his previous shot. That is the necessary statement that statisticians have asserted to try to prove this statistically significant. But it is also a very strict way of looking at this phenomenon. What if we instead said that the hot hand is a temporary period of high confidence during which players enjoy higher rates of success than normal? This confidence may be triggered by early success or may simply be the result of a clear mind that allows for a high performance level.

Now there is a statement that very few would argue with. Athletic performance is correlated with confidence, meaning that when you are more confident you perform at a higher level.

This is exactly the focus of sport psychologist Dr. John Eliot's work. He consults with both professional and college sports teams, helping their players achieve a confidence level that allows them to perform at their highest level. In fact, his work with the Tampa Bay Rays in 2007 helped turn around the entire franchise in 2008 as they made their first-ever world series, surpassing even Nate Silver's lofty expectations.

Eliot defines confidence in sports using brain waves. To perform well the athlete's mind must be quiet, meaning low beta waves and high alpha waves. Beta waves are very active when we are awake and asking questions or analyzing a situation. High beta waves when playing sports would cause an athlete to react slower to a situation and therefore perform slower and sub-optimally. The confident athlete, with low beta waves and high alpha waves, would use closed-loop processing to make their decisions on the field. This is the same loop that causes us to move our hand quickly after we touch a hot stove. We move our hand based on instinct and muscle memory, not on any analytical realization that the stove is hot.

Much of Eliot's work centers on taking athletes through repetitions or pre-game routines that reinforce these closed-loop patterns. These exercises are designed to reinforce routines, removing questions and therefore reducing beta waves while increasing alpha waves. As these movements are repeated they become the norm for the athlete, even in high-stress or high-stimulus moments. If they are confident and their brain is quiet, it is easy for them to continue closed-loop processing. Eliot believes that these are the keys to successful athletes.

So it is no surprise that as I sit down for lunch with Eliot he starts in on all the reasons that the statistical experts are wrong when they state their objections to the hot hand. "The problem with the statistical research that has been done is it asks, does one shot influence another shot?" he begins. "One shot does not influence another shot. One shot influences your psychology, and that psychology influences the next shot."

Eliot goes on to explain that making a shot may have different impacts on a player's psychology. For some it will bolster their confidence, but for others it could weaken their resolve. "Different people have different psychological reactions to success. The pessimist is surprised by unusual success and questions when it will end. They experience high beta waves as they question their own success." This is similar to the notion of choking in sports, where the gravity of a situation causes instinct to disappear and analysis causes paralysis.[5] There is a very real phenomenon here in which athlete success is correlated with not thinking too much.

Further, Eliot doesn't believe that the tests that have been done have done justice to the problem space of the hot hand theory.

"So if you could design a study to determine the existence of the hot hand theory, how would you do it?" I ask.

Eliot describes a potential experiment utilizing biofeedback in which basketball players would wear soft caps, monitoring their brain waves. The players would play a game against each other, and Eliot would monitor which players' minds got quieter during successful streaks. If the relationship between a quiet brain and successful shot making was significant over time, this would be evidence that during some streaks players feel more confident and therefore have more success.

But Eliot admits that this would by no means "prove" the existence of the hot hand. In fact, as I hear him talk about it, I'm pretty sure he feels similarly to Morey, that further discussion about the hot hand is really a waste of time. He is not focused on whether one shot influences another shot. He instead is focused on ways to analyze brain waves to help athletes get into a zone where they can perform at a higher level. That process is different for each athlete and may have nothing to do with whether they made their last shot.

It's really a pragmatic point of view that both Eliot and Morey take on, and to be honest, it seems a lot more useful than the academics' point of view on this subject. It certainly behooves those in the stats community to focus on practical problems rather than idealistic thought exercises. Is it more important to prove the existence statistically or to try to understand it from a psychological standpoint so that players can be coached to utilize it? The latter seems much more useful.

As I dove deeper into this thought process, I decided it was time to call the definitive source. I sent John Huizinga an e-mail to discuss his paper and findings. I was fully expecting a knock-down, drag-out fight with him, as I was sure that he believes in his work completely.

But the first words that came out of his mouth shocked me. "First of all, I want to say, that if you look at something statistically and don't find it, that doesn't mean it doesn't exist," Huizinga clarified. His enlightened and pragmatic attitude was definitely not what I was expecting.

I told Huizinga that his work had made Hollinger call himself an atheist of the hot hand theory and he chuckled. "Well if he's an atheist, I guess I'm an agnostic." And then Huizinga echoed an important sentiment. "When you do this kind of work you need to be humble. What I did was look at how much predictability there is in one shot. I did not prove anything else."

Huizinga went on to talk about noted psychologist Tom Gilovich, who began all this hot hand talk. "I think Tom was right when he started all of this. He was trying to show that people just don't understand what random patterns look like. They don't know how to process data very well." Huizinga was focusing on the more practical application of this work, which wasn't that there was no such thing as a hot hand but rather that people don't understand the true meaning of random and look for patterns in sequences where there simply aren't any.

As we continued to talk, it was clear that Huizinga actually thinks the more interesting part of his work is the fact that players believe in the hot hand and this belief actually changes their behavior. The fact that players are 16 percent more likely to shoot after a successful shot indicates that either they are forcing more shots up or their teammates are feeding them the ball more often. This is a more practical conclusion. With this information, a coach could tell his team, "Hey guys, just because you made your last shot, it doesn't mean you are going to make your next shot. So let's stay away from the idea that we need to force the ball to someone just because he made his last shot."

Again, Huizinga's preferred conclusion was a lot more practical than the one that consumes most observers. Rather than worrying about the question of the hot hand, he instead has focused on the player's belief in the hot hand and how it impacts their decision making. Our pragmatic friend Morey would look at this as an opportunity to tell Van Gundy that he should tell his team not to force the ball to Rafer Alston simply because he made his last shot.

This conclusion is incredibly more actionable than the alternative in this scenario. The statement that "there is no such thing as the hot hand in basketball" really has very little actionable value, and I would actually say it has negative value as it hurts the credibility of the church of statistics.

There has been a lot of valuable mental horsepower exhausted on the hot hand theory. And to what end? It does a tremendous disservice to the statistics community as a whole if you walk into an audience with anyone who has played sports and champion the theory that there is no such thing as the hot hand. It makes people discount what you say as statistical jargon that has no place in the real world.

While all this discussion of the hot hand may remind you of our streaky roulette wheel, there is a fundamental difference. Whether a roulette ball lands on red or black is completely random, and therefore any streaks are the result of variance. The same cannot be said of whether someone makes a basketball shot. This is the primary reason that I fall into the camp with Marathe and Beech. I believe that there are some shooters who at times become more confident due to early success, and this confidence leads to future success, that is, the hot hand. Unfortunately, these cases are few and far between and therefore difficult to isolate and even more difficult to prove statistically. In many respects, due to its complexity, it is an incredibly impractical problem to try to solve.

So building upon our lesson from the previous chapter of the importance of challenging convention and asking questions, we will add that those questions must have answers that create actionable lessons, that is, the questions must be practical. Continuing to debate the existence of the hot hand does not fall into that category.

In the case of the basketball hot hand, we found useful applications when getting beyond philosophical questions about existence. The finance analogy of the hot hand is a fund manager or stock picker who has put together a string of good returns in successive months. Is their short-term success indicative of future success or is it just another example of variance with little predictive power?

Again the existing literature would lead you to believe that, like basketball, there isn't a hot hand in finance. But like our basketball conundrum, I'm not sure if that's the point. If I were looking for a place to put my money, I would start with funds that had some kind of track record of success. Of course this isn't the only thing I would consider, but certainly it would be a start. However, rather than relying on recent success as the best predictor of future success, I'd go back to the lessons learned from our friend Dr. Bob. It's not how you did in your last few months but more how you've done over your last few years, over your career.

If I'm Daryl Morey and I'm making a key personnel decision, I'm going to look at a player's career, not just a recent subset of it. I'm also going to look at the player's underlying skills, his work ethic, and his mechanics. A fund manager should be placed under similar scrutiny. Are his methods sound? Do his strategies work? Have they worked over a long period? Perhaps this is why all this hot hand talk has become banal: It simply isn't that useful.

Back to the hot hand in basketball. As I researched this theory, I was frustrated with its impractical nature. Statistics should have practical applications. I talked with Morey about some of these practical applications of statistics in basketball, and we discussed which ones have found their way onto the basketball court. He highlights the "two-for-one strategy" as an example of analytics impacting on-court strategy.

The two-for-one strategy describes the optimal strategy at the end of each quarter in an NBA game. The NBA has a 24-second shot clock, meaning teams must shoot within 24 seconds of receiving the ball or lose possession and the ball is awarded to the other team. For the most part, the shot clock does not have a major impact during the course of the game as NBA teams often shoot well before the 24 seconds have expired. But at the end of each quarter there is an opportunity to use the shot clock to your advantage. Imagine receiving the ball with 45 seconds left in the quarter. If you use all of your allotted 24 seconds, then you will leave the other team with 21 seconds and they will be able to run the clock out, leaving you no more opportunities for that quarter.

But instead, if you shoot the ball with more than 25 seconds left, you are ensuring that unless you fail to get the defensive rebound, you will get the ball at least one more time that quarter. This is the two-for-one strategy. You are ensuring yourself two possessions to the other team's one.

It's not that simple, however. If you shoot the ball too early, say with 38 seconds left, you are giving your opponent a chance to do a two-for-one to you. So how do you know exactly when to shoot? Your gut would tell you that it is somewhere more than 30 but less than 40 seconds. But is your gut enough?

This is actually a relatively easy question to solve using statistics. So I decided to check the Internet for work that had already been done on this subject. To my surprise, I came up empty. For comparison's sake, when I Googled "hot hand theory basketball," I received 111,000 results.

I asked around, and the consensus from the basketball stat experts was that there had definitely been research done on this issue but the majority had been done at the team level and was likely not in the public domain. In other words, the smart teams had done the research but they weren't going to publish it anywhere—they wanted to keep their competitive advantage.

So without existing research, I consulted a talented friend of mine, Gabe Desjardins, who I've partnered with on research before, to do a simple study to determine the optimal time remaining in the quarter to take your shot in the two-for-one strategy.

Analyzing data from every game in the NBA starting with the 2003–2004 season, we focused on the last two minutes of the first, second, and third quarters. We omitted data from the fourth quarter since strategy caused by game score and timeout usage could significantly alter the data. Specifically, we calculated the mean points scored by the team with the ball and the mean points for their opponent for the remainder of the quarter by second. For example, if you have the ball with 80 seconds remaining, you would expect to score on average 3 points for the remainder of the period and your opponent would be expected to score 2.5 points. Of course since you have the ball at this instance, your expected points for the quarter are higher. The full results are shown in the chart below.

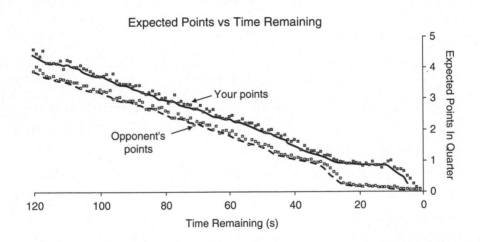

The difference between your future points and your opponent's future points, essentially the value of having the ball, is fairly consistent outside of 45 seconds remaining. It is at this point that effects of the two-for-one strategy kick in.

The next chart shows the difference in expected scoring after a change in possession at each second within the last two minutes of the quarter. Since the team with the ball will always have higher expected points going forward, we are trying to optimize for the time that makes this disadvantage the smallest. From the graph below we can see that number is 33 seconds. So the optimal time to shoot the ball to take advantage of the two-for-one is 33 seconds.

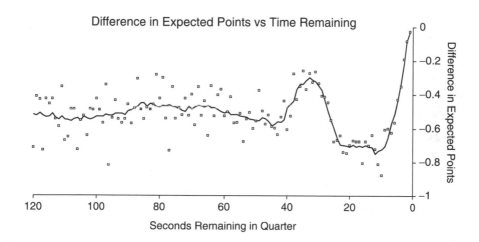

So a relatively simple statistical study yielded a relatively straightforward and practical result. The key word here is practical, since it really does have an application that every team would benefit from implementing.

This finding answers a very simple but practical question: When should I shoot the ball at the end of the quarter to maximize my points and minimize my opponent's points?

A valuable takeaway from this journey through basketball strategy is the importance of pragmatism in the face of the ideal world of statistics. Certainly this study would not grace the pages of the *Journal of the American Statistical Association*, and it's a strategy that coaches intuitively understand and implement, but it is an important result. While much of the progress in the world of statistics can be attributed to the academics, who ask difficult questions, the next forward phase of the statistical movement will come from those in the real world willing to create and implement practical solutions like the two-for-one.

And this lesson of pragmatism does not stop at the edge of the basketball court. It is a philosophical shift that is a valuable embrace for those wishing to gain the House Advantage in their business.

Recently at an analytics conference put on by Computer Sciences Corporation (CSC), leaders in helping "clients achieve strategic goals and profit from the use of information technology,"[6] CSC senior partner Alex Black echoed the words of my blackjack mentors, highlighting the need for pragmatism in analytics. Referencing the following quote from Professor Tom Davenport in his book *Competing on Analytics,* largely considered the bible on using analytics in business: "If a company has poor quality data for decision making, it should postpone plans for analytical competition and fix the data first."[7] Black made the point that this only applies in an ideal world.

"Companies should not delay using analytics to fix their data. Instead they should continue to move ahead with their analytics while making progress to improve their data concurrently," Black said. "The data will never be perfect so simply improving business decisions based on analytics is an important place to start."

Black's message was to be practical and not ideal. Yes, in the ideal world you would stop everything and focus on fixing your data, but the reality is that if you are making progress using analytics, why would you stop?

This message reminds me of an early conversation that I had with Billy Beane. We were discussing ideas of using analytics in sports outside of baseball, and Billy, as he often did in those days, brought the conversation back to soccer. I complained that soccer was such a fluid game that the data simply wasn't there yet the way it was in baseball.

I remember saying, "It just seems like it would be impossible to do something amazing [using statistics] in soccer."

Billy responded similarly to Black, "It doesn't have to be perfect or even amazing. It just needs to be better than what is out there right now. That will give you enough of a competitive advantage."

So much mental horsepower has been devoted to creating break-throughs or contrarian findings that will convince the world of the value of statistical analysis. Yet perhaps that is aiming too high. There are many opportunities where simple analyses using data and statistics will move an organization, industry, or individual forward. Focusing on the small practical questions rather than the large, idealistic problems will help you gain the House Advantage much quicker.

In business, as you look to incorporate analytics into your decision-making process, focus on manageable, practical problems. Don't think like an academic, trying to prove a universal theorem; instead, edge cases that apply to you and your situation can be enough. In Morey's case, simply understanding whether Rafer Alston's early performance in games was predictive of his later performance was a useful exercise. Similarly, understanding the success of a specific fund manager beyond a recent hot streak will help guide your decisions.

As you think about working with statistics and business analytics, don't worry about perfection. You will often face situations that seem impossible to model perfectly, yet this should not stop you from attempting to use math and statistics to improve your decision making. Think back to the lessons of the previous chapter. In both examples of fraud protection and football, the solution wasn't perfect, yet it created positive change for the business. Being pragmatic rather than ideal will help you create similar change. Even if you have had a recent hot streak.

6

USING NUMBERS TO TELL A STORY

Do not put your faith in what statistics say until you have carefully considered what they do not say.

—William W. Watt

THE REAL POWER of numbers lies in their ability to succinctly represent a broad range of information. The ability to quantify is one of the fundamental and most useful attributes of statistical information. This application has been growing in popularity since the mid-twentieth century, but it really took off with the work of Claude Shannon and his information theory. One of Shannon's major contributions is the use of a numerical measure to summarize a complex system or process. Related but simpler concepts can help in a multitude of business scenarios.

From horse racing to real estate, analysts these days try to fashion "single numbers" to answer difficult questions or to simplify what would otherwise be a highly complicated scenario. This is an incredibly challenging task that, unfortunately, often ends in failure.

The difficulty is answering questions that have many influential variables that themselves require subjective judgment. As each variable is added it becomes harder to manage how these variables interact and to measure their combined results because it requires a weighting system to determine how each of the variables needs to be combined.

For example, imagine trying to create a single number to answer the question, What car should I buy? If cost is your only concern, things are simple. It's very easy to compare the cost of, say, a Toyota Camry with a Ford Focus. But since you are also concerned with gas mileage, you add that as the second variable. Again, that single variable is easy to compare. But combining the two to answer the question of which car to buy becomes much more complicated. One person may be in a difficult financial situation and may be much more concerned with cost, while another may be more concerned with the environment and much more concerned with saving fuel. This dichotomy will yield different results in their weighting of the two variables. So this assignment can become very complicated, and pretty soon a fair amount of subjective opinion is required to make the decision.

It's a complex issue, and "decision analysts"[1] deal with this by saying one person has different "preferences" than another. That's not to say one person is right or wrong, in the same way nobody can be accused of being wrong if they say they prefer chocolate ice cream over vanilla; it's just that their preferences are different. So, consistent preference is a first step to creating objective measures and answering difficult questions. As card counters, we had a consistent and simple preference—to win money.

Our difficult question was, "How much should I bet on this hand of blackjack?" Because our strategy was predicated on betting more when the odds were in our favor and less or nothing when they were not in our favor, it was paramount for us to know at all times what our odds of winning were.

In my card-counting heyday, I would practice blackjack for at least two to three hours every day. When I got home from work, I would sit on my couch and practice, dealing hands of blackjack to myself. I'd eat, drink, watch television, and even talk on the phone while I was practicing. Any distraction was welcome, as I wanted to make playing in the casino the easiest, most natural space to play (if only by comparison). While I am not suggesting that numbers analysis in business needs to become an obsession, it is critical to live with the numbers that help you make decisions.

The true import of all the time I was spending in card counting was to make absolutely sure I could always keep the "count"—the most important statistic in counting cards. As we discussed earlier, card counting is a shorter, better-sounding name for keeping track of the number of high cards and low cards that you see. We counted high cards as minus 1, low cards as plus 1, and middle cards as 0.

So, if you saw ten low cards, two high cards, and three middle cards, the count would have been plus 8 (that is, $10 - 2 + 0 = 8$). The count was our signature number. It was the number we used to pass information from a spotter to a big player, and it told him whether the table was good or bad and whether the odds were in the dealer's or player's favor.

The count represented the truth. It was our key statistic. It told us everything we needed to know about the history of the cards, and it could be used to reliably make strategic decisions at the table. And it was by always knowing the count that we were able to make millions of dollars.

A count of plus 21 with three decks left meant we had a 3 percent edge over the casino. A count of negative five with five decks remaining meant we were at a 1 percent disadvantage to the casino. We knew these numbers backward and forward.

All of our training exercises were designed to make sure everyone could keep the count, no matter the distractions. We used to joke that at some point during our practice I would give someone a swift kick to the head just to see if they could keep the count under any conditions. Accurate tracking of the count was that important.

Most importantly, there was never any argument about what the count meant. It was a completely objective measure. Its creation was immune to bias. To be sure, when practicing, if two team members disagreed about the count, we could back out the cards and see precisely who was right.

The validity of our count was clear because the count's logic was so transparently obvious. The count was perfect because card counting is a perfectly mathematical exercise. It is based solely on numbers and data contained in the cards and, as such, represents a perfect application of analytics.

Yet such "perfection" in statistical analysis is the exception rather than the norm. Quantitative solutions to real-life problems are affected by multiple factors and can't be summed up with one number. In fact, often these solutions are counterintuitive and thus subject to scrutiny by what quants might call "non-believers."

It is not an easy thing to accept that numbers can and will tell a different story than what other, more traditional, methods of observation might. A perfect example comes from my work with the Portland Trail Blazers, a professional basketball team in the NBA.

I started working with the Trail Blazers in 2004. At the time they had a new director of player personnel named Kevin Pritchard. Pritchard had been the starting point guard on the 1988 Kansas University basketball team that went on to win the NCAA Championship. He had an NBA career spanning six years and five teams and even played briefly in Spain and Italy. After retiring in 1998, Pritchard tried a brief stint in the business world.

It was this work outside the baskeball realm that gave him an interest in the role analytics could play in his current job with the Portland Trail Blazers. He contracted my company, Citizen Sports, to develop a statistic that would use a player's college statistics to predict his likelihood of success in the NBA.

Using some pretty simple statistical methods, we created (with the help of a consultant named Ben Alamar) an equation that looked at a player's statistics in his last year in college and spit out a number that represented his probability of success in the NBA. The equation used different statistics for each position, which, based on the different demands and skill sets of each, made sense. Steals per minute and assists per minute were important for point guards. Field goal percentage was relevant for shooting guards, and blocks per minute were very important for power forwards and centers. None of this was counterintuitive.

Each year we sent the Blazers our list and rankings with explanations of why certain players ranked higher or lower than conventional wisdom might suggest. And every year they asked for more clarity on certain players in whom they were very interested. It was a great back and forth that represented a rare true collaboration between analysts and scouts. But it took a few years before this comfortable symbiosis really gelled.

After our second year working with the team, Pritchard (who had been promoted to general manager) invited me up to the training facility to meet with his scouts and present our methods. This was an exciting opportunity to get in front of real basketball people, but I realized what an important and delicate meeting it would be, as I was sure the people in that room would be predisposed to doubt all that I was prepared to sell.

I arrived at the Blazers' training facility and met with three of their scouts as well as their assistant general manager and Pritchard. I went through a pretty simple presentation that laid out the model we had built and explained how we generated our rankings each season. This first part of the presentation went over well as most of what was presented made sense to the basketball experts in the room. But as we dove into the next portion of the meeting, I knew there would be much more debate.

As I handed out our complete rankings for the past few seasons, the scouts and Pritchard immediately started pelting me with questions. "Why was Sean May ranked so high and J. J. Redick so low? Why were you guys wrong about Mardy Collins? And, why did you disagree with us so much on LaMarcus Aldridge?"

I tried to explain what the model said about each player and why statistically some scored well and some poorly. Sean May was an extremely efficient player in college. J. J. Redick showed very few skills in college aside from shooting, and even that was not as efficient as it could have been. Mardy Collins put up great college assist-to-turnover numbers and played almost 38 minutes per game. LaMarcus Aldridge was unfortunately a freshman on a veteran team and didn't get the opportunities to show his skills. It was a healthy back and forth until Pritchard, obviously a little frustrated, stopped the meeting and asked, "How do we get your rankings to look more like ours?"

Here was a guy who had been involved with the game at many levels, as a player and an executive. He'd played in the NBA for many years and had coached. He was now one of the hottest young general managers in the game. All told, he'd been in basketball for more than twenty years as a high-level player, coach, or executive. He clearly knew the game backward and forward and had confidence in his opinions.

I didn't doubt Pritchard's knowledge, but this question seemed proof that he didn't really get what we were trying to do or what our value was in this process. He wanted the numbers to be comforting, and, although he appreciated their value, he didn't want them to conflict with what his gut and scouts were telling him.

"We don't want our rankings to look like yours," I answered quickly, and then continued, "Our goal is to measure things in a different way than your scouts might. We hopefully are seeing different things in the numbers than you can with your eyes. And the reality is, you guys will see different things that the numbers can't. So we should be happy that our rankings don't look exactly alike.

"By watching the player in person and talking to the player, your scouts will certainly be able to see things that we can't. Likewise, numbers which take into account each game in an entire season will certainly uncover things your scouts can't.

"We use analytics because they help make smart decisions. They aren't supposed to mimic human observation; they are simply a tool to measure what human observation can't."

To his credit, Pritchard understood what I was saying, and the meeting ended on a positive note. We have had a good working arrangement since because he and his organization realize the numbers are not supposed to assuage or comfort. They are an unemotional tool used to make better decisions and nothing else. They represent information that cannot be unearthed by simple observation.

When Pritchard asked us to use statistics to help him predict success in the NBA, we first had to define "success." In order for this definition to pass something called the "clarity test," it had to represent one unique outcome.

Really, everyone might have a different definition of what success in the NBA means. Some might say becoming an All-Star defines success, while others might say being a starter. We defined success simply as a player ranking in the top ten at his position (based on a couple of advanced statistical measures) in his third year in the NBA. Aligning our preferences and choosing a single, consistent, testable outcome was the first important step to answering Pritchard's question.

Unfortunately, most people ignore the clarity test. They misunderstand the power or role of numbers and try to get them to say things that they simply cannot. Nowhere is that more true than in the media world, where the credibility of analytics is at the mercy of whomever happens to be presenting or discussing them on TV or otherwise. And when presented incorrectly or unclearly, numbers get a bad rap.

And sometimes, that's precisely the point.

Introduced in 1998, college football's Bowl Championship Series (BCS) selection system promised to replace fans' holiday squabbles with cool clarity and certainty. Statistics would now accomplish the seemingly impossible: crowning a legitimate "national champion" without requiring teams to sort it out on the field.

"I want to stress that it is not a poll," said Roy Kramer, then-commissioner of the Southeastern Conference (SEC) and the so-called "Father of the BCS."[2]

Kramer was playing to his crowd: millions of college football fans frustrated by the regionally biased Associated Press and the grudge-filled ESPN/USA Today coaches' surveys that dominated the debate.

In the 1990s, disputes over so-called champions—Colorado in 1990, Miami (FL) in 1991, Florida State in 1993, Michigan in 1997—were as prominent as the champions themselves.

But something better was on the way, something with numbers and computers and smart, objective Ph.D.s who, given the chance, would always side with truth over their alma maters. Kramer and his fellow alchemists sold the BCS as a "statistical rating system," and they sold it hard.

"Bowl Game to Be Chosen by Computers," screamed the Associated Press upon the BCS system's unveiling, three months before the 1998 college football season. The report quipped that "the new rating system is so complicated that it took [Roy] Kramer more than 10 minutes to explain it during a conference call."[3]

Kramer embraced this complexity and went along with the spin. But he also, if subtly, revealed what would be the real measure of the BCS's success.

"There's normally an adverse reaction to a new way of doing something, even if it's a better way and based on factual information and results instead of so much subjectivity. We're also hoping some people will accept it as just the way it is," said Kramer.[4]

To be sure, more than a decade after the BCS's creation, college football fans and coaches alike are still unsatisfied. Recent champions, coaches Mack Brown of Texas and Urban Meyer of Florida, have publicly bashed the BCS system; U.S. Senator Orrin Hatch (R-Utah) wants a Congressional investigation; and even President Barack Obama[5] suggests scrapping the system and instituting a playoff.

But fans still want to follow their favorite teams every which way they can. The whole BCS dissertation might make their eyes glaze over, but Kramer's hopes were realized—people no longer attacked the voters, instead they attacked the system.

While the BCS has been a commercial success, it hasn't been a statistical one, but that's because it was never meant to provide a true statistic. Despite how it was and still is represented, it isn't a black-and-white representation of college football performance at all; rather, the BCS formula is just a means to obfuscate the gray.

The secret is that the BCS isn't about numbers at all, and most of its detractors don't even realize that. It is actually a combination of three different parts.[6] The first two parts are the result of human voting and have nothing to do with statistics. In 2009, these two parts were the Harris Interactive Poll and the USA Today Coaches Poll. In both cases, they are simply humans voting subjectively on who they think is the best team. That doesn't sound scientific at all.

The third leg of this mysterious BCS triangle is indeed a computer ranking, actually a combination of six different computer rankings. It wasn't enough to water down the use of computers by combining them with human opinion; BCS system creators decided to combine six different methodologies, hoping that six was better than one but completely rendering impossible any hope of comprehending the methodologies.

In this case, statistics are just cover for the reality that college football's new system continues to make the sport just a nudge less subjective than figure skating. And much of the failure can be traced back to our concepts of preference and the clarity test. The BCS creators never established consistent preference in their definition of who was the best team. Likewise they never created a testable, unique outcome. Instead, voters, coaches, and fans alike are left to their own subjective opinion of who's the best team in the country and what that even means.

Who's to blame? The BCS formula, of course, is a number, a statistic. All dissension, disagreement, and derision are directed toward this formula and this math while the voters—the coaches—well, they stay unscathed.

What is the lesson here? Pseudo-statistics give the rest of statistics a bad name. The BCS has besmirched the concept of math for a generation of college football devotees.

So, what is a pseudo-statistic? Well, in order to define it, let's first look at the textbook definition of a statistic. Webster defines "statistic" as "a single term or datum in a collection of statistics (data)."[7] And then, "data" is defined as "factual information (as measurements or statistics) used as a basis for reasoning, discussion, or calculation."[8] So, combining those two definitions, a statistic is a single number representing a fact.

Hence, the problem with the BCS. Although presented as a single number, it is really a combination of many different numbers, some of which are not fact at all but a measure of public opinion. Yet, it is paraded around as a statistic of truth: a statistic that answers who the best team in college football is.

When Kevin Pritchard asked us to make our numbers agree more with his scouts' opinions, Kevin Pritchard was actually asking us to turn our statistic into a pseudo-statistic. We resisted and that prevented another misuse of numbers.

Objectivity is in high demand by sports fans regardless of whether it is possible. Because demand begets supply, we're served daily with a trove of meaningless numbers framed as something else.

Professional football's version of the BCS is a pseudo-statistic called the NFL passer rating. It is a number designed to solve the seemingly unsolvable question of who is the best quarterback in the league. Who doesn't want to know that?

There is no real statistical analysis behind this number. Rather, it is a compilation of performance data. Completion percentage, yards, interceptions, and touchdown passes are all factors included in the rating. But, absent from the formula are statistics like rushing yards, first downs, and, most noticeably, sacks. How can you measure a quarterback's performance without taking into account his ability to convert first downs or avoid statistics? Also, a quarterback who gains yards with his legs as well as his arm puts enormous pressure on the defense. That certainly should not be ignored.

In fact there is a belief among NFL insiders that certain quarterbacks will actually take sacks rather than throw incompletions in an attempt to keep their passer rating from dropping. One such NFL insider, Brian Billick, currently an analyst for Fox, went a step further in a recent Fox

NFL broadcast during the 2009 season, saying that quarterbacks he knew and coached would actually partake in this type of subterfuge.

So the ranking is an imperfect number because of its failure to measure important parts of the quarterbacks' performance. Worse, the passer rating was made even more imperfect by its creators when they decided (for some unknown, surely bizarre reason) to put the number on a scale of 0 to 158.3. Yes, a perfect rating is 158.3! Numbers are confusing enough even when grounded in logic, but the added complexity of this peculiar scale makes the passer rating even more absurd.

And this is the problem with the pseudo-statistics. They are often discussed ad nauseum in the media. They are classified as statistics and are thought to represent the advanced statistics movement. But often they are not created by anyone who knows anything about statistical analysis. In the case of the BCS, Kramer was the commissioner of a college football conference, not a trained statistician. Nor was the inventor of the passer rating, Don Smith, a math whiz. Actually, he was a recent retiree from his post as vice president of the NFL Hall of Fame when he conceived the passer rating.[9]

The problem with using pseudo-statistics in the media is their impact on how people think about statistics. At the least, the intentions of the aforementioned pseudo-statistics were in the right place: to dispell confusion and make lives a little easier. The same cannot always be said of many other pseudo-statistics in the media.

Take economic "statistics," for example, and, specifically, inflation numbers.

It has become a well-known fact that in the last 20 years inflation numbers were regularly manipulated. The government has myriad incentives to control the inflation rate. For one, increases in inflation mean a higher cost of living and put pressure on the government to raise interest rates and stifle economic growth. Also, government entitlement payments like social security and welfare are tied to the inflation rate. An accurate inflation rate would cost the government hundreds of millions of dollars.

But how can inflation numbers be manipulated since they are based on statistics, and statistics are numbers?

It's pretty simple, actually. The inflation rate is based on the growth of things like the Consumer Price Index (CPI). The CPI is defined as a "complex government statistic"[10] that tracks the cost of a "basket of goods and services." It was introduced in the 1920s, but, beginning in the Carter administration, federal economists began to manipulate the CPI.[11]

By removing expensive items, such as energy and food, from the basket of goods and services, the government was able to control the CPI's growth. Furthermore, a new variation of the CPI that measures "core inflation" was developed that excluded any items that "face volatile price inflation." Imagine trying to live without gas or groceries. That's what the government is telling you to do.

When removing expensive items from the CPI market basket of goods and services was not enough to depress inflation numbers, the Bureau of Labor Statistics innovated even more, changing the "weighted factors" used in calculating CPI statistics, so the results end up underreporting the true inflation people experience in everyday living.

The end result is that the inflation rate makes a mockery of the use of statistics and illustrates how human beings can manipulate a number until it loses both accuracy and relevance. Hence, the CPI has become a sad, abused pseudo-statistic.

Yet there is a true danger in the inaccuracy of the CPI, unlike that of the BCS. Incorrectly crowing a national champion is a far cry from creating fallacious government policy, a likely byproduct of an inaccurate CPI.

These repercussions are truly the problem here and the reason that it is so important to avoid creating and using pseudo-statistics.

Yet traditional media is more than a popular breeding ground for pseudo-statistics. In fact, the economy of television and radio is run by them: The price of most advertising is firmly based on pseudo-statistics.

The ratings system was developed in the 1950s by Arthur Nielsen and his company, Nielsen Media Rating. The ratings were built off a radio audience measurement system and were intended to measure the size and composition of television audiences. The ultimate goal was to create a single ratings number measuring audience size, release it to brands, and let them benefit from better-informed marketing decisions.

Since the Nielsen ratings were developed almost 50 years ago, it's no wonder that their methodology seems a bit antiquated. They are calculated by measuring the viewing habits of a small subset of the population, considered representative of the overall population. The data is gathered in two ways: either through "diaries," in which the target audience records its own viewing patterns, or by use of Set Meters, which are devices actually connected to televisions in the selected homes. In this day and age, the concept of people actually logging diaries to measure viewing habits is laughable.

The actual subset of the population used is quite small compared to the overall population. It is almost impossible to find out the number of Nielsen households, even after a call to the Nielsen public relations department. They are careful, though, to choose a representative distribution of different demographics within their sample population, and, from this subset, they extrapolate to produce a number that is supposed to represent the viewing habits of the greater population.

This all would seem to make sense if we were still in the 1950s when the overall population was much smaller, televisions were a rarity, and there were only three channels to choose from. But it's clear that in today's world those methods, while statistically sound, are likely to produce some large standard errors.

These standard errors are really only the start of the problems. Only recently did the rating try to take into account the viewing habits of college-age kids, and it still does not take into account viewing in group settings, such as bars and common areas. Add in the change in viewing behavior caused by the Internet and digital video recorders (DVRs) and you have a number that is way past its prime.

Yet, million-dollar marketing decisions are still based on the Nielsen ratings, and important programming decisions hang in the balance of what that small number of people decide to watch. Shows are canceled and careers ended based on a simple number that represents the viewing habits of a small group of people. More costly repercussions caused by a pseudo-statistic.

This is the true danger of a pseudo-statistic. It purports to accurately and succinctly represent complex information and in doing so discards or avoids numerous influencing variables that are core to the process. Nielsen simply doesn't have enough data to be accurate. Unfortunately, even as we are able to account for more measurements, pseudo-statistics rear their ugly head in different ways. Take Internet advertising and its ugly stepchild, the CPM.

CPM stands for cost per thousand (M stands for the Roman numeral for thousand), and from day one it has been the metric on which most advertisement campaigns are measured. It is a legacy of TV advertising, where advertising campaigns were priced per thousand viewers. However, in the Internet world it has morphed into CPM impressions. It ultimately measures only the number of times an advertisement has been served, while yielding very little information about the audience, yet it is the metric used to price most Internet advertising campaigns.

When a brand launches an advertising campaign on a website, it always knows the CPM they are paying. Yet CPM alone tells you nothing about the effectiveness of your campaign. More advanced metrics like CPC (cost per click) or CPA (cost per acquisition) are much more useful to the brand when attempting to measure performance but still only tell a limited part of the story.

Let's say that fast-food restaurant chain Sonic wants to launch an advertising campaign targeting sports fans. They decide to advertise on sports website A, spending $100,000 on a $10 CPM; their advertisement will be served one million times. But say the goal of the campaign is actually to drive people to sonic.com and get them to sign up for an offer of free tater tots. The CPM will tell Sonic nothing about the effectiveness of that campaign. Instead, Sonic will have to analyze the amount of people who actually sign up after seeing and clicking on the advertisement to measure performance.

Advertisers have a strong desire to measure the effectiveness of their campaigns, as witnessed by the creation of metrics like reach, frequency, gross rating points, and target rating points. However, in the offline world, there has always been a struggle to accurately capture the necessary data to properly measure the effectiveness of a campaign.

For example, how does a company like AT&T measure the effectiveness and value of placing an AT&T logo at a golf tournament? I asked Tim McGhee, who at the time was executive director of sponsorships for AT&T, about this very question.

"Well, we measure the amount of time our logo is seen in the broadcasts and calculate 30-second equivalents for those spots," McGhee explained. "But since we can't control the message, like we can with a commercial, we apply a discount to what we would have paid for ads in that time slot."

"Also, we measure increases in sales around times when we know the logo will be shown a lot," he continued. "But it is not a perfect science, and it comes down to a leap of faith that there is value to being associated with a brand like the PGA."

McGhee concluded, "What we always tried to do was make that leap as small as possible by doing as much evaluation and due diligence as we could. You'd rather make that leap across a crack in the sidewalk than a crevasse."

Again, the desire to "know more" about the effectiveness of their campaign is certainly there, but the struggle in measurement is with the data. However, that shouldn't be the case with Internet advertising. In fact, Internet advertising should actually be the model for measuring the effectiveness of a campaign. But the answer is more complicated than just a CPM.

This lesson speaks volumes about the practical application of analytics in business. It really is difficult to use or create a single number to make decisions. Even our glorious blackjack count was useless without one other small piece of information: how many cards were left in the shoe. Similarly, combining other metrics with CPM gives a much more complete picture with which to evaluate the effectiveness of an advertising campaign.

Let's go back to our friends at Sonic trying to determine the effectiveness of their ad buy. What they care about in this specific instance is how many people they can get to sign up for their free tater tot offer. So ultimately that is the "score." In this new scenario, they are running two campaigns, one with my company, Citizen Sports, and another with a sports website we'll simply call ABCD.com.

In both cases they have done a brand buy, meaning they have bought a certain amount of impressions priced on a CPM basis. Your natural inclination might be to ask why they don't insist that this campaign be priced on a CPC basis, meaning Sonic pays nothing unless a user actually clicks on one of the ads. This is problematic because once a user has clicked on the ad, there is no guarantee that they will sign up for the offer. And we might send Sonic far more qualified leads than ABCD. com because the demographic of our users is much more in line with Sonic's target customer.

Also, Sonic's goal from this campaign goes beyond the tater tot offer. They also hope to raise awareness among sports fans of the Sonic brand. CPC will tell them nothing of this efficacy.

So pricing on CPC is not the answer, either. Really the only answer is to track the user throughout the entire process, just like our retailers from Chapter 2 attempted to track their customers through their entire sales cycle. This would mean recording how many times a user saw an ad before he clicked on it. And once he clicked on it, finding out if he actually visited sonic.com. And how many times he visited the site before signing up for the offer. By finding these answers we can measure the effectiveness of both campaigns. While this might sound difficult, it is certainly easier than measuring the value of that AT&T logo.

And herein lies the true lesson of this chapter. Numbers can only be used to tell a story if they are given an opportunity to tell the *whole story.* And this is rarely the case as there is usually a fair amount of subjective measurement involved in the interpretation of statistics. The legacy of the CPM does a disservice to Internet advertising because it tells only part of the story. Wouldn't Sonic pay more to show their message to 1,000 carnivores versus 1,000 vegetarians? With hamburgers as one of their main menu items, I'd certainly hope so. Yet the legacy of television advertising leads us back to the CPM time and again. And that is problematic. Let's take a 50,000-foot view. Does Sonic ultimately care about how many people sign up for their tater tot offer? No. Again, that is just a proxy for their real goal—to sell more food. And of course that is difficult to measure regardless of whether the advertising campaign is on television or on the Internet.

But if we've learned anything so far, it's that more information is better than less, and Internet advertising gives you the opportunity to know more, to go beyond the CPM. The only way to get there is to demand more of our measurements. By creating new advertising metrics on the Internet, metrics that come closer to telling the whole story, we have a chance to hold advertising, wherever it occurs, to a higher standard. Maybe we'll even be able to give Nielsen a hand, eventually.

Statistics play a large role in our everyday lives. Interest rates, Internet marketing budgets, and the college football national championship are decided by them. The scary reality is that many of those so-called statistics are not really statistics but instead fall into the dangerous and misleading category of pseudo-statistics.

In blackjack, there was no room for pseudo-statistics. Our all-in number was the count, and it was the statistic that we used to make all of our decisions. We could always count on it to be objective and unbiased. And, crucially, it was always accurate. Yet the count did not exist on its own since, really, no number can.

As you look to obtain the House Advantage in your business, you need to find your version of the count—metrics that you can rely on to guide your data-driven decisions. But what is more important than finding that number is the avoidance of pseudo-statistics that will mislead you and, in the process, give real, useful statistics a bad name.

So how does one know how to create metrics that tell the whole story and avoid using or creating a pseudo-statistic?

First of all, statistics should be based on some sort of objective measure. The BCS is an example of this violation, as two-thirds of it is purely subjective. Really a statistic can only be as good as the data that feeds into it. The old expression "garbage in, garbage out" applies here. If the numbers that feed into the statistic aren't good to start with, the statistic itself has no chance. Think of the quarterback rating where important data points are omitted.

Second, a statistic should be easy to understand or at least should be presented in the simplest way possible. The quarterback rating and its scale of 1 to 158.3 clearly do not fit into that category. What if instead they made the scale from 1 to 100? Wouldn't it make a lot more sense if a perfect rating was 100? Numbers are hard enough to understand already. There's no reason to make them even more complicated by presenting them in a non-intuitive manner.

Third, statistics should not be manipulated or used to support lies. The way the U.S. government has manipulated inflation data may serve its own purpose, but it makes the general consumer less trusting of numbers. There are entire books devoted to the art of lying with numbers, and this behavior is one of the many reasons that people hate and don't believe what the numbers say. There is a certain level of ethics that you need to have when working with numbers. Because your numerical output carries more weight than a simple collection of words, you need to be careful that what you present represents some kind of truth.

Finally, a real statistic measures something useful, not just something that's easy to measure. In this sense it must have predictive value, which is the acid test of any statistic. If what you are really trying to measure can't be measured by your methods, you need to improve your methods, not measure something else that is less relevant. In the case of Internet advertising, the CPM measures audience but it doesn't measure the effectiveness of a campaign. To capture a truly accurate picture of the effectiveness of an advertising campaign, you simply need more information, more metrics. Or you need to compress the issue at hand down into a simple measure in one dimension that passes the clarity test. To answer complicated questions, this will always be the case.

The ability to use numbers to tell a story or represent information is an important part of gaining the House Advantage in business. By focusing on a statistic's accuracy, simplicity, and integrity, you will avoid using pseudo-statistics. This will allow you to truly harness the power of analytics and paint a complete picture.

7

NEVER FEAR

A good plan violently executed now is better than a perfect plan executed next week.

—George S. Patton

YOU KNOW YOU need to be fully aware of the external forces shaping the numbers that drive your business, and you know to approach them with a healthy skepticism, but there is an equally important point to keep in mind: Always know the worst-case scenario in order to avoid it.

As our success in the casinos spread, we began to look for new opportunities to make money, and that often meant new casinos, outside of Vegas. During the mid- to late nineties, casinos started spurting up in places like Black Hawk, Colorado, Albuquerque, New Mexico, and Lake Charles, Louisiana. Each of these represented a potential opportunity for us to ply our craft.

We evaluated each casino as it opened. Did it have blackjack? What were its table limits? What were the rules of the casino's blackjack table? How many blackjack tables did it have? These were all questions used to evaluate whether these remote locales warranted a visit from the MIT blackjack team.

As a team, we visited many of these casinos, with tremendous success at most. We'd hear reports from other card counters or teams that a certain casino in a certain area had become vulnerable to card counters, and we'd hurry to organize a trip to that casino. The problem was, after a casino was hit by card counters, the management would become paranoid about them and quickly make it hard to play there. This was the unavoidable risk in traveling to remote locales: We never knew if the trek would end up being a complete waste of time. Or, worse, a waste of money.

Midway into my blackjack career, we got word that Shreveport, Louisiana, had suddenly become a great place to play blackjack. Another team had won more than $100,000 there in a weekend, and there were four different casinos to choose from. Within the week, I was leading a group of four down to Shreveport in an attempt to replicate the other team's feat.

Shreveport is the self-proclaimed "Next Great City of the South," but to us, it was just another place to try and make our fortune. We arrived early on a Saturday morning and immediately made our way to the Horseshoe Casino. We'd heard this was the type of place where dealers would unblinkingly "take the action" (be comfortable with the large bets that we needed to make).

I was the big player. As big player, it was my responsibility to coordinate the trip. And, more importantly, I would be the one betting the big money. As we made our way into the casino, I noticed a few things. First, there were very few other Asians in this casino. Second, no one was betting big money. I sensed I was going to cause something of a stir.

But I refused to let all this bother me, as we'd made the trek from Boston, and our job was simple: Make as much money as we could and get back on the plane. So, we started playing. Everything went according to plan. Actually, it probably went better than planned. Over the next two hours, we won close to $60,000. Every time I stood up from a table, I left with more chips than I had when I sat down. Of course, this was by design, but seldom does it work out this well. After two hours, I walked through the floor of the casino and rubbed my hand on the back of my neck, signaling that it was time to end the session and head to our pre-planned meeting place.

I knew there were three other casinos in the area, so I thought it would be a good idea to take a break from the Horseshoe and move on to one of the others. Casinos were not built for winners, and to that end, we always had to take part in quite a bit of subterfuge. When you start to win quickly at a new casino, you tend to get noticed, so moving on to a new one was the prudent choice.

We met up at the rental car and headed over to the Harrah's casino across town. We talked about what had gone down at the Horseshoe, as I wanted to gather intelligence from my teammates. I was particularly concerned about whether they had noticed any "heat" from the casino employees. I personally hadn't been aware of any, but sometimes the big player misses nuances the spotters see.

"I didn't see any heat but you and your hot streak," my friend Robbie replied with a cheesy grin on his face.

None of my other teammates had noticed anything out of the ordinary, and they thought we'd be fine at Harrah's. Still, something didn't sit well with me, and I told my teammates they should go inside the casino first and see if they noticed anything off. And then, if things seemed copasetic, I would head in.

The Harrah's casino in Shreveport is actually on a stationary riverboat. When we arrived, I didn't board the boat immediately; I sat at the café just outside the boat's entry, waiting about a quarter of an hour before boarding. When I did step on to the boat, I didn't head straight to the blackjack tables. Instead, I walked around the periphery of the blackjack pit and looked for any signs of heat.

What I noticed right away was a burly man in a chocolate suit also standing on the periphery of the pit. After you've been in casinos as often as we had, you learn to judge people by visual cues, like the title on their nametag, the cut or fabric or tailoring of their suit, the frequency of a smile. This man was certainly a casino employee, and, by the look of his crisp, well-cut suit, he was a high-level one. Casino shift manager was my guess. My well-dressed friend was about ten yards in front of me and was clearly looking for someone in particular. I was sure I knew exactly whom.

He scanned the entire floor while I stood behind him; I knew he would soon turn around to see me. I stepped behind a pole so that if he turned around, he wouldn't notice me. But, before he had time to turn around, someone else in a boxy, ill-fitting suit swung up to him and tapped him on the shoulder. The cheap suit handed the expensive suit a piece of paper that looked like it had come from a fax machine. I stepped out from behind the pole and took a few steps closer to the man in the chocolate suit. I wanted to see what was on the paper. As I inched closer, I saw four dark rectangles on the paper. A few more tiny steps forward and I recognized the faces in those four rectangles—they belonged to me and my three teammates! I took a step back behind the pole and noticed the two men pointing across the pit at my friend Robbie. Robbie was sitting calmly at a blackjack table, completely oblivious to the trouble brewing. I had as much confirmation as I needed and ran off the boat. When I was safely off the property, I sent a page (this was before the prevalence of cell phones) to all of my teammates, "Heat. Get. Off. Boat!" I walked toward the parking garage and the rental car and waited for my teammates to show up. One by one they did, each with a different story of attracting attention in the casino. I was not seeing things: There was obvious heat.

We tumbled into the car and tried to figure out what to do. We had been programmed in a certain way by our mentors. We were in Shreveport to do a job: to use our statistical models to beat the casinos. We believed that any time we weren't playing was wasted time because the more we played the more we would win. In addition, in our haste to leave the Horseshoe, I had failed to cash out my chips, so I still had over $70,000 in Horseshoe chips. We decided to head back, assess the situation, and see if we could make a little more money over there.

In hindsight, this may not have been the best judgment. This was actually the first time in my career I had been the subject of this level of attention, and, to be honest, I wasn't sure how to deal with it. We didn't have a mathematical model that measured the amount of attention we were getting and spit out advice telling us what to do. Instead, this real-world scenario begged for a judgment call that I wasn't prepared to make.

So we found ourselves back at the Horseshoe Casino. We had discussed in painstaking detail what we would do if we got "heat." I would enter first because I still had those chips that I needed to cash out. If, when cashing the chips out, I noticed anything wrong, I would immediately walk off the property. I would then walk across the street, where my teammates would be waiting for me in the rental car.

As I entered the casino, I definitely felt uneasy. After what we had just seen at Harrah's, the idea of trying to play more did seem a bit stupid. But there was a lot of money at stake, and I brazenly decided to test the waters by sitting down at a blackjack table anyway. I was curious to see what kind of attention I would receive. As soon as I took my seat, I saw one of the supervisors run over to a phone. As she talked on the phone she stared hard at me. This was clearly more "heat."

Making a snap judgment, I got up from the table and headed over to the cage to cash out my chips. I quickly sent a page to my teammates telling them not to bother coming back. I stood at the cage placing my chips down on the counter and waited as the cashier counted out the chips.

"Any markers?" she asked.

"No," I answered quickly. "Just cash please." I handed her my ID and waited. I could feel a lot of eyes on me.

I continued to wait as the cashier walked away with my chips and my driver's license. It seemed like an eternity before she came back, handing me my ID first and then pulling out six big bundles of cash. She started to pull apart the bundles and I grabbed them, saying, "No need to count it out. I trust you."

I started out of the casino at a brisk pace. As I walked down the ramp out of the main casino, I heard a voice behind me calling, "Mr. Ma. Mr. Ma!"

I turned around to see an older man in a gray suit and equally gray mustache running after me. He offered his hand and I reciprocated, though a bit reluctantly. "Mr. Ma, I am the casino manager here at the Horseshoe, and we know what you are doing."

I tried to play dumb, although I knew there was no point. "Umm. I'm not sure what you mean, sir," I answered back in my best Eddie Haskell impression.

"You and your friends have had your fun. Don't ever come back to our casino," he said confidently and emphatically.

I turned away from him, knowing that one more word from me would have been too much, and I walked briskly off the casino property. As I stepped outside, I noticed two men in suits waiting in a pickup truck. As soon as I walked past them, they revved up the engine and started to follow me; their truck never moved any faster than my own quick pace and trailed me doggedly by about ten feet. I turned around and saw that there were two gleaming shotguns hoisted nonchalantly on a makeshift gun rack in the truck's bed.

It was at that moment that I wondered if anyone would notice if an Asian man disappeared in Shreveport, Louisiana. I hastened my pace but it didn't matter much, as the truck easily matched me and maintained our same ten-foot separation. When I got to the end of the driveway that led into the casino, I noticed my teammates sitting in the car across the street. If only I could get to them. But then, as I rounded the corner, I noticed a police car only a few yards away from our rental car. At first, I felt immense relief but, then, horrible doubt as I wondered, *Wait, are the cops in on this also?*

I wasn't sure what to do. Behind me I had a pickup truck with shotguns and in front of me a police car filled with local police. I had little choice, so I ran across the street, quickly jumping in the car and yelling "Drive!" to my friends.

Robbie sat in the driver's seat and immediately stepped on the gas; we raced away from the Horseshoe. I looked out the back of the car and saw the lights of the police car disappearing in the distance. The pickup truck also stayed put. Both were there to intimidate and dissuade us from ever setting foot in the Horseshoe again. Both were successful.

We called it quits for the rest of the weekend, leaving theoretical money on the table but keeping our collective piece of mind. I learned an important lesson that day. Even though we had a plan and strategy based on math and statistics, the actual execution of that strategy was subject to exogenous factors that, ex ante, could never be properly taken into account. Successful execution of that plan took more than math—it took judgment.

Blackjack had always seemed infallible to me. When we played it, we were invincible. But there was a real vulnerability that I encountered in Shreveport. And that vulnerability could not be modeled on a computer.

It's funny; I'm not sure if my life was ever really at risk back in Shreveport, but when I was there, it certainly felt that way. We had a very solid strategy that, when executed perfectly, was unbeatable. But problems encountered upon execution raised some important questions about our judgment: Had we been too greedy after we had a sense that we'd already been made at Harrah's? Instead of stopping after our run-in at Harrah's, should we have gone to one of the other casinos and tried our luck there? Had we wasted a chance to make more money at the Horseshoe by prematurely quitting before there was any real sign of heat?

This type of judgment played a large role in my success as a card counter. Looking back with infinitely more experience, I know that for the most part I made the right decisions in Shreveport. Sure, I could have played a little longer at the Horseshoe, but the reality is that they were on to us from almost the beginning. Heading over to Harrah's to test the waters was the correct thing to do because you never really know how much casinos talk to each other. Finally, getting out of the Horseshoe when we did was certainly the right move.

These judgments represent a very simple analysis. Is the opportunity cost of not playing more or less than the opportunity cost of pissing off the casinos so badly that they send my picture and name around to every casino in the world? I wasn't even aware of this at the time, but back then there was something called the Griffin Detective Agency, and their job was to protect casinos from the likes of us. If a casino really wanted to end your career, they would just send your information to Griffin and your blackjack career would be as good as over. I'm sure if I had continued to play that weekend I would have been caught by Griffin.

Throughout my career, my strategy in these situations was patience. There was no reason to allow greed or petulance drive my decisions. Blackjack is a game where the casino's death happens with a thousand cuts, not one. It's back to our lesson of large numbers and long-term perspective. Being too aggressive could ultimately spell your doom, ruining your chance to let your advantage take over.

There's a valuable business analogy here as many an investor or business person has been faced with a judgment call of how aggressive he should be when he knows the odds are with him or he has a winning strategy. He needs to choose between strategic alternatives: Does he go for broke or is he patient? Is he the tortoise or the hare?

There is no universal rule, but what's important to remember when faced with this situation is the lesson of Shreveport. Think about the opportunity costs associated with your actions and make sure your judgment is not being clouded by greed or impatience. The vision of those goons chasing me off their property will always serve as my reminder that slow and steady wins the race.

The reality is that being a truly successful card counter is about more than mathematical acuity. Social intelligence is worth its weight in gold, too. Similarly, successful implementation of statistical analysis in business is about more than just building a tight mathematical model.

The execution of your strategy or model in the real world takes elements like judgment, planning, and discipline. All were tested that day in Shreveport.

We've discussed the large role that judgment played in our success, but what of virtue number two—proper planning? In many ways planning, or rather counter-planning, was what set us apart from other card counters.

Planning did not simply mean figuring out in advance where someone should be and at what time. Our plan entailed so much more than that. We had well-orchestrated plans that had little to do with statistics and helped ensure maximum opportunities for success. One of those plans was the art of camouflage.

Camouflaging your play in blackjack is exactly what it sounds like. It is the art of masking or hiding your abilities and actions from the casinos. As mentioned previously, despite what casinos would lead you to believe, card counting (without the use of a device like a miniature computer or calculator) is not illegal.

At the core, card counting is simply using your brain to be better at a game than most others. Think of it as me beating you in Monopoly every time because I know to buy Boardwalk and Park Place and you focus on the Electric Company and Water Works. Finally one day you grow frustrated, throw the board up in the air, and declare my superior skills illegal. I know that sounds preposterous, but in essence that's what the casinos have tried to do.

One card-counting legend, Ken Uston, actually sued the casinos in Atlantic City for his right to play, represented himself before the state supreme court, and won.

Ken Uston was no academic slouch; he graduated Phi Beta Kappa from Yale University and received his MBA from Harvard. Instead of applying what he learned on Wall Street, like most of his classmates, he decided to attack the casinos. Building on the early work of our card-counting professor Edward Thorp, Uston was a true pioneer. He led some of the world's most successful blackjack teams and won millions of dollars in the mid- to late seventies. As you might imagine, Uston's teams were some of the very first barred from casinos in Atlantic City.

Uston challenged the notion that card counters could be barred from casinos and in a 1981 interview on *60 Minutes* said, "Basically I am just using skill in a casino. I'm not cheating; I'm not doing anything other than trying to use my brain. And, the fact that I'm not allowed to play bothers me." Uston even reasoned that banning him from playing blackjack was "sort of against the American Way."

To Uston, being prevented from playing blackjack in a public establishment was a violation of his civil rights guaranteed by the state's public accommodations law. In New Jersey, this law prohibits businesses offering goods or services to the general public from discriminating against or refusing service to people on the basis of preference. Uston started by taking legal action against the Las Vegas Dunes and Sands in 1975. He filed similar suits against the Flamingo Hilton, Holiday Casino, Las Vegas Hilton, Marina Hotel, MGM, and Silver City Casino in June 1976. Finally, in 1981, after Uston and his team were barred from the Resorts International Casino in Atlantic City, Uston filed the suit that would change everything. When the litigation first arose, the Casino Control Commission advised the resort that it enjoyed a common-law property right to exclude anyone, for any reason, so long as its exclusions didn't violate the state or federal constitutions (by, for example, excluding patrons for their skin color or gender). In 1982, the New Jersey Supreme Court disagreed and ruled that barring card counters was illegal.[1]

The court essentially balanced the property interest of the casino against the individual's competing right of access to public places and found that when property owners open their premises to the general public, they have no right to exclude people unreasonably. The court held that an incredible head for mathematics, as it were, is an *unreasonable* basis for exclusion. Henceforth, New Jersey casinos may not completely prevent card counters from playing blackjack. However, they are still able to create restrictions (up to the point of actually altering blackjack rules) that make it difficult for the card counter to win.

In Las Vegas, the legal restrictions are a bit different because Nevada courts consider casinos private enterprises and give greater weight to an ancient common-law right that entitles a property owner to kick anyone off his property, for any reason.[2] Banning a card counter is not considered discrimination (at least not for purposes of the state and federal constitutions) because the U.S. Supreme Court only prohibits discrimination against persons who are members of "suspect classifications" based on race, creed, sex, national origin, age, or physical disability. Card counters do not fit into any of these categories. Therefore, according to Nevada law, discrimination on the basis of the ability or intent to use a clever gambling strategy does not infringe upon any recognized constitutional right. More simply, card counters in Nevada can legally be banned from playing blackjack and even banned from the premises, although card counting itself is perfectly legal.

Beyond his efforts in the legal realm, for which every card counter is grateful, Uston is largely credited with the concept of team play, one of the greatest forms of camouflage. This is the very concept that my MIT blackjack team employed so successfully in the 1990s. In team play, groups of card counters play together but have different roles. The first role is spotter. The spotter's job is to simply track the count at the table. He can either stand behind the table or sit down and play the table minimum. He is supposed to remain as anonymous as possible. When the odds at his table get favorable enough to start betting real money, he signals to the "big player" with a simple fold of the arms or hand to the face. The big player will then walk over to that table. As the big player arrives, the spotter will use a code word to tell the big player the table's count.

Typically a spotter would simply utter the code word loud enough for the big player to hear, but other times the spotter would actually try to use the word in a sentence directed at anyone other than the big player. "Man, you just took my whole *paycheck*," a spotter might utter to the dealer as the big player walked up. The big player would then know the count at that table was 15. In another instance, a spotter might turn to the dealer and ask, "Do you know where that lady who sells *cigarettes* is?" The big player would touch his nose to signify that he understood that cigarettes signified the count was 20, and the spotter would eventually get up and leave the table.

This was the type of team play that Uston more or less invented, and, really, it was our best form of camouflage. We had tremendous success deceiving the casinos with team play simply because they weren't looking for it. It was not a novel concept, but by the time we started playing in earnest, casinos had all but forgotten Uston. They had one profile of a card counter and that was someone who sat down for long stretches at the table, betting less money at the beginning of the shoe and more at the end. They weren't looking for someone who would jump into a table in the middle of the shoe.

And, of course, executing team play took a lot of planning. But it was invaluable time spent as it allowed us to ply our craft for much longer than we would have been able to otherwise. When implementing a winning strategy, you cannot open your kimono and let the whole world see what you are doing. We had to have a plan that hid our actions from outsiders. Unfortunately, the outsiders eventually caught on, and that led to our downfall.

An exposed strategy contributed to the downfall of another collection of MIT geniuses. Founded in 1994, Long-Term Capital Management (LTCM) was a collection of some of the best and brightest in the finance world. The founder, John Merriweather, was one of the pioneers of bond trading, revolutionizing the industry while building one the most successful trading groups at Salomon Brothers. After being forced out of Salomon for reasons beyond his control, Merriweather assembled finance's best of the best at his new firm, LTCM. His team included Ph.D.s, finance professors, and even two future Nobel Prize winners in economics. And, yes, it included many people either with MIT degrees or associations to my alma mater, along with others from high-profile institutions like The University of Chicago and Harvard.

The story of LTCM has become a cautionary tale taught in business schools and finance classes alike. In summary, LTCM used complex mathematical models and financial theory to create trading strategies that allowed it to buy low and sell high. They often did this in pairs where the two parts of the pair were similar but for some reason were priced differently. They would sell the more expensive part of the pair short and buy the cheaper part of the pair. As long as the market eventually realized that these parts were indeed similar, the two prices would converge and LTCM would make a profit equal to the difference in price.

For its first four years, LTCM was incredibly successful, producing gross returns of 28 percent, 59 percent, 57 percent, and 25 percent.[3] But in its fifth year, 1998, LTCM hit a snag. In August of that year, Russia experienced a financial crisis, causing it to default on its newly issued government bonds. This was not a third-world country, it was Russia, a nuclear superpower, and this unprecedented event triggered hysteria in the global financial markets.[4]

Fundamental to traditional economic theory is the notion that human beings behave rationally, and rational behavior was what LTCM counted on as they waited for the market to finally price their two paired parts equally. Temporary hysteria causes irrational behavior, and extended periods of irrational behavior were not good for LTCM. Legendary economist John Maynard Keynes said it well with his famous quote: "*Markets can remain irrational* far *longer* than you or I can *remain* solvent."[5]

And here was the difference between the LTCM models and the reality of the real world. Jim Simons from Renaissance Technologies again plays the role of sage with his wise words: "A trouble with convergence trading [the name of LTCM's strategies] is that you don't have a time scale. You say that eventually things will come together. Well, when is that eventually?"[6]

The first day of the hysteria, LTCM lost $550 million. But that was just the beginning. Eventually LTCM would lose more than 91 percent of its capital. They started 1998 with $4.7 billion, but a difficult year had left them with only $3.6 billion in mid-August. And then a horrendous five weeks of hysteria would leave them with a mere $400 million and a tremendous need for a helping hand.[7]

During this five-week armageddon, in order to find this helping hand, LTCM had to reverse a history of secrecy and camouflage—the same secrecy and camouflage that had allowed them to execute winning strategies for four years without their competitors catching on. Since LTCM was looking for help in the form of a cash infusion from their competitors, they were left opening the kimono for all to see.

Soon, LTCM's worst fears were realized. Roger Lowenstein writes in *When Genius Failed,* "Rival firms began to sell in advance of what they feared would be an avalanche of liquidating by Long-Term . . . Hilibrand [an LTCM partner] had not been wrong: when you bare your secrets, you're left naked."[8]

It's like playing a game of poker where your cards are dealt face up and everyone else's face down. If everyone knows the cards you hold, you are doomed. Naked was what LTCM was, and naked was what we would have been without our camouflage.

In business it is vital to have an element of surprise. Not just in the obvious case of your competitors but in other, less straightforward cases it helps to play things close to the vest. Recently I was helping a friend with a public relations strategy for the launch of his new company. For six months, his company had been operating in stealth mode, that is, not talking with the press and keeping their operations under wraps. We were discussing how they planned to announce the company to the world. They expressed a desire to get the word out gradually via the bloggers and then eventually pitch the story to a bigger publication like the *Wall Street Journal* or the *New York Times*.

The problem here is that once you are "naked," the *Times* and *Journal* no longer want to write about you. I advised them to keep their story quiet until they were ready to engage the major papers. Keeping a certain level of anonymity would put them in a much better position to close a major publication down the road.

LTCM's problems ran much deeper than any sort of loss of metaphorical clothing, though. At the core of it were very real human problems that mathematical models did not account for. The markets had always expected the United States to bail Russia out because America could ill afford a nuclear superpower going bankrupt. But Bill Clinton may have been a bit distracted. He was being impeached over the Lewinsky affair and had far more pressing matters to deal with, not the least of which was his wife. The net result was that Russia had a lower priority and ended up overlooked—a worst-case scenario that was difficult to plan for.

And herein lies the larger problem—the need to manage risk for a worst-case scenario.

As a blackjack team, we were experts in managing risk. First, we needed to follow a very strict money-management plan. Even though we had an edge against the casino, that edge was relatively small. And remember our coin-flipping analogy from the first chapter—when you have a small advantage, you need to make sure that you have a lot of opportunities to realize that advantage. Since we didn't have an infinite amount of money, the amount we bet was always based on a calculation that took into account our overall bankroll.

We followed the same money-management strategy discussed by Thorp in *Beat the Dealer*, the Kelly Criterion. Named after Bell Labs scientist Jon Kelly, the Kelly Criterion is used to determine the optimal size of bets based on overall bankroll and advantage on each hand.[9] Simply put, the larger advantage the larger the bet, the smaller the advantage the smaller the bet. Ed Thorp calls this one of the greatest financial analogies to come from card counting. "The bigger the edge the more you bet."[10] Likewise, if there was no advantage, the Kelly Criterion would tell you not to bet at all, meaning if you followed the Kelly Criterion to a tee, you would never play slots, roulette, or craps because you have no edge. In all cases, the amount to bet was a percentage of the overall bankroll. If we had an unlucky streak and our overall bankroll diminished, our Kelly calculation would tell us to reduce our bet size in relation to that smaller bankroll. Following Kelly, we had very little chance of going bankrupt.

Bankruptcy is the ultimate sin for a card counter. Whether it is the middle of a trip, session, or shoe, running out of money means that you don't have a chance to let your advantage work for you. Even worse, if you run out of money in the middle of a hand, you might not even be able to follow basic strategy. Imagine that you put your last two $1,000 chips out on a hand and get 11 on one and a pair of aces on the other against the dealer's 5. If you don't have any money left, you would have to simply hit that 11 and completely give up the chance to win another $1,000. Even worse, you would not be able to split the aces and would have to play the hand as 2 or 12—a tremendous basic strategy mistake.

This is an extreme case, but even the tamer version of bankruptcy, or "tapping out," is horrible. Imagine that you are counting cards and play through a big streak of low cards. And as you play through those low cards, you hit an enormous losing streak. This is actually likely to happen when you play through low cards, as we know these cards are good for the dealer and bad for the player.

Now, imagine you haven't managed your money effectively and after your seventh losing hand in a row, you run out of chips. The odds are now highly in your favor because most of the low cards have already been dealt. But you're out of money and out of the game. So, you played seven hands where the odds were very much against you and, even though you know going forward that the odds will be in your favor, you can't do anything about it. This is not good.

Philip Maymin was a trader at LTCM starting in the summer of 1996 and was with the firm though April 1999. He was there in the good and bad times. "My greatest lesson from LTCM is attention to risk management. You have to make sure you have enough capital to withstand the worst-case scenario," Maymin explains to me. These words bring me back to our statistical commandments and Dr. Bob's bankrupt clients. If they understood this statement, they would have been able to withstand his "worst-case" losing streak.

In our blackjack world, we made sure the worst case never happened. We made sure that our individual bets were small compared to our overall bankroll. And if we lost, those bets grew smaller since our bankroll was smaller. Unfortunately, due to lack of liquidity, LTCM did not have a similar option. They were forced to face a worst-case scenario that they had not prepared for. They simply did not have the capital to stay in the game.

But that didn't have to be the case. At the end of 2007, before any of this adversity, in an act that may have seemed prudent at the time, the LTCM partners reduced the size of their fund by giving $2.7 billion dollars back to investors. The partners wanted to ensure that they were getting the same relative returns on their own money that they had through the first four years of LTCM, and the only way to do that was to reduce their overall fund size by giving back money to the outside investors.

We actually faced a similar situation where our early years of success at the tables, not unlike LTCM's great run, provided us with excess capital. We began to limit investments only to those who were active players within the team. But at each point we made sure that the overall money we had was liquid and was sufficient to withstand the worst-case scenario. Also, since we followed the Kelly money-management strategy, our bets were always in relation to the size of our bankroll.

The action of giving money back to their investors shows that LTCM's focus was on anticipating success rather than failure. Risk management must be focused on the worst-case scenario, not the best, and strategies need to be developed with this worst-case scenario in mind.

As we faced situations with excess cash or not enough opportunities, we had to maintain our discipline. Playing with a bankroll in excess of $1 million, we knew that we could make bets averaging $2,000 to $3,000 and capping out around $10,000 on special occasions. But if we doubled the bankroll, we would have to come close to doubling our bet size. There aren't that many casinos that will take those large bets without some serious scrutiny. So rather than push the envelope, we stayed disciplined and kept our bank size near $1 million.

Even as our run grew to a close, we had to stay disciplined. With the number of opportunities (playable casinos) shrinking, we remained focused on the few casinos that offered the best blackjack game. We did not look for opportunities in games we knew little about simply because we needed more action. And we didn't start a craps team because we knew there was no advantage for us there.

Unfortunately, LTCM traders did not possess similar discipline. The large size of the firm resulting from their early successes caused traders to lament the lack of opportunities in their traditional strategies and they eventually branched out into areas that may have been out of their expertise. This is called "style drift," and the results of it were predictably bad.

The story of LTCM teaches us much about the problems that geniuses can face when their ideal world of math and computers collides with the real world run by rational and irrational human beings. The unfortunate reality of Shreveport exposed similar challenges with our blackjack strategy.

Planning is core to being successful in business. From having a strategy that helps you "keep your clothes on" to managing your resources for the worst-case scenario, the importance of obsessive planning cannot be underestimated.

Finally, discipline in business may be the most important lesson from Shreveport and LTCM. And obviously this is easier said than done, whether you are winning hand over fist or losing your shirt, but in both cases you need to exercise discipline and stick with your system, stick with what you know works. Don't let the emotion—good or bad—of a situation affect you.

As you think about me running away from the bad guys in Shreveport, you will hopefully be reminded of these lessons and will avoid ending up like Merriweather and his boys.

8

MAKING THE RIGHT DECISION

Winning isn't everything; it's the only thing.

—Vince Lombardi

REMEMBER THE CUBS fan from Chapter 3? He didn't want me to come into his table in Chicago and tried to convince me not to. If I had listened to him, I would have cost the team $6,000. If I had listened to him and stood on my ace 7 rather than doubling it, I would have cost the entire table. Of course it's not really fair to judge these decisions on the results; rather, they should be judged on what they cost theoretically.

Judging the merit of a decision can never be done simply by looking at the outcome. A poor result does not necessarily mean a poor decision. Likewise a good result does not necessarily mean a good decision.

This is something that few people intuitively understand. In fact most people believe that if the result turned out positively, then the decision must have been the right one. But taking an extreme example, one can see how flawed this thinking can be. Let's assume I decide to drive home from work tonight. This is the right decision since I can't get home any other way and I have to get home at some point. If on the way home

I have an accident, which is clearly a bad result, it cannot be inferred that my original decision to drive home was a bad one.

Similarly, in blackjack, if someone decides to hit on a 20 and happens to receive the only card in the deck, an ace, that will help them, but this does not justify the decision. The positive outcome does not make the decision a good one.

The decision and the outcome are separate entities. The quality of the decision can be evaluated by the logic and information I used in arriving at my decision. Over time, if one makes good, quality decisions, one will generally receive better outcomes, but it takes a large sample set to prove this. Hitting a 20 will cause you to lose instantly 12 out of 13 times (each time you don't receive an ace); there is no sound logic short of knowing definitively that an ace is coming that would render this a good decision.

Remember my friend Brian from Chapter 2? He was convinced that because the roulette wheel had served up several red results, he had a better chance that the next spin would land on black. If he had won his bet on black, it would not have meant that he had made the right decision. We know that his bet on black had less than a 50 percent chance of winning, and since his payoff was even—betting one dollar would win him one dollar—this was a bad bet, a bad decision.

So instead of looking at my result while next to the Cubs fan, that is, the $6,000 I had won, instead I need to look at what theoretical gain I would have given up by not playing. Assuming we had about a 2 percent advantage on that hand and I bet $4,000 total, by not playing I would have cost the team about $80—still a relevant amount of money in an evening's work.

Ignoring the Cubs fan was easy. But it's not always that easy to make the right decision. Early in my blackjack career, I faced a much more difficult test of my ability to ignore external factors. I had been with the team a little over a year and found myself playing at the MGM Grand during Super Bowl weekend. In that year, we had so much success and were so confident in our system that a single bet of $5,000 was not at all uncommon.

Back in its heyday, the MGM Grand ran at an almost frenetic clip. It felt huge, like the Costco version of a casino. But it was a fantastic place to play blackjack because it had a lot of tables, was always busy, and had implausibly alluring $10,000 betting limits at most tables on the floor. Again, we had experienced tremendous success and were flush with cash going into the weekend. Our betting unit was higher than it had ever been. In addition, Super Bowl weekend brings in more high rollers than almost any other weekend, so the bets all around us were exorbitant anyway, making ours less noticeable.

It was exciting to enter the casino knowing that this session would likely have a very large outcome. The only thing that I wasn't sure about was whether that outcome would be good or bad. As I've mentioned, our edge over the casino was small and the variance was large. So with even larger bets than normal, the evening's potential swing was huge.

It was Saturday night, January 27, 1996, and I had close to $150,000 in cash and chips in my suit. Some were $100 bills stuffed into the pockets of my black blazer. Some were $5,000 chips crammed into the pocket of my pants. But all were in play for me to bet that night. As I started my walk around the floor of the casino, I noticed my friend Paul standing behind a table with his arms folded—the signal that he had a hot shoe. I quickly walked in front of him and he blurted out the word "paycheck." This meant the count at this table was 15.

I sat down at the empty spot at the table and glanced quickly at the discard rack. With two and a half decks remaining, a count of 15 and a $1,000 betting unit called for a bet of $5,000 exactly. I put down a $5,000 chip into each betting circle.

"Chocolate action!" The dealer called out. She was referencing the brown-colored $5,000 chips that I had just put down on the table and was trying to get the attention of the pit boss. The pit boss was a man named Larry, and he knew me well. He looked up for a second from the clipboard that had previously held his attention, saw it was me, and called out, "Hey, Mr. Lee. Go ahead, Janet." I waved to him with a smile. Mr. Lee was one of my favorite aliases.

I broke even on that first round, winning with a 20 but busting by drawing an 8 on my 14. But, the count did the unexpected and kept rising. With a little over two decks remaining the count was 20, which called for me to bet two hands of $8,000. I added three yellow $1,000 chips to each $5,000 chip already in the betting circle and waited as the dealer dealt me a blackjack on one hand and two 10s on the other. The dealer had a 6 up. Quickly glancing around the table, I calculated that the count was now 17.

With less than two decks left in the deck and a count so high, the correct mathematical play was for me to split these 10s. Yes, you heard me correctly. I needed to split these 10s. I had never actually split 10s before in my brief blackjack career, and I started to fidget.

The math behind splitting 10s is relatively simple. With a 20 against a dealer's 6, you have roughly an 85 percent chance to win the hand. So your expected value is 0.70 (0.85–0.15) times whatever you have bet, in this case $8,000. My expected value of standing on the 20 was $5,600.

If you split the 10s, putting another $8,000 down on the table, your new expected value is the sum of the expected value of each new hand. Starting with a 10 against the dealer's 6, you will win roughly 64 percent of the time. So in this case your expected value is simply .28 (.64–.36) times $16,000 (the sum of the two bets). My expected value of splitting the 10s was $4,480.

These numbers apply to normal conditions, facing a deck with a standard ratio of high cards to low cards remaining. However, when the deck gets rich in high cards, your odds of winning in each scenario— splitting versus standing—both increase. And the more the deck gets skewed toward high cards remaining, the more the probability of winning in each scenario increases.

Let's take the extreme case when you know there are only high cards remaining in the deck. If you stand your 20, you will have pretty close to a 100 percent chance to win, and your expected value will be $8,000. But if you split your 10s you will also have close to a 100 percent chance to win, and your expected value will be close to $16,000, two times your expected value for standing.

Of course this is merely a theoretical ideal scenario, but it illustrates the value of splitting 10s. In a favorable situation it allows you to put more money on the table and therefore win more money.

Splitting 10s is something called a "numbers play" and is something you only do once you have mastered all other aspects of card counting. Numbers plays are deviations to basic strategy based on the count at your table. On that night in Las Vegas, numbers plays were something I had just learned.

Based on the math this was not even a close decision—splitting the 10s was the only correct move. And as I contemplated this decision, I remembered something that one of my blackjack mentors once told me and that made me resolute. As the dealer finished paying my blackjack, she started to pass over my 20 and I had to stop her verbally: "Hold on a sec, ma'am, I think I want to split these."

Everyone at the table looked at me, aghast. Here I was, a 23-year-old kid who had just made $12,000 on one hand, contemplating splitting a beautiful 20 to make even more. If only Cubs fan could see me now.

When you split 10s in a casino it is a major production, even if you are only betting $5. You can only imagine what it was like with eight grand on the table. I knew that the people to my left would be incredulous if I lost and angry if my stunt caused them to lose. This was a $100 minimum table; everyone at the table had real money wagered on this hand.

"I'm going to do it," I said as I put another $8,000 in chips next to the original stack.

"Larry, splitting 10s!" The dealer called out to my friend.

This time he put down his clipboard and walked over to the table. He looked at me with a very disappointed eye. "You sure you want to do this, James?" (Yes, my alias was James Lee.)

"Yup. I got a good feeling," I replied.

The dealer dealt me an ace on my first 10. I waved that off and she then dealt me a 9, giving me 19 and 21 on my two hands. I felt pretty good about myself, but I needed the dealer to bust or there was a chance that everyone at the table was going to lynch me.

The dealer flipped her hole card and revealed a 10, giving her 16. She then did the right thing and dealt herself a queen, giving her a total of 26 and making everyone at the table a winner.

Our table breathed a collective sigh of relief, and I collected my chips as the shoe was over and the dealer was about to start shuffling. In roughly five minutes, I had just won $28,000. But what stood out to me was how I felt when I faced the difficult decision about whether to split those 10s. It really wasn't a difficult choice from a mathematical standpoint. It was actually only wrenching from an emotional standpoint. How could I give up a nearly sure thing with my 20?

The answer lies in my blackjack mentor's words. "You can't be afraid to lose," he once told me. "This game can be tough, but we are on the winning side, and you have to play as if you expect to win. You should never worry about losing because it is going to happen—a lot."

So, at that moment I decided to simply do the right thing without fear of failure, ignoring the opinions of those around me: the dealer, Larry the pit boss, and everyone else at my table. I knew what was right mathematically and had the discipline to make a data-driven decision. In this instance, it worked, and in a lot of business scenarios the same principles apply. Fear of failure will prevent you from the most daring but possible wins.

There were a lot of factors in play that made me reluctant, though, to make the right play and split the 10s. First of all, there were the social pressures of those around me—the other players at the table, the dealer, Larry. What I was doing was so unconventional in their minds, it couldn't be right. The unconventional never seems right.

Being a contrarian is never easy. It is much easier to go with the flow and make decisions that you think everyone will agree with. That way if the results turn out badly, you escape the blame. And if the results are positive, many will lump praise on you since that is what they would also have done. People are inclined to think that you made the right decision if it agrees with them.

But simply because things are only done one way does not make them right, and having the conviction to challenge convention, especially in business situations, is an incredibly important step to gaining the House Advantage.

Take the plight of one Bill Belichick. Belichick, currently coach of the New England Patriots, is the most successful NFL coach of the last decade, having won three Super Bowls in that time. Beyond his obvious success and acknowledged genius, Belichick is known for his surly manner, poor sportsmanship, and polarizing behavior.

But lately more than ever, Belichick has become known as a contrarian. Tracing back to his early days in Cleveland, he's always been willing to make the unpopular choice. While a first-time head coach of the Cleveland Browns, Belichick signed and then chose quarterback Vinny Testaverde over favored son Bernie Kosar in a move that one of Belichick's friends equated to "beheading the Browns' mascot."[1]

Before the 2002 season, Belichick made the bold move to jettison long-time starter Drew Bledsoe in favor of Tom Brady even though Brady had only proven himself for less than a season.

But then in the first week of the 2003 season, Belichick made what was likeliest his most unpopular decision. Facing the prospect of a salary commitment to a popular but aging player, Belichick cut safety Lawyer Milloy. Milloy had been a favorite of Belichick since his rookie season in New England, but this decision was all about business—all about dollars and cents. Milloy was due to count for $4.5 million against the NFL salary cap, which in Belichick's estimation was simply too high for a player of his performance.

"Guys were outraged," former Patriots guard Damien Woody said, and the lack of cohesion showed on the field as the Patriots lost 31–0 to Milloy's new team, the Buffalo Bills. In what has become a popular practice, media pundits relished Belichick's misfortune.

ESPN analyst Tom Jackson said that Belichick had lost the respect of players in that locker room, stating, "Let me very clear about this. They hate their coach."[2]

Yet somehow, these Patriots that lacked cohesion and hated their coach managed to win 17 of their next 18 games, cementing Belichick's second Super Bowl victory. Clearly, the difficult decision worked out alright.

Belichick's long track record of success has finally given him a certain level of faith from the fans and media. The term "In Bill We Trust" refers to the high level of confidence fans have in Belichick's decisions even when they don't seem to make sense at the time. For the most part, Belichick has become beyond reproach.

That is, until he made a decision so unconventional that even his staunchest supporters decided to jump ship. In week ten of the 2009 NFL season, Belichick's Patriots were facing a fourth and 2 at their own 28-yard line. With a little over two minutes remaining, the Patriots led the game by only six points. A touchdown would have given their opponents, the Indianapolis Colts, a lead for the first time that evening.

So Belichick's only choice was to punt and try to put as much distance between the Colts and the end zone as possible, hoping that his defense and time would eventually win the game for the Patriots. Every other NFL coach would have done the same.

But Belichick's opponent was not any old team, and they weren't led by any old quarterback. They had already scored 28 points in that game and were led by one of the greatest quarterbacks of all time, Peyton Manning. Manning had already led the Colts on two touchdown drives that quarter, the first taking 2:04 and the second taking 1:49. A third with two minutes remaining did not seem out of the question.

So Belichick did the unthinkable. He decided to go for it. As a Patriots fan, I sat in shock as I saw the Patriots' offense go back onto the field. It was with equal shock that I watched Patriots quarterback Tom Brady snap the ball and complete a pass for one yard—one yard short of the first down, giving Peyton Manning and the Colts' offense the ball at the Patriots' 29-yard line.

What ensued next was incredibly predictable. The Colts marched down the field, scoring a touchdown with 14 seconds left, effectively winning the game. All the pundits and fans lined up to pile on Belichick.

Ron Borges from the *Boston Globe* compared Belichick and his decision to something the Three Stooges would have done.[3] Recently retired Rodney Harrison, a fixture in the middle of the Patriots defense during their Super Bowl run, said, "This is the worst coaching decision I've ever seen Bill Belichick make," during the NBC postgame show.[4] And ESPN analyst Trent Dilfer said, "my vocabulary is not big enough to describe the insanity of this decision," concluding that there was "no justification for this call being made."[5]

Belichick's utterly unconventional decision defied traditional logic. That we can all agree on. But had it been the *right* decision?

Making a decision is simply about choosing between alternatives. At first glance, he only had two alternatives: He could punt, or he could go for it. But on closer inspection, he had numerous alternatives as he could run, or pass, or fake punt, or try to draw them off-sides, and each type of run or pass play represented a unique alternative. Clearly this was far from a simple decision.

But going back to our framework of asking simple questions to help frame the problem, there are three questions that Belichick should have asked of the data to help make his decision:

A. What are our chances of converting fourth and 2?
B. What are our chances of stopping the Colts from scoring a touchdown from our 28-yard line?
C. What are our chances of stopping the Colts from scoring a touchdown from their own 34-yard line (the average result of a punt from the Patriots' position on the field)?

Since A, B, and C all essentially end the game in the Patriots' favor, the analysis is pretty simple. If you go for it, your chance to win the game is the sum of converting the fourth down (probability A) plus the chance that you don't convert the fourth down (1-A) times the chance of stopping the Colts from your own 28-yard line (probability B). In summary, $A + (1-A) \times B$ is the chance of winning when you go for it. And probability C is the chance of winning when you punt. So if the former is more than the latter, then you should indeed go for it.

The statistical geniuses ran through this analysis and to a man came back with the same conclusion. Belichick was right. Brian Burke, a football coach, self-proclaimed closet math enthusiast, and the founder of www.advancednflstats.com, wrote, "Statistically, the better decision would be to go for it, and by a good amount."[6] Wayne Winston, the John and Esther Reese Professor of Decision Sciences at Indiana University's nationally ranked Kelly School of Business, commented that the decision was "at worst…a tossup."[7] And *Freakonomics* author and renowned economist Steven Levitt said, "The data suggest that he actually probably did the right thing if his objective was to win the game."[8]

Case closed, right?

Not so fast. The pundits fired back at the stat people. ESPN writer Bill Simmons attacked Belichick's decision, calling it "reckless" and attacking the use of historical data to describe a situation this unique. Matt Lau, one of my former MIT blackjack teammates, said: "All of this 'proof' by statistics is ridiculous. People are pulling whatever relevant numbers they want from whatever source….There are far too many variables (and far too much variance in them) for the numbers to have any real meaning."[9]

And then it hit me. In this case, the data was only a tool. It did not make Belichick's decision right as much as it didn't make it wrong. It simply gave us a platform to say he could have been right and certainly was not off his rocker, as many pundits would have led you to believe.

So data and statistics were the tool used by the "Belichick was right camp." But the "Belichick was crazy camp" jumped on history also. Their history was the large collection of poor decisions made by previous NFL coaches.

That NFL coaches make poor decisions and do not go for it nearly enough on fourth down has been a well-known fact since the work of

University of California, Berkeley, economics professor David Romer.[10] In fact, Romer's conclusion is that these poor decisions significantly hurt a team's chances of winning.

Using play-by-play data from 1998 to 2000 and something called dynamic programming, Romer analyzed this fundamental coaching decision of whether to go for it or kick on fourth down. His general conclusion is that NFL coaches are far too conservative when it comes to fourth-down decisions.

He isolates one particularly telling situation, where a team faces fourth down and goal at the opponent's two-yard line. We'll assume that a team kicking from the opponent's two-yard line has nearly a 100 percent chance of success, so a decision to kick is worth three points. Based on his data, a team in this situation that goes for it will succeed roughly three times in seven (he uses third-down success as a proxy for fourth-down success due to the small sample size of fourth-down tries). So assuming a 100 percent chance of a successful extra point, the decision to go for it is also worth three points.

But here's where the extra value in going for it comes in. If the team goes for it and does not get the touchdown they are leaving the opposing team with very poor field position, likely inside their own two-yard line. The average field position after a kickoff, the consequence of a made field goal, is close to the 30-yard line, a 28-yard difference. No matter whether a coach believes in statistics or not, he will readily admit that that is a huge difference.

So in this case it is clear that going for it would give you the best chance to score the most points and eventually win the game. Yet in the three years of data that Romer looked at, no team faced with this situation actually went for it.

So operating under the premise that historically NFL coaches have not been aggressive enough on fourth down, it seems folly to use this collection of poor decisions as proof of anything.

Which is exactly what ESPN writer Simmons does. Drawing on his personal experience of watching "12 hours of football every

Sunday dating back to elementary school," he makes the statement that, "when a football coach tries something that I cannot remember another team doing...that's not 'gutsy.'...It's not 'revolutionary.'...It's reckless."[11]

This defense using groupthink principles is problematic. Simply because everyone thinks or does things a certain way does not mean it is correct, and those who are able to divorce themselves from this type of decision making often are the winners.

Take the case of financial commentator and stock broker Peter Schiff. The constant contrarian, Schiff went on record as early as 2006 stating that the U.S. economy, specifically the real estate sector, was in danger. In most cases, he was laughed at by the pundits the same way that Belichick was. Commentators called him the "eternal pessimist," comparing his contrarian view to someone ready to conduct an exposé on Santa Claus.[12]

"The United States economy is like the Titanic and I am here with the lifeboat trying to get people to leave the ship....I see a real financial crisis coming for the United States," Schiff said in August 2006.[13] Later that year, Schiff predicted in a debate on Fox News that "real estate prices are going to come crashing back down to Earth."[14] With the Dow well over 12,000, real estate prices at all-time highs, and neither showing any sign of weakness, both statements looked like splitting 10s or going for it on fourth and 2 at your own 28.

Yet we know now that Schiff turned out to be a sage and dead on with both predictions. Schiff's ability to see what no one else saw and, more importantly, his conviction to act on it despite societal pressures provide an enormously important lesson.

So how does one get this ability?

Well, in order to understand how to harness this ability, let's first examine what makes each decision so hard to make in the first place. In other words, rather than focus on the groupthink deterrent of doing the right thing, let's instead focus on the reason these decisions are hard to make in the first place. Let's focus on the root of the problem.

Splitting 10s is difficult for many psychological reasons. The first is something called "loss aversion." Loss aversion refers to a cognitive bias where people are more affected by a potential loss than they are by a gain of equal value. In other words, people don't like to lose.

As the cards come out and you see your 20 and the dealer's 6, you have essentially already put that money in your bank account. You see that money as yours. To split the 20 puts that money, *your money,* at risk. It doesn't matter to you that there is greater potential gain to splitting those 10s. Your new frame of reference has made you subject to "loss aversion," a principle first discussed by Amos Tversky and Daniel Kahneman.[15]

Understanding how to avoid loss aversion is an important business lesson because it creates tremendous pitfalls beyond the blackjack table. As an investor, imagine that you are more concerned with avoiding loss than gaining profit. Loss aversion might cause you to hold on to a bad investment simply to avert loss. Similar reasoning might cause you to quickly sell an investment that shows small profits since the potential incremental gain is not worth as much to you as the potential loss of your profit.

To some degree, it's a problem with your frame of reference. At the blackjack table, our goal at all times was to maximize profits. It didn't matter whether we were up or down for the trip, the day, or the hand— the ultimate goal was to make as much money as we could. We couldn't change our frame of reference or our behavior based on our profit or loss for the day. If we were loss averse, we might quit in the middle of a weekend when conditions dictated we should continue playing.

The fourth-down dilemma can also be explained by loss aversion. The case of kicking a sure field goal rather than going for a risky touchdown is very similar to our splitting 10s dilemma. You'd have to imagine that most coaches have banked that field goal and three points in their minds. To risk it and go for a touchdown would be risking those three points—risking a potential loss.

One way to avoid loss aversion is to look at everything from a true zero frame of reference. Rather than looking at our blackjack dilemma as giving up a 70 percent chance to win $8,000, instead evaluate both options with relation to zero. It's easy in that case to take the bet with a higher expected value.

Similarly, if a football coach ceases to think about a field goal opportunity as money in the bank, they can instead focus on the overall goal of their team—to score as many points as possible. With that in mind, a 60 percent chance for seven points would always seem better than a 90 percent chance for three.

In business and in investing, having a true zero frame of reference will keep you from suffering from loss aversion. Imagine you've made some risky but sound business decisions that have helped you grow your business and expand your market share. You are now faced with a similar set of risky but sound decisions. The businessman suffering from loss aversion would worry about protecting the gains his company had already made and would shy away from this new set of risky decisions. But the true zero analysis would tell you that these new decisions are necessary to grow the business regardless of previous gains.

Another interesting bias illustrated in the reluctance to split 10s is omission bias. Omission bias is a desire to favor failure or bad consequences by inaction rather than action. You actually don't have to look at a polarizing decision like splitting 10s to see this bias in most blackjack players.

In a study entitled "Fear and Loathing in Las Vegas: Evidence from Blackjack Tables,"[16] Bruce Carlin of UCLA and David Robinson of Duke University analyze the decisions of blackjack players and find that people make two types of mistakes when deviating from basic strategy— those of inaction and those of unnecessary or suboptimal action. They found that errors of inaction occurred four times more than errors of incorrect action. In general, most people were too conservative, deciding not to take a card in order to avoid going over 21. Instead they waited and hoped that the dealer would bust.

The cost of inactivity in this study was significant, as the players who played optimally won 20 times more often on similar hands than the players who played scared. Our blackjack team used to call this "playing not to lose."

Again, this lesson transfers well to our football coaches. The idea of going for it is very proactive, while the idea of punting or kicking a field goal seems much more passive. Omission bias would say that choosing the less active choice will cause less regret in the case of failure.

In business, awareness of omission bias should help you feel comfortable with action and inaction equally. The message is not that you should constantly micromanage a situation—that is, hit every hand until you either get 21 or bust. Instead, the key takeaway is to consider action and inaction—hitting and standing—equally. Maintaining status quo should not carry more weight simply because it might produce less regret if unsuccessful.

In fact, an important lesson that Belichick and our blackjack researchers teach us is that deciding not to make a decision is actually equivalent to making a decision. It is important to recognize that maintaining status quo is a decision to do exactly that, maintain status quo. Therefore, it should be treated with the same weight as making any kind of change.

This type of thinking certainly carries over to the business world, where our recent economic crisis has made employment a gift, not a birthright, and maintaining job security often trumps innovation. In 2000, my friend Karie was hired by one of the largest hospital groups in Chicago and charged with nurse recruiting. Her specialty was online recruiting—everything from building websites to placing job ads.

For hospitals, recruiting and keeping nurses has always been a big deal. It is very competitive—they have to constantly hunt for people because, if they don't, they'll immediately have a shortage.

Her boss was the head of human resources and had been there forever. One of the first things Karie did was conduct an analysis of their advertising. Where were they spending? And how was it working?

At the time, they were spending 90 percent of their budget—a considerable one—on the *Chicago Tribune* print. This is what they had done for years, of course, since historically print newspapers were the only way to recruit.

This was early on in the emergence of Monster.com, Careerbuilder.com, and other Internet job search companies. They were only spending 10 percent of their budget with these companies.

Karie's analysis showed that that 10 percent was resulting in more than 90 percent of the nurses they were hiring.

She showed the results to her boss and went about trying to convince her superiors: Why wouldn't you go with something that works better?

The answer in most cases: because different equals risk, and while taking risks is what you have to do as an entrepreneur, for many in such a corporate setting it only looks like a way to potentially get fired.

In business, as in blackjack, all decisions should be considered equally, independent of any biases. And the way to make the right decision is to focus on the data. If Karie's boss had been presented with two new recruiting strategies, one that was almost ten times as cost effective as the other, her decision might have been easier.

It's similar to the classic question of whether to hold on to a stock or sell it. Again, these are two very clear alternatives, and you must choose between them. If you sell it and it goes up, you experience more regret than if you simply held on to it and it went down. In both cases you are losing money, so both actions should be considered equally. The decision of whether to hold on to or sell a stock really comes down to whether you think the stock is overvalued or undervalued. Try to divorce yourself from ownership. If you didn't own the stock, would you want to buy it at its current price? The answer has to be yes, otherwise, you should really think about selling.

But even if a blackjack player or football coach could personally get over both of these biases, splitting 10s and going for it on fourth down would still be incredibly hard to do simply because nobody does it. The above biases have caused a groupthink mentality where conflict and innovation have been stifled in the name of reducing conflict.

The classic example of groupthink occurs in a company where group decisions are made not to optimize value creation but rather to reduce internal conflict and maintain consensus. This happens because the group values group harmony over making the most productive decision. By focusing on a group's cohesiveness, healthy conflict disappears. Yet healthy conflict is important for any group or organization to flourish.

In general avoiding groupthink is straightforward. Certainly if an individual in the group is truly committed to data-driven decision making, groupthink can be avoided. Let's think about our friend Coach Belichick. He didn't care if his decision strayed from conventional thinking and caused conflict. In fact, by all accounts conflict is something that Belichick thrives on.

Likewise, we made our decisions at the blackjack table as individuals. We did not believe that the other players at the table were a part of our group and needed to buy in or even agree with our decisions. We were simply making the best decision we could with the data available. If people in business did that, there would be no groupthink.

Yet groupthink is pervasive and can infect entire industries. We've seen the job it has done on NFL coaches; not going for it on fourth down isn't the only situation where coaches shy away from a difficult decision that could help them win more games. Trying surprise onside kicks is another example of a risk that coaches should take more often but don't.

Every time a team kicks the ball off, they have the option to attempt an onside kick that, if executed correctly, will give them possession of the ball. Unfortunately, if they are unsuccessful, the receiving team will have tremendous field position. It is an incredibly risky strategy. The average onside kick gets recovered at a rate of 25 percent. The lion's share of those kicks, however, occur at the end of a game in a desperate time, where the receiving team knows that the kicking team will be onside kicking and has prepared accordingly by putting more men on the front line. In these cases, the receiving team actually puts in some of their most skilled position players, like wide receivers and running backs, to increase the likelihood that they will recover the onside kick.

And it works. The difference in recovery percentage between surprise onside kicks and non-surprise onside kicks is striking.

Using an advanced statistic called win probability, Brian Burke was able to separate surprise onside kicks from their non-surprise counterparts. Win probability is a measure of a team's chances of winning at any point in a game. There are many different versions, but the general formula takes into account such things as score, time left in game, number of timeouts left, yard line, possession, and down and distance to go.

Burke's theory was that onside kicks are expected when a team has a low likelihood of winning, that is, during desperate times. So to determine the recovery rate of surprise onside kicks he throws out any attempts where a team has a lower than 15 percent chance of winning. Doing so raises the recovery rate to 60 percent.

So does that make it worth the risk?

In order to answer this question, Burke employed yet another advanced statistic called expected points (EP). EP utilizes many of the same inputs as win probability, but its output is the number of points that you would expect on that drive based on the situation. Armed with this metric, Burke was able to calculate that if a team can recover an onsides kick at 42 percent, it is worth the risk.

Yet you can count the number of surprise onside kicks in one season on one hand.

Obviously the caveat here is once you become known as a team that tries surprise onside kicks, it ceases to be a surprise, but the reality is very few teams even attempt the surprise onside kick. The reason? There's just too much potential downside. Even with a 60 percent chance of recovering, there is a 40 percent chance of not recovering. So you will fail four times in every ten times you try it. And the operative word here is "fail" because that is something NFL coaches are afraid of doing. Failing in a case like this leaves an NFL coach open for all sorts of scrutiny, from players, fans, and owners alike.

John Maynard Keynes was an incredibly influential British economist central to many of the theories we have described in this chapter. His work is detailed in the modern masterpiece *Against the Gods* by Peter Bernstein. Keynes, after describing an investor with Belichick-like courage as "eccentric, unconventional and rash in the eyes of the average opinion," says that that investor's success "will only confirm the general belief in his rashness; and...if his decisions are unsuccessful...he will not receive much mercy." This is similar to the lack of mercy showed to both Belichick and Schiff by their detractors. Keynes concludes with the statement: "Worldly wisdom teaches us that it is better for reputation to fail conventionally than to succeed unconventionally."[17]

The NFL coach who tries the onside kick won't be seen as a genius if he succeeds, he'll be seen as reckless and lucky. If his attempts fail, he will simply be seen as reckless. From a reputation standpoint, it's simply not worth the risk. Similarly, the blackjack player who splits 10s and wins will be seen as an idiot no matter whether he wins or loses. Fortunately, popularity is not a casino game.

Finally, the trader who says "sell" when everyone else is buying is likely to be the target of scorn and derision.

Ultimately this discussion comes back to Bill Belichick. His ability to make difficult, contrarian decisions is transcendent bordering on absurd. His one decision caused weeks of conflict in the media among the football pundits. But how is he able to make these difficult decisions time and again?

Actually, the answer is pretty simple. There is no coach in the league with more job security than Belichick—three Super Bowl wins in the last decade will do that for you. Since Belichick does not have to worry about job security or his legacy, he can instead focus on the only thing that matters—the results. His preferences, which focus only on winning, allow him to focus on optimizing his decisions to that end.

We should all be so lucky to have this luxury. If we did and afforded this same luxury to those who work for us, we'd all make better decisions. It's a very empowering concept and is important to remember to ensure innovation. Imagine if Karie's boss hadn't been worried about getting fired. It would have been much easier for her to tell Karie to reallocate the budget away from the underperforming *Tribune*. Unfortunately, her fear of rocking the boat stifled innovation within their organization.

Of course Belichick's result in this isolated event was not positive, and his detractors will always point back to that. But they are falling for another bias called hindsight bias, the final point in this discussion.

Everyone has heard the expression "hindsight is 20–20," meaning that you can always see the past perfectly from the future. And the simplistic hindsight analysis of Belichick's decision is that, because it didn't ultimately work, it was the wrong decision.

This is obviously a relatively uninformed view on the situation, but the real problem is the legacy of Belichick's failed decision. Coaches facing similar decisions will now remember all too well the result of Belichick's risky but sound decision. In fact, they will not only remember the result but they will remember all the negative reviews his decision received.

And when they are faced with a similar situation, the vivid memory of the aftermath will hold an inflated space in their brain. This is an example of a psychological phenomenon called the availability heuristic.

The availability heuristic has a very complicated name, but it is pretty simple to understand. Think of it this way: Every day you face a decision about which way to go to work. One way involves highways and is a bit longer from a distance standpoint. The other way is shorter but involves only surface streets and usually takes longer due to traffic. On almost every day you take the highway route since it is on average ten minutes faster.

So today, like every other day, you are driving to work and need to decide what route to take. You are pressed for time and need to take the route that will get you there faster. Every day so far this year you have taken the highway route, but yesterday there was a huge accident on the highway and it took you 45 minutes longer than usual. You decide to take the surface streets because the memory of sitting in your Prius in that ridiculous traffic is ingrained in your mind. Because you can picture it, you are assigning the possibility of an accident a much higher probability than it deserves.

And this is likely to happen with NFL coaches. The unfortunate result of Belichick's brazen decision is that NFL coaches are probably going to be less likely to go for it on fourth down than they ever were.

But you don't have to fall into the trap. The next time you face a difficult decision, try to picture all scenarios before making your decision. In our driving example, you should try to imagine the other 99 days that you traveled on the highway and it was smooth sailing. Faced with a difficult business decision, close your eyes and imagine all scenarios equally and try to do it with as much detail as possible. That will help you give even the unconventional choice equal consideration.

The company Altman Vilandrie takes this one step further, actually simulating worst-case and best-case scenarios for their clients. "We often help our investor clients by simulating the business model for a prospective investment under all sorts of risks—market risks, competitive risks, labor conflicts, and even vendor rifts. Our best clients take risks—but they're very well calculated," Ed Vilandrie explains.

When I played blackjack, I tried to think about the joy of winning rather than the anguish of defeat. Defeat always leaves an indelible mark on us, so winning needed to be given a fair chance in the analysis. A focus on imagining success and a full understanding of the cost of failure will help you make business decisions without fear. That people will forever look back on Belichick's decision as a bad one is simply a testament to how difficult it is to make good decisions. For one, as we discussed at the beginning of this chapter, it's difficult to combat flawed human nature, which would lead us to believe that a negative outcome means a poor decision.

In addition, unlike blackjack, where a decision can be tested hundreds, even thousands, of times, this exact football scenario occurs only once, and therefore there is no way to truly test the decision. To evaluate

Belichick's decision, we need to imagine that it occurred hundreds or even thousands of times. One trial simply isn't enough.

Finally, the idea of probabilities can be hard to understand. If the weatherman says there is a 70 percent chance of rain tomorrow, he is also saying there is a 30 percent chance of no rain. If it doesn't rain, he is not wrong. But if he says a hundred times that there is a 70 percent chance of rain and it rains only 20 of those times, well, then we know to find a new weatherman.

Making better business decisions is difficult, but if you can look objectively at the problem, understand all of your alternatives, and then choose the one that gives you the highest chance of success, you will end up on top more often than not. And that's really all we can hope for.

9

WHEN I WON, WE ALL WON

Greed is good.

—Gordon Gekko, *Wall Street*

A consistent set of goals and a unified commitment to winning were two of the keys to our success as a blackjack team. We had a large pile of cash and chips that every weekend we tried to grow into a larger pile of cash and chips. It was that simple. This simplicity created transparency and alignment. We were always on the same page and working toward the same goal.

We ran our blackjack team like an investment fund. First, we started by raising capital to establish our fund. This was easy, as all the people who played on the team previously had made good money playing blackjack. They realized how great an investment it was and therefore wanted to invest. There was never a lack of available funds. Regardless of all that, we still had to go through an official process so people could declare how much money they wanted to commit to the new fund, which we called "the bank."

After we established the bank, we set a win goal based on the size of the bank. That win goal would change based on the time it was taking us to reach it. The logic was that when it took longer than expected, the goal would increase because we had tied up the investors' money for longer than originally anticipated. When it took less time than expected, the surplus was paid out as bonus to both the investors and players.

This bonus structure created a consistent set of goals between the players and investors. Both players and investors wanted shorter banks because that would mean larger bonuses for both. In the investors' case, they would see a higher percentage return. In the player's case, they would receive higher compensation. You can easily see this played out in a business scenario, such as sales commission goals or hedge fund management fees.

Reaching our win goal was called "breaking the bank" and was a much-anticipated event by players and investors alike. Think of it as a liquidity event similar to an IPO or an acquisition of a start-up company. When we broke the bank, we would allow players to take their salary and expenses out and would allow investors to cash out their returns. At the start of every trip, every player knew to the dollar how much money we needed to break the bank.

I remember one particular weekend we were in Vegas and had been playing on the same bank for more than six months. We were way over the anticipated time, and everyone was extremely anxious to reach our win goal. We had a decent start to the weekend, but as of Sunday morning we still needed to win about $57,000. As I sat down to play at the Mirage that morning, I knew how much money I needed to win and how many people were counting on me.

I battled and played for close to four hours, finally getting to a point where I was pretty confident I was over $57,000. It's always hard to know exactly how much money you have won until you get up to the room and can spread out all the cash and chips to get an exact count of your profit/loss for that session. Nevertheless, I felt pretty good about my total and called an end to the session. Rubbing the back of my neck to signify that I was done for the time being, I headed up to my room. When I got upstairs, I sat down at the desk in my suite and counted out my chips and cash. When I was done, I realized that I had not only broken the bank but I had actually won $67,000 total. I sent a group page to all of my teammates with the announcement, "I broke the bank!!!" Wiped out, I laid down for a nap.

An hour later I was awakened by a heavy clank near my head. Startled, I looked up at the figure standing over me. It was Wes, one of my teammates. I was a bit groggy but was proud of my morning's accomplishments. "Hey Wes, I broke the bank."

"Oh really, that's great, Jeff. How much did you win?" he asked.

"I won $67,000," I said almost boastfully.

"Oh, that's great. I actually did pretty well also," he started. "I won $167,000, and it's all in here." He pointed at a lump near my head, and I realized the clank had been a pillowcase full of chips and cash.

It was a healthy competition that resulted in Wes besting me by $100,000, but in the end we both won because all of our winnings were pooled. There was no self-interest other than the pride of being the biggest earner. That made it easy for us to constantly make the right decision not just for ourselves but for everyone on the team. We had a consistent currency for winning—big piles of money that we wanted to make bigger. The competition helped drive us while the win unified us even more.

One weekend soon after Wes and I sat by the Mirage pool. We had had our biggest weekend ever, wining $450,000 total. It was the middle of the summer, and Vegas was sweltering as usual. As the last two members of the team in town, we had all the weekend's winnings with us in a duffel bag. We did not want to leave the money up in the room as we had heard horror stories of money disappearing, even out of safes, so we sat with all of it, including the money we had originally brought out with us, in that duffel bag under the lawn char.

Sitting by the pool, the heat eventually got to me. I turned to Wes and asked jokingly, "You think we can leave the money here and go for a swim?"

He looked at me, reading my smile, and asked, "How much is in there?"

"It's the money we brought out here, $540,000, and the money we won, $450,000, so it's about $990,000," I responded.

"I don't see why we can't just leave it here," he started. "It's not like it's a million dollars." Wes began to laugh as the words came out of his mouth, and I joined in.

Establishing this unity was paramount to our success and was achieved only by our solitary commitment to winning. Winning is an extremely simple yet powerful goal. Organizations that are truly committed to winning have an easy path to common goal setting and aligned incentives among employees.

As elementary as this may sound, there are many examples where self-interest trumps the desire to win and the success of the organization suffers. This happens in places you would least expect.

In the previous chapter, we discussed the plight of the NFL coach. Although I understand the psychological reasons and biases that cause coaches to make their decisions, the idea that professional sports team coaches would knowingly make decisions that don't give their team the best chance to win is still crazy to me.

In sports, this goal of winning is transparent, making this analogy so striking. Imagine a CEO or even a manager of a business unit knowingly making a less-than-optimal decision. Surely this would not be tolerated by a boss.

Unfortunately, there aren't many people in coaching positions within professional sports who believe in statistical analysis. Most professional coaches and field managers resist the use of numbers and data, preferring to rely on gut and intuition. Their tendency to shy away from data-driven decision making is not shocking. But they have bosses. And those bosses, typically general managers of the teams, are increasingly becoming more and more educated as to the value of statistical analysis and less and less subject to groupthink.

At the forefront of this new breed of general manager is my friend Daryl Morey. Morey is a highly educated man; he has a bachelor's degree in computer science with an emphasis on statistics from

Northwestern University, as well as an MBA from the MIT Sloan School of Management.[1] He got his start in sports with the Boston Celtics, working for three years as the senior vice president of operations. During his tenure with the Celtics, Morey began introducing statistical analysis into both the player personnel and game management decisions.

His work did not go unnoticed, and in April 2006 he was hired as assistant general manager of the Houston Rockets. At the time of his hiring it was also announced that Morey would eventually succeed Carroll Dawson as general manager. That day came a little over a year later, and Morey was named general manager of the Houston Rockets in May 2007.

In Morey's first two seasons with the Rockets, the team compiled a 108–56 record, and Morey himself won numerous accolades for his work as general manager. It was actually Morey who gave me my start in sports, ironically by deciding not to hire me. At the time I was working as the chief technology officer for a technology start-up in the finance space called CircleLending.com. I had started to gain some notoriety from the success of *Bringing Down the House,* but I wasn't sure what to do with that notoriety until I read *Moneyball.*

After reading Michael Lewis's account of how Billy Beane and the Oakland As used statistical analysis to compete in the game of baseball, I realized that there were some real similarities between what they did and what we were doing in blackjack. With that in mind, I decided that I wanted to work in sports.

So I talked to each and every one of my friends that had anything to do with sports, and I found one who worked for the Celtics. She knew that Daryl, who was in his first year with the Celtics, was looking for help. She thought I'd be perfect for the job.

I went in to interview and quickly was convinced that sports was where I needed to be. Walking through the Celtics office at the Boston Garden and seeing the trophies, pictures, and memorabilia was a fan's dream. I sat and talked with Daryl that day for a couple hours, and he cautioned me that the job was little more than an internship. It might not even be paid, he explained. I told him I didn't care. I simply wanted to work in sports. I didn't care if that meant quitting my job as CTO to take an unpaid internship with the Celtics.

A week later, Morey called me to tell me that he would not be offering me the job. He explained that it had come down to me and one other candidate, and the other candidate simply had a better skill set for what he needed. He also explained that the other candidate seemed to be a more permanent fit for the Celtics. He envisioned me wanting a bigger challenge within a short time frame and using the job as an entry point, and he thought the other candidate would be with Celtics for a long time. In hindsight he was right, as that candidate, Mike Zarren, is still with the Celtics and has flourished within the organization, currently acting as the team's assistant general manager.

While Daryl snubbed me, I understood why and we have kept in touch since. And as I struggled to understand how NFL coaches could continue to ignore such compelling evidence from the data, he seemed a logical place to start looking for answers.

When Morey and his Rockets came in to San Francisco for their game against the Golden State Warriors at the beginning of the 2009–2010 season, we sat down for lunch. As we got caught up on the last year or so of our lives, we eventually got on the subject of which other NBA teams were actually using statistical analysis.

"Teams that use the two-for-one strategy are a good indication. Also teams that understand the value of the corner three both from a defensive and offensive standpoint," Morey explained, referring to two practical basketball strategies, one of which we discussed extensively in Chapter 5.

These strategies share similarities with our football strategies from Chapter 8: going for it more often on fourth down and trying more surprise onside kicks. They are all coaching strategies that are supported by data. But there are some big differences. The two-for-one and corner three are intuitive. In fact, many coaches instinctively tell their teams to do both without knowing what the statistics say. Meanwhile, our football strategies are incredibly counterintuitive and hence carry a disproportionate amount of downside.

So to explore my point, I shifted the conversation to football and David Romer's paper, which statistically advocates going for it more on fourth down. Morey immediately understood what I was getting at, showing his familiarity with the study by referring to Romer by his first name. "The problem is that people want to keep their jobs and they coach that way. Coaches get unfairly tagged as the easiest thing to change and because of that it's impossible not to think about your own career. You'd be stupid not to," Morey explained.

I was naively surprised by Morey's words, but as they sunk in they made sense. The problem is that ultimately the coach's goal is not always to win. Instead coaches are making decisions based on the self-interest of keeping their jobs—classic self-preservation. It certainly explains the herd mentality of NFL coaches. With so few jobs to go around, why take an unnecessary risk? Better to do the thing that is seen as safer and more conventional. In the case of kicking a field goal, this poor decision is even seen as a small success versus the fatal failure of going for it and failing.

And herein lies the real problem. Coaches actually have a responsibility to the team's stakeholders—the players, fans, and owner—to try to win a championship. Morey recognizes that responsibility. "It's not like I'm a hedge fund trying to beat the S&P every year. I'm trying to be the one of 30 teams that wins the championship. In order to do that you simply need to take more risks."

This is a classic case of misaligned incentives. A coach feels compelled to make safe decisions that he believes will help him keep his job while most everyone else that matters, essentially the shareholders, wants him to take more risks and bring them a championship. His decisions are based on the following decision criteria or preferences: My first priority is not to get fired; my second priority is to win a championship. In this sense coaches ironically often make the correct personal decision even though it may hurt the results of the team. They maximize their chances of remaining employed, but this comes at the cost of not making more sound but also risky decisions.

Again, the business parallel here is obvious. Employees and even CEOs who must choose between self-preservation and building long-term shareholder value are often going to make the selfish choice. And who can blame them?

And that's a problem because our sports stakeholders and our business shareholders have little ability to make an impact on the direction of the team or company. Sure the owner can fire the general manager and the coach or the board can fire the CEO. But the fans and the shareholders can do nothing.

For this reason, Morey believes that having an active owner is actually a blessing since they are the only cog in the wheel with the time horizon to make the right decisions. Building a championship team might take longer than the tenure of the average coach or general manager. In that case, it's the owner's job to help those in his organization make the right decisions for the fans. He's the only one without the pressure of keeping his job and the only one who really can have a long-term outlook. Likewise, a company's board of directors needs to fill this role, understanding that building real long-term value in a company is more important than any short-term blips.

Self-preservation is a powerful motivator behind decisions. Coaches are more worried about keeping their job than they are about winning championships, and achieving the former might be done at the expense of the latter. Ideally, a coach would be compensated on how much his team is improving—how much closer it is to becoming a championship-caliber team. And likewise all those in the organization under the coach would receive incentive in the same manner. Unfortunately, in sports and often in business there isn't this consistency. And in our previous chapter, we see the result of this inconsistency, as coaches are inclined to make the decision that may not ultimately help the team win but will leave them less open to criticism. It is self-preservation at its finest.

This concept of inconsistent time horizons is also problematic. Since the coach's career shelf life is often so short, there is tremendous pressure to win now. A coach producing great results in his inaugural campaign buys himself a certain amount of job security, but those short-term results may be at the expense of the ultimate goal of winning a championship. The quintessential example of this is the decision whether to play the veteran or the rookie at quarterback. Often a veteran quarterback will give you a better chance to win games in the short term, but giving a young quarterback immediate on-field experience may be better for the future.

This time-horizon dilemma is not limited to the football field. Think of salesmen who get bonused quarterly or even annually. Will they choose to sell to the customer with the most long-term revenue potential or will they instead choose to devote their time to the sale that has the highest likelihood of closing in the short term? The former might be the best thing for the company, but the latter would clearly be a better thing for the salesman and his family.

Tom Woo, a rising star in Google's compensation department, stresses the importance of compensation plans that align the goals of the individual with those of the company. "You really can't rely on the goodness of mankind. Any individual is going to be motivated by self-interest. It's just human nature."

Specifically for his salespeople, Woo preaches some simple rules for compensation plans. First off, the plans should be transparent and easy to understand. Too much creativity in the incentive package may make it too complicated and leave employees unclear on how to attain their goals, thereby killing the notion of incentive and motivation.

The goals must appear attainable, otherwise the salesperson will lose hope and the incentive will disappear. Woo cautions that this is the problem with incentive packages based on longer time horizons. "If someone gets behind early, they may give up," he comments. "You need to give them a restart every quarter."

Bonusing must occur as close to the sales event as possible, and this further accentuates the problem of inconsistent time horizons. In industries where there is huge variability in lifetime customer value, this presents a difficult dilemma. How do you compensate a salesperson based on an uncertain lifetime value? You can't wait until the customer's value is known, otherwise the immediacy of the incentive will be gone.

Google has experimented with a sustainability metric that tracks a salesperson's accounts over time. A small portion of the salesperson's bonus is based on this sustainability metric, which helps give the salesperson a bit more of a long-term perspective.

At the end of the day, the only surefire way to ensure that salespeople make decisions in the best interest of the shareholders is to truly align their incentives with those of the company.

Our blackjack team was a great case study in compensation plans. First off, all of our players had job security. They understood their roles and that if they and the team performed well they would be compensated handsomely. Our concept of time horizons was always consistent. There really was only one that mattered—the length of the bank. And everyone was compensated if and only if we broke the bank. There was no payout or golden parachute based on short-term gain. Everything was based on building real "value" in the bank, that is, growing that big pile of chips and cash into a bigger pile of chips and cash. Finally, we were all accountable to our shareholders because in essence we were the shareholders. We actually had a policy that every player had to be an investor, and as we all made enough money that we did not have to accept outside investment, we made the reverse requirement—all investors had to also be players. This ensured that there would never be an inconsistency with the goals of the players, essentially the management, and the investors, essentially the shareholders.

The 2008 mortgage crisis is a good example of misaligned incentives. While there's plenty of blame to go around for an industry that caused the worst financial crisis in 75 years, misaligned incentives are a good place to start pointing the finger. The ability to earn substantial fees from originating and securitizing loans, coupled with the absence of any residual liability, skews the incentives of originators in favor of loan volume rather than loan quality.

While there are many layers to the sub-prime crisis, and I would hate to oversimplify, certainly an important aspect of the crisis was the origin of the loans themselves. Mortgage brokers who were simply trying to make a living and keep their jobs, just like our NFL coaches, were paid and evaluated based on the number of loans they were able to originate. Compensated per loan with transaction and commission fees, these brokers were under tremendous pressure and incentivized to originate as many mortgages as possible. They had zero incentive to care about the quality or risk of these loans and, frankly, no interest. Whether these loans defaulted or grew to maturity was of no concern to the brokers, and so naturally many loans were given out that shouldn't have been.

I'm confident that if the mortgage industry had taken a cue from our blackjack team, they may have avoided some of these issues. We had our own version of mortgage brokers called spotters. These team members scoured the casino floor for good tables for the big player. Like the mortgage brokers, there was pressure on the spotters to find a lot of good tables because without good tables there would be nowhere for the big player to play and thus no money to be made.

But here's where our team differed from the mortgage industry: Our spotters had incentives aligned with both the big players and investors in the blackjack fund. They would only make money if we won. If they found tables that were less than optimal but reported them as optimal they knew we would not win, and if we didn't win they would not be paid for their work. So they only found tables that were truly good bets.

So how does one apply this analogy to the mortgage industry? Imagine if mortgage brokers were only paid their transaction fees if the mortgages that they originated did not default. Certainly, they would have been a bit pickier to whom they loaned money.

The mortgage crisis, and indeed the entire financial crisis, also recalls the inconsistency of time horizon. While shareholders cared about building long-term value in a company, executives were compensated based on building short-term value, and often the short-term value was a mirage. Think of highly risky mortgage-backed securities. They seem much riskier if you are thinking of holding them for years as opposed to months. The executives making the decisions needed to think on a longer time horizon—one consistent with that of their shareholders.

Finally, shareholders were not able to hold executives accountable during the crisis. It was such a glaring omission that it was one of the first things that Treasury Secretary Timothy Geithner tried to address. In his statement on June 10, 2009, Geithner writes:

> First of all, we will support efforts in Congress to pass "say on pay" legislation, giving the SEC authority to require companies to give shareholders a non-binding vote on executive compensation packages. "Say on pay," which has already become the norm for several of our major trading partners, and which President Obama supported while in the Senate, would encourage boards to ensure that compensation packages are closely aligned with the interest of shareholders.[2]

The lesson of misaligned incentives is an important one as they cause problems whenever they appear. Whether it is a vice president of sales more concerned about making a quarterly number than building long-term shareholder profit or a football coach more interested in keeping his job than winning championships, the misaligned incentive is something we all should look to eradicate from our business models.

The main problem is that self-interest inevitably surfaces and fundamentally guides our decisions in ways that may be hard to understand initially. The only way to truly eradicate self-interest is to align everyone's interests so that self-interest becomes group interest.

Our blackjack team was able to avoid self-interest by setting up a consistent compensation plan. Players were paid only when we won and were paid more the more money we won. It didn't matter if you were the big player or the spotter. Your pay was always based on the same metrics.

One of the reasons I've always enjoyed working for start-ups is the highly aligned compensation goals. Since nearly everyone in the organization has some equity, there is a unified focus on building shareholder value. This is easier to do in a small company, but employers can look at our blackjack team as a model for aligning incentives in all situations.

When Wes won, I won. When I won, our investors won. And when our investors won, our spotters won. It really was and can be that simple if everyone's goals are aligned.

Our team's uniform approach was integral to our success, and any organization with consistent goals will be that much closer to winning big in business.

10

WHY PEOPLE HATE MATH AND WHAT TO DO WITH THEM

Be nice to nerds. Chances are you'll end up working for one.

—Bill Gates

I REMEMBER THE first time I ever tried to tell my parents about my new career in card counting. My dad is an incredibly intelligent man who graduated at the top of his class in both high school and college. He was, in fact, one of the only students in Taiwan who didn't have to take the national college admissions test; he simply chose the college that he wanted to attend and they welcomed him with open arms. He certainly understood numbers and statistics, having studied chemical engineering as an undergraduate, master, and doctorate student, and he made his living as a professor in that field.

So it was with cautious optimism that I approached this learned man with my blackjack story. I had just started playing and was fascinated by the math behind it. I hoped he would be, too. I began by explaining the statistics and the mathematical beauty of what we did. I continued by discussing the complex ways we applied simple principles to beat the game of blackjack and concluded with an explanation of how we used financial principles to ensure that over the long haul we would win money.

But my very intelligent, mathematically inclined father did not want to hear any of this nonsense. "You can't beat the casinos. They use multiple decks. You can't win over the long haul when you are gambling. Nobody beats the casinos."

I persisted, but he would have none of it. I remember feeling a bit relieved since his dismissal of our endeavors allowed me to change the conversation and not discuss the full extent of our actions. Nobody really wants to tell their dad that they are a professional gambler. But I was disappointed in my dad's response as well. He simply didn't understand the power of statistics and analytics outside his comfort zone—academia—and had a limited perspective on the power of numbers. To him that power did not extend into the casinos.

The ability to beat the casinos is always something that is hard for the average person to understand. But that's because the average person never really takes the time to understand the math behind what we did. They are dismissive of our actions because they don't really understand that math governed our actions—in essence, they don't believe what they don't understand.

This doubt of statistics is prevalent in all types of people—even the very intelligent, like my father. So as we started PROTRADE and began looking for thought leaders to help us spread the gospel of statistics, we were cautious to pick the right people.

Early on we were fortunate to begin working with Billy Beane. Billy's appreciation for the use of analytics and statistics has already been discussed thoroughly in this book. That commitment to analytics made Billy the perfect baseball thought leader. Billy was signed early on as an adviser to our company.

Next up was football, and we looked for another iconic name. Jeff Moorad, one of our main investors, had a strong relationship with NFL coaching legend Bill Walsh. Walsh was certainly an icon, having been the head coach of three Super Bowl champions. He pioneered the West Coast offense and is largely credited for identifying such Hall of Fame talents like Joe Montana and Jerry Rice. Walsh was not what many would consider to be a stats guy, but he had an appreciation for the analytical approach and to that end had a great admiration for our effort.

So Coach Walsh joined our company as an investor and adviser. So we had our baseball face and our football face, but we still needed a basketball face. However, this one wasn't as easy. We spent a good deal of time brainstorming who would be the right person, and the answer came to us as we stared at the NBA logo.

Jerry West was a Hall of Fame player for the Los Angeles Lakers and was named to the All-Star team 14 times in his 14-year career. He went on to become the Lakers' general manager, and during his tenure the Lakers won seven NBA championships. He was twice named NBA executive of the year. West eventually left the Lakers and, at the time we approached him, was the general manager of the Memphis Grizzlies. And yes, his silhouette is the model for the NBA logo.

Two days after our brainstorming session, I was on a plane to Memphis with Mike Kerns. Our goal was to recruit Mr. West to join our movement to use statistics to revolutionize sports. I remember sitting across the table from Mr. West in his office, wide-eyed, bushy tailed, and excited to tell him how math was going to revolutionize basketball. He looked across the table at Mike and me with a deathly serious face and uttered the simple words, "Boys, I need to tell you one thing. I hate statistics."

This seemed like an inauspicious beginning to our recruiting session, and I almost gave up and just asked Mr. West recommendations on where to get the best barbecue in Memphis. But as we talked more, it became clear that he didn't hate statistics so much as he hated how they were used in the NBA. He hated the fact that Allen Iverson was considered a good player because he averaged 30 points a game yet needed 35 shots to score those 30 points.

As we continued to talk, Mr. West warmed up significantly. He took us on a tour of the facilities and was extremely engaged. Toward the end of our time together, Mr. West was on the phone calling his scouts, asking them if they were tracking all rebounds equally. He echoed our earlier discussion, telling his scouts that they should not consider a rebound of a missed free throw equal to an offensive rebound that gets the team another possession. He told his scouts that he didn't think assists that lead to jump shots should be valued equally with assists that lead to dunks. We had just concluded this exact discussion with Mr. West before he got on the phone with his scouts.

All in all, we spent over two hours with Mr. West, and at the end of the meeting he agreed to be our basketball adviser.

I remembered Mr. West recently as I read an Accenture report discussing the use of analytics to make decisions in "large US companies."[1] This report stated that while two-thirds of the companies surveyed believed that they needed to "improve their analytical capabilities," 61 percent of the companies did not believe they had sufficient data with which to make decisions.[2] Sound familiar?

These company executives sounded exactly like Jerry West. They didn't so much hate statistics—in fact, 66 percent believed that their organizations needed to use more statistics. But 61 percent also believed that the data they were collecting was deficient.

Statistics get a bad rap by those who don't fully understand or embrace them. Here we had a brilliant professor in chemical engineering, an NBA legend, and a group of executives from large companies all saying that they didn't fully believe in numbers. In my dad's case, it was a failure to accept that the power of numbers could extend into something like blackjack. But in the other two cases, it was a frustration with the misuse of numbers.

It is not uncommon to encounter very smart people who hate numbers. However, it is extremely important to work with these people to convert them to believers. "Being able to analyze situations with statistics is extremely important and hard, but convincing other people that it will work is just as hard and probably even more important," my good friend Paraag Marathe once told me.

Marathe is one of the pioneers in the use of statistics and data in the decision-making process in the NFL. He has held various offices within the San Francisco 49ers' organization and currently serves as their vice president of football and business operations. Marathe has a bachelor of science degree from the Haas School of Business at University of California, Berkeley, and a masters in business administration from Stanford University's Graduate School of Business.

But his path from Stanford MBA to high-level NFL executive has been anything but smooth. The NFL is a tight-knit community in which those who are not considered "football guys" are often outsiders looking in. Marathe has never been and will never be considered a football guy.

His arrival in football was met with much skepticism. Portrayed by the media as a numbers geek, Marathe was even asked once by a reporter if it bothered him that nobody in football knew how to say his name. But in talking with Marathe, you realize he is personable, likable, and about as American as apple pie. His meteoric rise in football owes as much to these personality traits as it does to his ability to use statistics and analytics.

Says Marathe, "I try to help people in the organization understand how different strategies that I'm espousing would have worked in the past or how they've worked for other organizations. By giving them anecdotal success stories, they can understand the value of what I'm trying to sell. And helping them understand is the key."

Similarly, basketball analytics pioneer Roland Beech shared his early thoughts with me about working directly with the Mavericks coaching staff. "No one here really hates math. They are so competitive and want to win so badly that if you can give them anything that will help them they will be receptive. That is, as long as it is well formed."

Roland went on to explain that he is trying to develop relationships with the coaching staff and has tried not to "ruffle too many feathers initially."

But again Beech is the exception in the basketball statistics world, and as we begin to discuss his role at the Mavericks, it is clear that he has an ulterior motive. I have known Roland Beech for more than five years. He was one of the first "stats" guys I reached out to when we started PROTRADE. Even at that time, he struck me as one of the truly unique stats guys. Certainly his grasp of statistics was second to none and his passion for sports was evident, but Beech never had the idealistic notions of an academic and was always fascinated by the side of the game that he couldn't understand—the side of the game that could not be quantified or, at least, has not been quantified to date.

"I'm always a guy that wants to see more data and try to find ways to model the seemingly impossible," Beech explained.

For many years in sports, there has been a chasm between the basketball stats people and the non-stats people. Beech blames the stats people for that chasm as much as the basketball people. "The stats people don't have a great understanding of the sacrifices that people in the organization make. They say things like, 'You're wrong because my numbers say so and your 30 years of experience mean nothing.' Of course, that type of interaction is not going to go over very well."

Beech preached that it was important for the stats people to acknowledge what they don't know and has realized over time how much there is for him to learn about the game of basketball itself. He was so committed to narrowing the chasm between the stats and non-stats people that he uprooted his life in a remote beach town on the central coast of California to pursue a nomadic existence traveling with the Mavericks for their full 82-game season.

"It's really the only way I'm going to learn about the impact of things like team chemistry and real interactions on the court," Beech explained.

It is this type of effort and understanding that makes a guy like Beech successful around the real basketball types. If you meet Beech, Morey, and Marathe, you will notice a consistent theme of pragmatism. Also, they all have a real appreciation and respect for the people they work with who know nothing about statistics. And that makes them the recipients of the same type of even, fair treatment.

The importance of this even treatment cannot be overlooked. Nobody wants to be told that they are wrong or that they don't know anything. This only puts them on the defensive. But even more than that, there is a real psychological barrier that the stats people must overcome. Nowhere is that barrier more prevalent than in sports.

In a lunch conversation with author Michael Lewis, he calls this the geek/jock conflict and explains that the majority of the people with power in teams were jocks growing up. They were the popular people and have always held the power in the geek/jock dynamic as it pertains to sports. That power imbalance has persisted in professional sports.

And team owners are largely responsible for the lofty positions that the jocks enjoy. Throughout history most team owners either inherited their teams or were so rich that they did not need to be overly concerned with the health of the organization. George Steinbrenner, the current owner of the Yankees, paid a reported $10 million.[3] The Yankees are now worth more than $1.2 billion.[4] These teams were toys for the owners, and part of the benefit of owning that toy was the opportunity to hang out with the jocks who would have stuffed them in their locker in high school.

It's the only explanation why guys like Matt Millen, Michael Jordan, and Kevin McHale are hired to run organizations when they have little to no previous experience beside what they did as players. Millen, a former NFL linebacker with four Super Bowl appearances to his credit, was hired as the president and CEO of the NFL football team the Detroit Lions. Millen had zero previous experience in an NFL front office and instead spent his post-football years in the broadcast booth. Yet the Ford family felt compelled to give him the keys to the franchise. What resulted was the worst eight-year record of any NFL team since World War II (31–97) and Millen's eventual termination.

Michael Jordan, arguably the best NBA player ever, has held not one but two different front office positions. His first stint with the

Washington Wizards was an unmitigated disaster, resulting in a 110–179 record and an eventual unceremonious exit for Jordan. Among Jordan's "brilliant" moves was hiring longtime college coach Leonard Hamilton, despite the fact that he had no professional experience. After a 19–63 season, Jordan showed Hamilton the door. That next year, Jordan tried to go back to the well that made him rich, returning as a player for the Wizards. Again the results were mixed, and in 2003 Jordan retired as a player, hoping to return to his role as team president. The Wizards ownership decided they had finally spent enough time hanging out with this basketball icon, announcing, "While the roster of talent he has assembled here in Washington may not have succeeded to his and my expectations, I do believe Michael's desire to win and be successful is unquestioned."[5] Not exactly a ringing endorsement.

But unlike the real world, where getting fired can make you less hirable, new suitors lined up for Jordan's services, wanting him to run their franchise. Robert Johnson, the principal owner of the expansion Charlotte Bobcats, pounced on Jordan, offering him partial ownership in the organization and the position of managing member of basketball operations.[6] In the press conference announcing Jordan's hiring, Johnson said, "I'm thrilled to have my friend, Michael Jordan, join me in my business and sports pursuits."[7] Johnson, an incredibly savvy and successful businessman outside of basketball, may as well have said, *I'm thrilled that I'm going to get to hang out with Michael Jordan for the foreseeable future.* Who can blame him?

The Michael Jordan Charlotte experience has been no better than the Michael Jordan Washington experience. In his first three seasons at the helm, the team has a record of 100 wins and 146 losses with no playoff appearances. And due to a litany of laughable draft picks, the Bobcats are no better off than when Jordan arrived.

The allure of the ex-athlete is unquestionable. But in the last few years, that is changing. With a new breed of owner has come a new culture within sports where the voice of the geeks is getting louder.

But imagine the chagrin of the jock now being told by the geek that everything they think about sports is wrong. That's not going to go over very well and is likely to get the geek stuffed into another locker. Instead it is important for the geek to acknowledge this dynamic and act accordingly—that means don't be a snot-nosed know-it-all.

This analogy transfers well from sports into business as the same power dynamic is true of most CEOs. Take our friend Jack Welch. Working his way up from junior engineer to CEO and having close to 40 years of experience certainly gives him a large amount of entitlement. He has been successful for a reason and rightly has abundant confidence in his knowledge and experience. To discount that knowledge and experience is tantamount to telling a jock that he doesn't know anything about sports.

Even my dad had a similar perspective. Certainly his 21-year-old son could not be teaching him something new about numbers. He was predisposed to doubting me.

So what are the important ways to convince the metaphorical jocks that they don't actually hate math or those who think they know everything there is to know that there are actually more applications?

The first step is your approach. There's absolutely no reason to lead aggressively. If, after Mr. West told me that he hated statistics, I had countered with, "Well you're wrong," he likely would have thrown me out of his office, and we never would have had an opportunity to see our common ground on things like rebounds and assists.

There is a certain arrogance attributed to the stats community. Much of this arrogance comes from that geek/jock dynamic. Geeks have always believed that they are smarter than the jocks, so as their work becomes more relevant their sense of entitlement becomes greater. Unfortunately, that attitude is counterproductive.

The resistance that Marathe encountered early in his career caused him to shy away from the limelight and keep as low a profile as possible. He was happy to give others credit for any of his successes and was the consummate team player. This ego-suppression facilitated his meteoric rise from business school intern to vice president of football operations. Even to this day, Marathe stays out of the limelight, instead allowing the owner and general manager to handle all press opportunities. He has almost become afraid of attention and wanted to read every word that I wrote about him in this book.

Of course, being humble is easier said than done because certainly when you have a great idea you want people to know about it. And of course we all have tremendous pride in our work. But there is a subtle difference between being smart and acting smart, and in this dynamic acting too smart can be the kiss of death.

Leigh Buchanan, editor-at-large for *Inc.* magazine, said it well in an article entitled "The Office: Too Smart for Comfort."[8] She states that bosses are threatened by employees "who seem more intelligent than they are," and that when interviewing for a job, the smart candidate will show off their intellect only enough to impress—but not intimidate—their potential boss. Essentially act smart but not too smart.

As a blackjack team, we devised an entire strategy, called "guerilla big players," to mask our intelligence.

Big players were the livelihood of our team. They were the most advanced players and had gone through the most rigorous training. They were the ones who ultimately decided our profit and loss, so their skill level was uncompromised. The problem was that it took a lot of time, commitment, and intelligence to be a big player. And therefore big players were a limited resource.

So we created a new strategy in which we would train different recruits to be guerilla big players. A guerilla big player didn't need to be as skilled as a big player. In fact, they didn't even need to learn to count. They simply had to memorize basic strategy. When playing in a casino, they would always play with a "signaler" at the table. A signaler was someone who knew how to count and had the same basic skills as a big player but for whatever reason didn't work as a big player. The signaler would do all the hard work—counting, calculating, and estimating—and then would make a signal to the big player, telling them what to bet.

The signals were subtle. A hand placed under the chin, chips stacked in a certain location, or fingers stretched in a certain direction would tell the guerilla big player what to do.

The beauty of this strategy was that guerilla big players didn't have to focus on anything, only occasionally glancing at the signaler. This allowed them to play different roles to deceive the casino. One of our guerilla big players named Steve McClelland played those roles well.

Steve has been a close friend of mine for nearly 15 years. He is a big, jolly man who has perhaps the world's most infectious laugh. He is incredibly intelligent, having graduated with a biomedical engineering degree from Duke University, but he leads with a light, approachable personality. It was this levity that he took to the casinos in his role as a guerilla big player.

My favorite recollection of Steve's tenure was one Sunday morning at the Bellagio. Steve was playing his role of guerilla big player and walked around the casino gnawing on an apple. The reasoning was that people who eat apples in casinos are eccentric, and eccentric people aren't smart. Next, whenever Steve wasn't playing blackjack, he would stand behind the roulette wheel and stare, occasionally putting a small bet down. Roulette has the worst odds of any game in the casino, so certainly if Steve played roulette he wasn't very intelligent.

The clincher was the effort that he went to at the tables to convince the casino personnel that he wasn't a threat. He used to sit down at the handicapped tables, lower tables to accommodate patrons in wheelchairs, and ask if the rules were the same at that table. After the casino staff explained that the rules at those tables were the same, he would simply say, "So the same but lower."

That morning at the Bellagio, he pulled one of my all-time favorite stunts. Sitting at the blackjack table with his signaler, as soon as the dealer started to deal, Steve crouched down under the table to tie his shoe. While he was under the table, the dealer finished dealing his cards and waited for Steve to resurface. Steve did not oblige. Instead, he remained under the table.

Growing impatient, the dealer finally asked, "Sir, I need to know what you want to do with your hand."

Steve kept his head under the table pretending to have trouble tying his shoe. "What do I have?" he asked from below.

"12, sir," the dealer answered.

"What do you have?" Steve asked.

"I have a six showing sir," the dealer stated, growing exasperated.

Knowing that the dealer would not accept only an audible signal, Steve reached his hand above the table, still keeping the rest of his body below and waved it back and forth, letting the dealer know that he did not want any more cards. Certainly someone who had trouble tying his shoes and didn't even care to see his cards could not be very intelligent.

With this act, Steve was able to fly under the radar for some time. The casino personnel were not threatened by him because they didn't think he was smart. In fact his lack of perceived intelligence was endearing to them, and even when some figured out Steve's act and he was eventually thrown out of the casinos, you sensed that they still didn't believe he was a threat.

"I once overheard a floor person ask one of the dealers about me. He asked, 'Do you think that guy's on some kind of medication?'" Steve recalled with a smile. "They didn't think I was a card counter because they barely thought I could count."

As a team we always attempted to seem less intelligent. We obviously never mentioned MIT, always making up stories about where we went to school. We knew that a high level of intellect would just put the casinos on the defensive and would make our job harder.

For some reason, the stats community has always taken the opposite approach, trying to make what they do seem complicated. Perhaps it is a badge of honor or perhaps it's a defense mechanism. If using statistics is too simple, then anyone could do it and the need for smart statisticians would diminish. But making analytics seem complicated makes them even less approachable. It puts people on the defensive, so that they're less inclined to give statistical analysis a fair chance.

This quote by Dr. Stanley Gudder, a mathematics professor and author, sums up my thoughts on the matter well: "The essence of mathematics is not to make simple things complicated, but to make complicated things simple."[9]

In fact, when I talk to people in sports or business I try not to even use the words analytics or statistics; instead I talk about using information from the past to help make decisions about the future. No one would tell you that they don't want more information with which to make decisions, but in the same breath they might tell you that they don't need to hear any more statistics.

Making statistics approachable is about more than just your attitude. Similar to our incentive package for salespeople, our incentive for using math to make decisions needs to be simple and transparent. Presenting the value proposition of data-driven decision making in a clear, concise manner is a great way to win over the most reluctant converts. The average gambler actually fits into that category, and I've had to convince many of them of the merits of card counting.

After *Bringing Down the House* came out, I had a variety of different press opportunities to promote the book. One such appearance was on a local affiliate of National Public Radio. During that show, I told our story to all who cared. About 15 minutes into the interview, the host asked if I would mind taking some calls. I obliged and we started taking questions from the callers.

The first few callers asked the typical questions. Is card counting illegal? Nope. Are you allowed in Vegas? This was one of my favorites. Of course I'm allowed in Vegas. It's not like they have someone waiting for me on the jetway at McCarron airport telling me I have to go home. And I'm allowed and welcome in just about every casino. Am I allowed to play blackjack? Well, that's another story.

The third call was a bit more interesting. The caller started in by boasting of his card-counting prowess. "I'm a pretty good card counter and I know all about that system you guys used. But card counting is boring. It takes all the fun out of it."

This was actually the first time I'd heard someone criticize the entertainment value of card counting. I asked him to expand upon what he meant by boring.

"Well, I mean, you just always do the same thing and you don't ever get to use your gut. It's too mechanical. I like to get out there and gamble a little bit," the caller answered.

The caller's name was Jim and I was actually interested in what he was getting at. "So you can count cards but you'd rather not do it because you don't think it's fun?"

"Yup."

"Well, Jim. Let me ask you one thing. Is it more fun to win or lose?" I asked.

He paused for a second. "Well, it's more fun to win," he answered.

"Well, when we count cards we win," I declared.

Jim paused again and then finally blurted out, "Oh. I get what you mean."

Even Jim came around when I put it in such black-and-white terms. And really, that's how simple it needs to be. The reason that we counted cards is that we wanted to win. The reason that more professional sports teams are finally starting to incorporate data into their decision-making processes is their similar desire to win. And the reason that every business should embrace analytics is that it will help them win.

But sometimes even this simple message isn't enough. Sometimes there are psychological factors working against you as you try to introduce analytics into an organization, and it is important to be aware of these obstacles as you try to effect change.

Because analytics are often the work of people who are not in the inner circle of management, bringing analytics into an organization subjects it to the "not invented here" syndrome. In these circumstances, resistance to new ideas is higher simply because the ideas were invented outside of the organization's core group.

In one of my first conversations with a Major League Baseball general manager, I sensed an attitude of "not invented here." So rather than pull out the long presentation that I had prepared, I instead created a dialogue where I gave him ample opportunity to suggest the answers that would have been included in my presentation. Giving him a chance to feel like he was inventing the ideas made the conversation much easier.

Even the first time we met with Coach Walsh, we spent a lot of time talking about his ideas and thoughts rather than flooding him with our newfangled way of looking at things. Fortunately, many of his thoughts coincided with ours, so the process went smoothly, but certainly giving him a chance to feel ownership of our ideas was helpful to receiving his buy-in.

Sometimes buy-in isn't even needed, and simple visibility is enough. Take the case of the publicly traded Dutch company Vistaprint. Vistaprint is an e-commerce business supplying "high-quality graphic design services and customized printed products."[10] Their affordable pricing makes them perfect for both small businesses and the average consumer. With better technology on the design and printing side and improved infrastructure, Vistaprint is able to offer cost-effective solutions in a competitive space. The company has been profitable for many years and saw revenue grow from $90.9 million in 2005 to $515.8 million in fiscal year 2009.[11] That's a whole lot of business cards.

But one of the main reasons that Vistaprint has been successful is a commitment to analytics. They list as two of their guiding principles: "Analytics-driven decision making" and "Culture of test before invest." With guiding principles like these, it's easy to see the high level of trust that Vistaprint has in data. What makes them successful is how they have instilled this culture of data trust in the employees; they have made analytics approachable, allowing even those who hate math to have visibility into the numbers.

Senior Director of Marketing Todd McClain explains Vistaprint's philosophy to me: "We are a very transparent organization when it comes to data and analytics. It's all out there for people to see and use. We do have dedicated analytics teams, however everyone throughout the company has an analytic and quantitative mindset in some way or another. Because of this and to create scale, we've built numerous internal tools over the years which allow a non-technical person to be able to get at and use data. We have our marketers digging into numbers themselves for their campaigns every day, and they don't need analytics support every day to do this. This allows our analytics teams to be focused on bigger things and be more proactive when it comes to analysis and guiding decision making and strategies."

While McClain highlights the resource advantages of his organization's transparent approach, the clear message is that allowing everyone to have access to the analytics is an important step to gaining acceptance for these methods. Vistaprint has helped their non-analytics people to feel like those numbers were invented at Vistaprint.

But as my radio caller Jim pointed out, there is a certain swashbuckling machismo to making decisions without real analysis, and certainly making data-driven decisions takes more energy than simply flipping a coin. I talked about this with one of my former blackjack team members. We were in the midst of a friendly poker game with some friends, and I noticed that he made a very odd play—a play that someone versed in statistics likely wouldn't have made. During one of the breaks, I asked him about it since I thought there must be some logic behind it. He simply smiled at me and said, "With all the money we've won and lost playing blackjack, you really think I care about dollar ante poker? I'm just here to have fun. I don't really care if I win or lose. Calculating pot odds just seems like too much work for me right now."

Using math to make decisions is not always easy, but if you are really committed to winning, it is well worth the effort. And by winning I'm not just talking about at a blackjack table or on a football field. I'm talking about winning in business.

But people are predisposed to resist the use of analytics unless it is presented in the right way, with simplicity, humility, and a sense of collaboration. Unfortunately, many great analytical ideas fail to see the light of day because they are presented incorrectly.

As you think about how to introduce analytics into your business or life, don't think of it as math or numbers. Instead think of it as a new way to make decisions, a way that allows you to systematically incorporate more information than you had before, a way that allows you to look objectively at the decision, and a way that allows you to win more often.

11

THE BRAIN CELLS IN YOUR STOMACH

Intuition becomes increasingly valuable in the new information society precisely because there is so much data.

—John Naisbitt

PEOPLE WHO HATE math often eschew data-driven decisions because they rely on their gut—their intuition. Famous swashbuckling General Electric CEO Jack Welch didn't write a book called *Straight From the Brain*. His book was instead called *Straight From the Gut*. Much cooler sounding.

As a believer in data-driven decisions, but wearing my practical hat, I have always wondered what role intuition should play in the data-driven world. It's a difficult question for me because my blackjack background would lead me to believe that it should play absolutely none.

In the movie *21*, there is a scene where Ben Campbell, the character based on me, loses his cool and starts to "gamble." Coming off a bad run, he becomes emotional and starts to bet big money even though he knows it is not statistically sound. His teammates watch in shock as he loses hundreds of thousands of dollars. Hollywood's version portrays this as a bad decision as Campbell loses everything and eventually realizes the error of his ways.

When I read the script for the first time and came across this scene, I was bothered by its incredible inaccuracy. I actually asked the writer if he could take it out, explaining that as card counters we were emotionless and something like this would have never happened. It simply couldn't. We understood that there was no room for gut or intuition. In fact if we had made a mistake like Ben had in *21,* we would have been kicked off the team instantly. Every decision we made was black and white—there was no gray.

This black and white started with any new player memorizing basic strategy, which allows only one answer to every decision. They had to know it perfectly and their test was to play through close to 360 hands of blackjack, making no mistakes. If they made one mistake, they failed and would have to start over. After they were finished with this portion of the test, they would then need to write out the basic strategy chart (see Appendix) perfectly to prove the thoroughness of their knowledge.

Every hand had a clear-cut answer. A pair of aces was always split. Elevens were doubled against everything but an ace. Soft 17 was always hit against a 10. Learning basic strategy was the first step to understanding that there was no room for intuition in blackjack.

After a player learned basic strategy perfectly, we would introduce the concept of counting cards. Using our very simple system, where each card had a point value, players were drilled for hours. Tens, face cards, and aces were worth minus one. Twos, 3s, 4s, 5s, and 6s were all worth plus one. Sevens, 8s, and 9s were all considered neutral. These were the rules, and they were non-negotiable.

Players were tested on their counting abilities and again were allowed to make virtually no mistakes. Players had to pass several different counting tests. Sometimes they were asked to simply stand behind a table as people played in front of them. Other times, they had to sit at the table and play two hands while counting perfectly. The tests were approximately 24 decks long, and players were allowed to make at most two mistakes. If they were ever off by more than two from the actual count, they would fail and would have to start over.

Once they passed the counting tests, they were taught how to use the count to determine what to bet. Based on the count there was a simple mathematical equation that told you what to bet on the hand. In between hands a player would actually do a quick calculation based on the count and the number of cards yet to be dealt. They would then bet accordingly. At no point did they have a decision that did not have math as its basis. If a player had a bad feeling about a dealer or someone else at the table, they would have to ignore those feelings. If a player was feeling unlucky because they had lost three hands in a row, well, really there was no room for them to feel unlucky: They simply followed the system and made decisions based on the data.

There was a great comfort in the structure and safety of this world. In fact, although I know it sounds odd, I've struggled to find something outside of the world of blackjack that has this level of certainty. My work in trading certainly failed me on this point. Every other avenue I explored outside of blackjack simply fell short.

I can honestly say that I understood why every decision I made at the blackjack table was right and that I never made a wrong decision. That is not to say I never made a mistake or never lost a hand, but the basis and intention behind my decisions were always "right." I'm not sure if there's anything else I can say that about.

It is this reliance on math that makes blackjack truly unique and a game where every decision is backed by data. Through the blackjack lens, intuition has no place in the decision-making process.

Poker, like blackjack, has a memory and is subject to conditional probability. If I have an ace in my hand, the chance that someone else has an ace has certainly decreased. Also, similar to blackjack, I can calculate pot odds and make bets based on expected value and probability, knowing that there is data behind my decisions.

But there are some obvious differences between the two games. In blackjack you play only against the dealer. The other players at the table are of no consequence. And to make things even simpler, you always know what the dealer is going to do. It is implicit in the rules of the game. A blackjack dealer has to hit until they get to a total equal to or greater than 17 and stand on any total 17 or greater. If the dealer has a 12, you know the dealer has to take a card. If you have 18 and they receive a 5, giving them a total of 17, even though they don't have you beat, they cannot take another card. They automatically lose.

With that knowledge, when the dealer has a 5 showing and you have a 15, basic strategy says you should stand because the dealer has to take a card, and your best chance to win is to hope that he will bust. Basic strategy depends on the certainty of the dealer's actions.

But this is not the case with poker, as your opponents are not bound by specific rules. They can play their cards any way they want, and one of the keys in poker is figuring out your opponent's tendencies. Two players may play the same two cards very differently. The ability to read people and predict their behaviors is a key skill that is necessary in poker and useless in blackjack. Data-driven decision making in poker is not as simple as it is in blackjack.

But if you could somehow simplify poker and make it more like blackjack, you might be able to create an optimal strategy—a basic strategy for poker. In other words, if you could make your opponents follow certain rules and behave in predictable ways, like a blackjack dealer, you would be able to devise a data-driven framework for playing poker.

In order to model complex situations, you often have to oversimplify the situation. You need to make some assumptions that make the problem manageable. And that's exactly what Andy Bloch did to create a data-driven framework for making decisions in poker.

Bloch is one of the most successful professional poker players of the last decade, having won more than $4,000,000 playing tournament poker. He has cashed in more than 20 World Series of Poker events and has won countless tournaments, including the 2008 Pro-Am Poker Equalizer, the $10,000 buy-in Ultimate Poker Challenge II, and the 2002 Seven-Card Stud event at the World Poker Finals. Beyond his tournament success, his other claim to fame is his advanced level of education: He has received two electrical engineering degrees from MIT and a JD from Harvard University.[1]

Bloch started playing casino poker at Foxwoods Casino in Ledyard, Connecticut. Originally founded as a bingo hall, Foxwoods added table games in 1992 and with its proximity to both Boston and New York City became a popular destination for highly educated gamblers like Bloch. Bloch entered into $35 weekly poker tournaments, making the two-hour trip from Boston once a month, and his poker career was born. But it wasn't until a year later that gambling became more than just a hobby for Bloch.

While unemployed that year, he came across a new game at Foxwoods called "Hickok 6-card Poker," an obscure version of poker played against the house. After observing the game he hypothesized that it might be beatable. Bloch wrote some computer programs and developed a strategy for "playing Hickok that gave the player a pretty substantial edge of about 6 percent."[2]

Bloch played in a weekly poker game and through that game met some fellow MIT alumni who were members of the blackjack team. They joined forces and put together a team of MIT students and others to beat Hickok. This new team won consistently for a few months, but the casino caught on fairly quickly and changed the rules so that Hickok was no longer beatable.

On average the Hickok team only won about $30 an hour and in total they had won less than $100,000, but more importantly this experience gave Bloch an introduction to the MIT blackjack team and the world of professional gambling. He started going to MIT team practices in late 1994 and went on his first blackjack trip to Las Vegas with the team in early 1995. Meanwhile, growing bored with his engineering job, he quit and began playing blackjack and poker full time while deciding what to do next. He has gone on to become one of the most successful poker players of the last decade.

So Bloch, with his analytical background and experience in blackjack, was the perfect person to create a purely mathematical, optimal strategy for poker. Looking at poker with the eye of a card counter, Bloch sought to create a framework that would give him blackjack-like conviction in his poker decisions.

In order to build this framework, Bloch sought to create a purely objective ranking of every two-card hand possible in Texas Hold'em. With this ranking, players could consistently devise a data-driven strategy to play before the flop (before any community cards have been turned over).

In order to do this Bloch needed a computer, but he also needed to simplify the problem. With so many more factors than those present in blackjack, this was not an easy problem.

The first thing he did was reduce the number of other people at the table to one. So in the game he would simulate, he was playing heads up against only one other player. Next he needed to make that player behave in a predictable manner. So he gave his opponent only two choices—to fold or go all in.

With these simplifications, Bloch was able to create a ranking system for all 169 possible two-card hands. Combining that knowledge with the frequency of those 169 hands gave Bloch some data-driven information on what was successful.

So there it was. Andy Bloch had his basic strategy for poker.

When I spoke with him, I suspected that this basic strategy could not be followed as religiously as that of blackjack. What Bloch's exercise gave him was a basic ranking of all starting hands and an overview of how to play those hands. But the situation was based on an oversimplification, and poker still has many moving parts that weren't accounted for. It's not a basic strategy in the blackjack sense of the word.

Even if there really was a basic strategy for poker, it would have a lot more variables: how many people are at your table, what position are you in, how much money you have relative to the big blind, how much money is in the pot already, etc. Then add in the fact that every poker player is a different person with a different skill level, strategy, and knowledge of the game, and you have a situation that seems utterly impossible to model. There can't be a basic strategy that could cover every case.

So if this strategy was an oversimplification and therefore did not cover every possible situation, how did Bloch make decisions in the edge cases? Certainly poker, unlike blackjack, allowed for and even demanded that Bloch use his intuition. But if that were true, how did that need go over with a guy like Andy Bloch—a truly analytical mind who had created and implemented purely mathematical winning strategies?

I asked many questions about intuition in poker while I talked to Bloch on the phone. "So how often do you deviate from your poker basic strategy?" I asked him.

"I try to follow it pretty consistently, but of course depending on the type of players at the table I'll vary. I'll play tighter if I know there's a really aggressive player in the big blind, raising every time he's in the big blind. Or if there is a really loose player to my left, I'm going to tighten up a lot. But even those variations have a framework behind them." Bloch's thoughtful answer reinforced my trust in him as an analytical thought leader. Everything he did at the poker table was well thought out, well planned. It was clear that Bloch was incredibly disciplined and did approach poker in much the same way that he approached blackjack.

Yet even in Bloch's answer there was a certain amount of subjectivity that you would not see in a discussion on blackjack. So I decided to just outright ask him the question that was consuming me: "How do you balance intuition with math when playing poker?"

Bloch paused for a second and then started by saying, "I use intuition but I'm careful about it. If you listen to your intuition too much, you start listening to things that aren't really intuition. Like having pocket 4s and saying, I think there's going to be a 4 on the flop, so I'm going to go all in. That's not intuition. That's just a guess.

"You have to use the right intuition—intuition that is based on some kind of fact. Like if you notice an opponent's tell that makes you call in a situation that you wouldn't normally. You might not be conscious of exactly why you make that call, but your intuition was based on some kind of fact," Bloch concludes.

This was certainly a different type of intuition than most people talk about. Bloch continued explaining his version of intuition: "I use intuition when I face a situation that I've never seen before—a situation that I haven't had a chance to model."

This statement was of great interest to me. Since intuition played no part in our blackjack strategy, I struggled to understand what role it should play in the data-driven world, and perhaps this would give me a clue. Intuition is defined as "direct perception of truth, fact, etc., independent of any reasoning process."[3] But Bloch's version was different because it always had a reasoning process—conscious or not.

Bloch was defining a new type of intuition—one that clearly had data behind it. His intuition was a non-conscious data-driven decision. The reasoning might not have lived in a computer or spreadsheet, but it certainly was there.

This exchange with Bloch reminded me of my first meeting with Coach Bill Walsh. At the time we were trying to build a new framework for valuing the performance of football players. Our premise was that traditional football statistics were not accurate in painting the whole picture.

Aggregate statistics in football certainly have their shortcomings. If you pick up a paper on a Monday morning during the football season, you will often see a list of the 100-yard rushers from the previous day's games. But who really knows if any of those performances were that exceptional? Certainly 100 yards on 20 carries is a great day for the running back. What if the running back needed 30 carries to rush for those 100 yards? Would that still be a good performance?

So the next natural step in looking for the truth would be to look at rate-based statistics rather than aggregate statistics—in this specific case, yards per carry. But what is an exceptional yards per carry? In our first case, the running back averaged 5 yards per carry and we deemed this good. In our second case, the running back averaged only 3.3 yards per carry and we were pretty sure that was bad. So the acceptable number of yards per carry must fall somewhere in between.

Unfortunately the answer isn't even that simple. Let's split the difference and say that, based on our aforementioned examples, the acceptable yards per carry is a little over four yards per carry. But not all four-yard carries are created equal. A four-yard run on third and 3, yielding a first down and a new set of downs, is clearly a success. On the contrary, a four-yard run on third and 5, leaving you with fourth down and a punting situation, is clearly not.

So rather than focus on rate or aggregate statistics, we decided instead to focus on contextual statistics. We decided to judge each play individually and rate whether each play was a success and to what extent. So in our system a five-yard run on third and 4 would be much more valuable than a five-yard run on third and 6. For the edge cases this was pretty straightforward, but things got a bit more complicated on first and second downs where plays can certainly be successful even if they fail to yield a first down. So the challenge was to create a metric that could measure success on a play-by-play level.

In order to answer this question we built a statistical model based on play-by-play information from every NFL game over three seasons. Using this data we created a new statistic called expected points (EP) (similar to the system that Bryan Burke used to prove that more NFL coaches should attempt more onside kicks). EP was a framework that could tell you, based on the situation at the start of any play, how many points the offensive team could be expected to score. For example, the EP of first and goal at the one-yard line would be just under seven points. Based on the data, in this situation you were highly likely to score seven points on that drive. Even though you hadn't done it yet, the value in your situation was worth nearly seven points. Let's say that you committed a holding penalty and lost ten yards. Now you were first and goal at the ten-yard line and your EP fell to five points since the likelihood of scoring a touchdown had dropped considerably. That holding penalty cost you two expected points.

Here we had a new measure that would tell you the EP of any situation in a football game, and we therefore had our new metric for measuring the success of individual plays. On each play, we could measure how much the play changed the team's EP. If the change was positive, the play had been a success. If it was negative, clearly the play had been a failure.

An important part of any mathematical modeling process is called the laugh test. It's when you look at your results and ask people who have industry insight what they think. It's called the laugh test because you are hoping they don't just laugh at your results. It represents a sanity check that you are on the right track with your method.

And that's where Coach Walsh came in. As an advisor to our company, Coach Walsh was generous with his time and agreed to meet with us to help us validate our results. We prepared a presentation with the goal to see whether our statistical findings were in line with his observations from having been involved with the game for sixty-some odd years.

Meeting with Coach Walsh in his office at Stanford University, there was a certain sense of anxiety. Walsh was a genius and legend but was not a statistics guy. We had spent a lot of time working on this method, and if Walsh didn't agree, we were likely going to have to start all over again.

The first question we asked Coach Walsh was a simple one: "What are the number of yards that you need to gain on first down for it to be considered a success?"

Coach Walsh thought about the question for a second and then answered, "I think somewhere around four yards. Five is definitely a good play. Four is probably okay. Three is definitely not good enough."

"How about on second down?" I continued.

"Well obviously it depends on the total yards you need but at least half of the yards."

In both cases, Walsh's years of wisdom echoed what our months of number crunching had told us. Of course his analysis was founded on a lot more than a few seconds of thought. It was founded on a lifetime of work in the sport—a lifetime of observations, a lifetime of data.

As we went through more of our results, Walsh's intuition was perfectly in line with our data-driven findings. While many would call his thoughts instinctive or intuitive, you could tell that he was recalling observed data as he made those judgments.

Paraag Marathe had a similar experience with Coach Walsh. Marathe had been hired to help the 49ers take a second look at their draft card. A draft card is a guide that gives point values to every possible draft position in every possible round. It is used to evaluate how to trade picks. For example, if a team wants to know if trading their third- and fifth-round pick for another team's second round pick is a good idea, all they need to do is look at the draft card and add up the points. The original draft card used by most teams at the time was developed by Gil Brandt in the 1970s when he was the Dallas Cowboys' personnel head.[4] Coach Walsh's intuition disagreed with that card.

In fact, Walsh had always believed that the 49ers' draft card was incorrect and did not always follow the card. So he decided to hire some analytical people to help him confirm statistically what was in his head. Marathe and his team spent three months on the project and came out with a new draft card.

Marathe used this new draft card to evaluate the way Walsh had traded draft picks in the past and to his surprise found that Walsh's trades actually followed the point system of the new card. As they looked at his trades through the lens of their new and improved draft card, they noted that Walsh had actually been trading along their new guidelines before they had ever been created. His intuition produced results that they had needed three months to figure out using analytics.

In both cases, Walsh's intuition matched what the analytics said, in many ways confirming Walsh's genius. He didn't need a computer to tell him what success was in the NFL or what relative values of draft picks were. Likewise, he didn't need numbers laid out in a spreadsheet to tell him who to draft—he just knew. But were Walsh's decisions truly based on intuition in the strictest sense of the word? Were they, as the dictionary says, "independent of any reasoning process"[5]?

Or were they like Bloch's version of intuition? Simply, decisions based on sub-conscious reasoning—reasoning that Bloch hadn't had a chance to model or that Walsh hadn't felt the need to model. At some level Walsh believed in data-driven decisions, otherwise he would have never hired Marathe and his crew to confirm what his intuition was telling him.

At the time of Walsh's death, he had been involved with organized football for more than 60 years. It's hard to believe anyone that smart would simply ignore that much information when making decisions on whom to draft. Also, Walsh was known for his excessive preparation, even scripting the first 25 offensive plays of the game. He did this so he would be prepared for any situation and wouldn't have to just make a quick, gut decision. So I'm not ready to make Coach Walsh the poster child for "gut-based" decisions.

Yet Walsh's genius made me wonder, are there just certain people who don't need data and are better off making gut decisions? And, if so, where do these decisions really come from? The last time I checked, there were no brain cells in the stomach.

My journey to find a truly intuitive thinker led me to another industry in great flux due to the data revolution, an industry where decisions are often life and death—literally. The impact of the data revolution on medicine has produced mixed results. It has created advances via techniques like data mining yet has spawned the controversial evidence-based medicine (EBM).

The debate over EBM is a heated one. In many ways, EBM is the poster child for why people hate statistics. Many misinterpret EBM to mean practicing medicine by numbers and nothing else. The idea that a doctor could make life-and-death clinical decisions solely based on past clinical studies and meta-analysis sounds ludicrous, but some opponents of EBM have shaped its definition in just that way.

Dr. Michael Blum, a cardiologist and the medical director of information technology at UCSF Medical Center, defines EBM as "the provision of clinical care based on current guidelines and data generated via scientific research (i.e. clinical trials)."[6] He explains that "EBM incorporates the provider's clinical judgment, so it is not supposed to be a blind application of a guideline, but that is sometimes how it is portrayed in politicized discussion."

Blum explains, "Strict adherence [to EBM] is not necessarily a problem if the evidence/guideline is strong (i.e. multiple, well-done trials in tight agreement) and applied appropriately. The challenges are that the data are often weak, conflicting or altogether lacking, apply to populations and not necessarily the individual that you are treating right then, and don't take into account the preferences and culture of the individual patient.

"For example, a female patient with coronary artery disease (CAD) comes into my office but is also experiencing some heartburn (not due to the CAD). By CAD guidelines she should be on aspirin. However, the aspirin could make a potential ulcer worse. Additionally, the data that support aspirin for prevention in CAD are mostly derived from studies in men and exclude patients with active or suspected peptic ulcer disease. So, following this very basic guideline could be inappropriate and harmful in her case." Blum illustrates here a case where a doctor needs to use judgment and can't simply follow what the data tells them, since the data really doesn't apply.

So EBM, or rather a strict adherence to data, can potentially oversimplify the situation, like Bloch did in his basic strategy for poker. "The inclusion/exclusion criteria in the clinical trials that generate the evidence and guidelines are critically important and frequently lost in the discussion. Real patients often don't fit into neat tidy categories and it is often arguable whether the evidence would apply," Blum further explains.

The main issue here is that no matter how great the research study is, and as Blum would tell you most research studies at this point are not great, it will most often fall short of a perfect fit for the given situation. Most of the research is performed on a very specific population. Assumptions like "a person of perfect health" are achieved when researchers are able to screen their subjects, choosing only those who fit that criteria. But doctors in the clinical world do not have that luxury and often have to deal with patients who don't quite fit in to the existing research.

In cases like this, doctors must call on their own database, the one in their head, to make the most relevant diagnosis or treatment for their specific patient.

So if the data doesn't fit, are doctors left to make decisions with their gut? Blum doesn't think so. "Doctors, like all individuals, make decisions based on their own preferences, biases, and anecdotal experience. Unfortunately, it has been shown that most individuals, doctors included, make decisions based on their personal anecdotal experience rather than data (regardless of how available the data is). Clinical judgment is an interesting cross between individual anecdotes and a synthesis of data that allows a good physician to prognosticate a patient's likely severity of illness, risk, and course—they know who to worry about."

This is math in the real world, where the number of variables are often too numerous and the sample size too small to create perfect models. But that doesn't mean you should ignore the data. It just means that you always strive to find the best data—the most relevant data with which to make the best decisions.

I call this data-driven intuition, and it is a process that many successful people implement when faced with a situation where using a purely data-driven statistical model is impossible. A world-famous professional poker player, an NFL coaching legend, and an extremely accomplished cardiologist all practiced this new form of intuition.

Yet the question still perplexed me. Were there people who made purely "gut" decisions? Decisions independent of any "reasoning process"?

Split-second decision making in sports, like a quarterback calling an audible at the line of scrimmage or a pitcher deciding to throw a curveball, happens continually throughout a game and must happen quickly. With so little time to make these types of decisions, the opportunity to have a reasoning process seems low and the likelihood of classical intuition seems high.

Yet conversations with two major league pitchers led me to think differently. Craig Breslow and David Price are both successful, left-handed pitchers in the major leagues, but that is where the similarities end. Physically they are diametric opposites. Breslow is officially listed at a generous 6′1″ but could easily walk under a six-foot doorframe without ducking. Price stands a full 6′6″ and would likely destroy that same doorframe if he tried to walk through.

I was first introduced to Breslow by a mutual friend. Breslow was interested in recruiting me to work with his charity, the Strike 3 Foundation,[7] and wanted me as the keynote speaker at the annual dinner. After meeting Craig, I accepted immediately. He was truly a unique and thoughtful individual—someone I wanted to be associated with.

Breslow graduated from Yale University with a degree in molecular biophysics and biochemistry. Because of this pedigree, Breslow has been dubbed the "smartest man in baseball."[8] Yet his career has had its share of ups and downs. In a seven-year professional career, Breslow has been with six different organizations. But in 2009, he seemed to find a home with our friend Billy Beane and the Oakland A's, posting a dominating 2.60 ERA while finishing second in the league in appearances.

"My career really turned around after I started changing my preparation," Breslow recalled. "I used to just think I could go out there and throw my curve or my fastball and get people out. But when I was in Minnesota, Dennis Reyes, who was a situation lefty like myself, pulled me aside and showed me how he prepared.

"I started using a computer program called BATS that let me watch different past at bats of the batters that I was going to face. You can actually select specific types of at bats that you want to see. I would watch all of their at bats against lefties that I considered similar to me and look at their approach. How did it change during the course of the at bat? What pitches were successful against them? What pitches weren't?

"Also, going into any series we would have pitchers' meetings with our coaches and scouts, and we would be given data of how different hitters performed against different pitchers and even more specifically how they performed against different pitches.

"From this data I was able to come up with an approach for each hitter." Breslow was describing a data-driven process for pitch selection. By gathering data from both scouts and video archives, he was able to look for patterns that gave him an advantage over the hitter.

As Breslow finished his explanation, I asked him, "So do you always do what the data says?"

"Well, to be honest, and this may not be what you want to hear, even if the data shows that a hitter has had a lot of success against the curveball, I still might throw my curveball to him if I think that's the best pitch for me to get him out," Breslow answered.

"Interesting. Is there a reasoning process behind that kind of decision?" I asked, thinking that I'd finally found a truly intuitive thinker.

"Actually, there is a strong reasoning process. I'll do that if I've had recent success getting that hitter out with curveballs. I'll trust that smaller sample size because I think my curveball is different than the other pitcher's curveballs that I either saw on film or were in the data the coaches presented to us."

So in point of fact Breslow was ignoring data he thought might not be specific enough for the situation and instead was focusing on more relevant data—his personal experiences.

"Back when I was with the Padres, Trevor Hoffman stopped coming to our pitchers' meetings," Breslow started. Hoffman is a certain future

Hall of Fame pitcher and is the all-time leader in saves. He has made his career off essentially one pitch—an incredibly deceptive change-up.

"He was like, 'What am I going to learn at these meetings that I can actually use? If they tell me that I shouldn't throw change-ups to Manny Ramirez because that's what the numbers say, I'm still going to throw change-ups. One, because I have no other choice, and two, because I think my change-up is better than everyone else's.'"

Essentially, Hoffman was echoing Breslow's sentiment that he didn't think using the success or failure of other pitchers was strong enough data to get him to alter his approach; instead he preferred to rely on the more relevant personal data. It's very similar to doctors deciding that their patient does not fit the criteria of the latest study/guideline they are looking at.

This sentiment of "it doesn't apply to me" can be a very dangerous viewpoint as it gives people a way to avoid using data to make decisions. But in Breslow and Hoffman's case they weren't ignoring data altogether. Instead they were using what they considered to be more relevant data.

So Breslow was a clear believer in data-driven decisions and did not use his intuition in the classical sense. But what of his antithesis, David Price, a pitcher who, due to a surplus in physical skills, would likely not need to rely on guile in the same way that Breslow does?

See, while Breslow was drafted in the twenty-sixth round by the Milwaukee Brewers, Price was drafted first. No, not just in the first round; Price was actually the first player chosen overall. That difference belies a tremendous difference in talent. Surely, Price and his wealth of can't-miss talent would not worry himself with data to make a decision.

As I talked to Price, though, I was struck by how similar our conversation was to the one I had with Breslow. Price talked about the pitchers' meetings and the scouting reports and all the data that he is presented with. He talked about countless hours of watching video, looking for clues in the way the batter holds his hands and lifts his foot. He mentions conversations he has with pitchers who more recently faced the team he is going up against, collecting information from them on how they got different hitters out. And he laughed as he talked about one of the crowning moments of his data-driven approach.

Knowing that I am a Red Sox fan and relishing the opportunity to rub my face in his shining moment, Price said, "I'd have to say that fast-ball away I threw to J. D.," referring to the moment that he, as a rookie pitcher for the Tampa Bay Rays, ended the Red Sox playoff hopes with a strike out of Red Sox right fielder J. D. Drew (in the same season that our sage Nate Silver predicted they would win 88 games).

"Everything I heard told me that was a pitch he couldn't hit," Price concluded. By "everything" Price was referring to the scouting reports, the video, the words of other pitchers—the data.

As I listened to him recall this story, I wasn't sure if I truly believed him. David Price is the type of player that kids want to be. He throws the ball hard and with so much movement that even if a batter knew what was coming there would be little he could do. Surely Price had the Jack Welch machismo and had times when he went with his gut.

"So are there ever times where you just throw a pitch without a reason because that's the pitch you want to throw, that you think you should throw?" I asked, hoping to lead him into an admission of classic intuition.

"Nope. There's a reason behind every pitch I throw. I actually visualize the pitch before I throw it and imagine success with that pitch before it comes out of my hand," Price answered unequivocally.

So even the swashbuckling, ultra-talented David Price eschewed the classical gut version of intuition. Instead, his approach was even more measured than Breslow's.

So my quest to find a successful individual who truly used their gut and nothing else to make decisions had come up empty. This was reassuring since I'm still looking for those brain cells in the stomach.

But what I did have to show for my efforts was a new definition of intuition. Instead of intuition being defined as "direct perception of truth, fact, etc., independent of any reasoning process," I came to see it as, "direct perception of truth, fact, etc., independent of any *documented* reasoning process." No one successful truly makes decisions without some reasoning process. They may not want to spend the time to explain that reasoning process or they may not have the sufficient information to document that reasoning process, but it's clear in all cases I explored that there was a method behind the madness.

There has been a fair amount of work in terms of the predictive value of expert intuition. And the results should be a little troubling to those who tend to believe expert intuition above all else. In his book entitled *Expert Political Judgment: How Good Is It? How Can We Know?*[9] Berkeley economist Philip Tetlock suggests that experts actually aren't as good at making predictions as one might think. He posits that experts tend to be good at articulating their views and presenting them well, but often their value is in the cosmetic aspects of decision making, and, when measured objectively, they generally come up short. This is usually a result of overconfidence and not examining the actual case at hand, that is, ignoring the data and instead relying more on base experience than thoughtful examination.

And that really is the lesson here. Every good decision has some data behind it as well as a thorough examination of the specific case at hand. It might not be data that sits in a spreadsheet or an analysis performed by a computer, but it is science much more than art.

Blackjack gave me a unique view on data-driven decisions. That view looked only at what the hard numbers would tell you. But sometimes the numbers aren't so available or applicable, and in times like this you need to make decisions with less data and unfortunately less structure.

I don't think this new definition of intuition should scare even the staunchest numbers guru. It is an important part of creating a world that is more like blackjack than poker. We should strive to make blackjack-like decisions because certainly those decisions will be right more often than they are wrong, like they were for us at the tables. But again, sometimes this level of certainty is not always possible.

Helping people understand what they are doing when they make what they think are intuitive decisions will help them appreciate the true value of using analytics. Imagine giving a doctor a clinical study of 100 different subjects who fit their exact patient to a tee. Or handing Bill Walsh a spreadsheet that includes every decision he ever made in his coaching career. Or handing Andy Bloch a complete log of every table and every person he'd ever played poker against. Or handing David Price a collection of simulated data of what J. D. Drew would do against his outside fastball. They all would have embraced this data and would have used it to make better decisions.

In the end, if you look at any successful person, whether it is in sports, gambling, or business, data is at the core of their decision-making process. And as you face difficult decisions in your business life, remember this consistency and use it to inspire yourself to eschew classic intuition for modern data-driven intuition, where you incorporate any data available to make decisions. This data may not always be packaged up in a nice statistical model, but striving to make your world more like blackjack than poker will help you make the right decision more often.

EPILOGUE

We should favor innovation and freedom over regulation.

—George Allen

PEOPLE OFTEN ASK me how it all ended.

Was it like the movie? Did we really get beat up? Did we get to keep the money? Did our MIT professor really steal the money? Why don't casinos just make it impossible to count cards? Why did you quit? Can you still do it today?

No, we didn't get beat up. Yes, we did get to keep the money. No, our professor didn't steal anything.

As for why casinos don't make it impossible to count cards—well, that's a study in human psychology. Blackjack was introduced in casinos in the 1930s but really didn't become popular until our friend Mr. Thorp showed the world it was beatable. Blackjack is popular because of the illusion that it can be beaten. It doesn't matter if people really can beat it; just the notion is enough for people to try.

Casinos play lots of tricks to convince people that they can win or that the best bets they offer are fair. Remember Brian, the roulette expert? He was a victim of the casino's subterfuge as he fell prey to the "magical" lights and history above the roulette wheel.

Poor Brian. This wasn't the only trick he fell for that weekend.

After his devastating roulette loss, Brian decided that he would follow my lead at the blackjack table and win all of his money back. We sat together at the Hard Rock and started playing. Almost immediately, the count started to climb, and his bets started getting correspondingly larger. Brian, playing with his hard-earned money, decided to bet two hands of $500. Since the count was 9 with a little under two decks left, he had roughly a 2 percent advantage over the casino and, based on his overall bankroll, this was a good bet. I gave him the nod and the dealer started, giving Brian a 20 on one hand and a blackjack on the other. There were three other people at the table: One of them also had blackjack and the other two had 19s. The problem was the dealer had an ace as his up card.

In that hand, the count had dropped by 9 since there were nine high cards, two neutral cards, and zero low cards. The count was now 0, meaning it was of standard composition. Basically, the same as it was when we started the shoe.

The dealer looked at Brian and asked him if he wanted even money on his blackjack. Brian started to nod, but I quickly butted in. "Hold on. He doesn't want even money," I said.

Brian looked back at me sharply. "I have $500 and blackjack and he has an ace. Of course I want even money."

"Hold on a second," I said, hoping I could keep the dealer from clearing his cards and giving him his even money. "Brian, if he has blackjack, I'll give you your $500. If he doesn't you can give me the $250 you would have given up by taking even money."

Brian begrudgingly agreed. Then the dealer asked the rest of the table if they wanted insurance. Insurance is a bet offered by the casino when the dealer is showing an ace. It is a two-to-one bet that the dealer has blackjack. In other words, you are betting that the dealer has a 10, J, Q, K underneath his ace, and if you bet $100 and he does, you will win $200 net. If he doesn't, you lose your $100.

The problem is that like just about every other bet in the casino, those odds are not fair. Just do the math. If the composition of the deck is standard, the dealer will have blackjack four times (10, J, Q, K) for every nine times (ace, 2, 3, 4, 5, 6, 7, 8, 9) he doesn't. So the true odds are actually 9 to 4, meaning for every $100 you bet you should actually win 9/4 times $100 or $225.

Most people realize insurance is a bad bet and don't take it. That is, unless they have a good hand—"a hand worthy of insuring." Of course, this is folly since a bad bet is still a bad bet. It doesn't matter what your hand is. It's not like you are deciding to insure the new beautiful house you bought and are making a fair exchange in the case of disaster. This exchange is far from fair.

Luckily, Brian knew enough about insurance to wave the dealer off, saying he was fine gambling with his 20 and blackjack, especially as he muttered, "Since I have Jeff's personal insurance."

The dealer revealed a 7, giving her a total of 18, and everyone at the table won. Brian handed me the surplus $250 he had made on his black-jack and smiled at me. "How did you know?" he asked.

"I didn't," I answered as I handed back his $250 and smiled.

Of course I didn't know that the dealer didn't have 21, but I was play-ing the odds. The "even money" payment the dealer was offering Brian was simply an insurance bet dressed up with lipstick. Essentially, they were wagering his surplus $250 for him without telling him. In other words, they were implying that Brian was betting $250 on insurance. If the dealer had blackjack, his original $500 would be returned to Brian since his blackjack tied the dealer's blackjack. And he would win $500 on his two-for-one insurance bet. If the dealer didn't have blackjack, he would lose his $250 insurance bet but would win $750 on his original $500 bet for having blackjack. So his net winnings in either case would be $500.

But the sneaky thing that the casino did was the positioning. The dealer marked the bet as "even money." Who wouldn't take even money when facing a dealer's ace? It's loss aversion at its finest. Brian had already banked that hand as a winner. To end up tying that hand would have felt like a loss, and anything he could have done to avoid that loss was well worth it.

One of my former teammates used to say that "Vegas exists because people suck at math." If one examines the inherent logic in the Kelly Criterion, it's amazing that casinos exist at all. Kelly tells us if you don't have an edge, you shouldn't bet. Casinos make their fortune off exploiting incomplete or faulty reasoning. We made our fortune throwing that right back in their face.

Since they always have an advantage, when casinos model out their business, they realize that time is on their side. The more times a patron gambles, the more money they will eventually lose. For the casino, determining the expected revenue per hour at a particular table is relatively easy. You only need to know two things about the table—the amount of money wagered per hour and the average house advantage at that game. The latter is relatively easy to estimate. Start with the inherent casino advantage and then add in some padding for the fact that no player actually plays optimally. You can pretty easily model the strategy of a typical player and come up with a good estimate of the house advantage. Take blackjack: We know that, depending on the rules at the table, the casino's inherent advantage is about 0.5 percent—that's if a player is playing perfect basic strategy. But very few players actually do that. Therefore, the actual disadvantage is probably something like 3 percent.

The amount of money wagered per hour is the next input for the casino model. Casinos keep track of the betting behavior of every player that sits down at a table. Specifically, they track what their average bet per hand is. Casino employees will watch what you are betting and will actually take notes during the course of your time at the table. This information is important to them for many reasons. First off, casinos have some of the most comprehensive loyalty and incentive programs. They give their best customers free rooms, food, and even merchandise in some cases. These loyalty programs are based on the amount of money they expect to win off that player and also, in extreme cases, the amount of money that player actually loses. They are basically paying you back a portion of your losses to keep you happy and to keep you coming back. Think of it as a gambler's rebate.

So the casino knows what players are at each table and how much these players bet per hand. To determine the amount of money wagered on the table per hour, they simply need to know the amount of hands that they are able to deal in an hour. This information is used in a linear relationship, meaning the number of hands per hour multiplied by the amount wagered per hand will give you the total amount wagered per hour. Therefore, maximizing the amount of hands dealt in an hour will maximize the total amount wagered per hour—pretty straightforward stuff.

When a table has downtime for any reason, that is, when hands are not being dealt, it has an impact on the casino's bottom line. Any time dice are not being thrown, roulette wheels are not being spun, or cards are not being dealt, the casino is effectively losing money. So casinos are always looking for ways to minimize downtime.

Before the advent of the automatic shuffler, blackjack tables were a constant source of downtime. Every time a dealer neared the bottom of the deck or shoe, they would need to stop for a time to shuffle the cards. For single- and double-deck shoes, this was a pretty quick process, and the most important thing for the dealers was to make sure they really mixed up all those cards so they were truly distributed randomly. But for six- and eight-deck shoes, the problem was a bit more cumbersome.

Put down this book and try it yourself. Grab six full decks of cards and see how long it takes you to shuffle them in a way that makes you feel comfortable that they are randomly distributed. How long did it take? Five minutes? Ten minutes? More?

Of course you are not a professional dealer, but the sheer number of cards that you are trying to shuffle would require a few minutes for even the best dealer to shuffle sufficiently. So casinos were faced with a dilemma—sufficiently shuffling six decks of cards was losing them money.

So what did they do? Most casinos realized that thorough shuffles were the cost of doing business in blackjack and stuck with a fairly complicated process that took four to five minutes. But a few casinos decided that reducing downtime and optimizing revenue was paramount. They had their dealers learn very simple shuffles.

The problem with these simple shuffles was that they did not distribute the cards enough. In fact, if you watched the shuffle closely enough, you could track packets of cards through the shuffle and would know where they were going to end up in the next shoe. The location of approximately 39 cards (three-quarters of a deck) could be determined reliably in the next shoe. Specifically, the shuffle would distribute these 39 cards randomly within a group of approximately 78 cards (one and a half decks) in the next shoe.

The reason that this laziness—or greediness, depending on how you look at it—was such a big mistake was that if a card counter has knowledge of the distribution of cards within a shoe, they can shift the odds to their favor. Let's say you notice that in the first 39 cards (three-quarters of the deck) of the shoe there were a lot of 10-valued cards and aces. If you were counting, you might know that within that first three-quarters of a deck there were ten more high cards (10, J, Q, K, A) than there were low cards (2, 3, 4, 5, 6).

Let's assume you are playing at one of those lazy/greedy casinos and because their shuffle is so simple, you are able to track this packet of cards into the next shoe. Because of the simple shuffle you see the exact deck and a half that this special three-quarters of a deck ended up in. In the next shoe, when the dealer gets to that deck and a half you would know that there was a high frequency of 10s, face cards, and aces. And in that special deck and a half you would bet more. And you would win more.

This strategy is called shuffle tracking and was something we perfected during our card-counting run. In the mid-nineties, three casinos—the Rio, the MGM Grand, and the Tropicana—introduced simple, quicker shuffles. All three were infiltrated by card counters immediately. And all three eventually scrapped their simple shuffles for more complicated, time-consuming shuffles, essentially admitting their mistake.

Those three casinos had made an error in judgment primarily caused by a failure to consider the whole picture. In some respects, you could say that their decision was driven by analytics and data. They had modeled their business and were simply optimizing that model to increase revenue. The problem was their limited viewpoint.

This is not an uncommon problem in business, as even those focused on analytics can experience tunnel vision and miss obvious clues. Dennis Yu, a 15-year veteran of Internet advertising, experienced a similar tunnel vision early in his career. Tasked with the goal of building out the website for American Airlines, aa.com, Yu applied analytics to customer behaviors, trying to optimize the airline's advertising spend. What he found was that a disproportionately large amount of airline tickets were actually purchased in the evening and very few tickets were purchased during the day.

In what he believed to be a very rational, data-driven decision, Yu decided to cut all advertising spend during the day, instead focusing all the company's resources on the evening hours—the hours when tickets were being purchased. This seemed like a pretty sound decision until he noticed a tremendous drop-off in traffic to the site and with that drop a large decrease in revenue.

Quickly, he reversed his decision and reallocated advertising spend back to the daytime. After talking with more consumers, he realized that the sales cycle for an airline ticket doesn't occur only at night. People spend time during the day at work pricing tickets, comparative shopping, and planning their trip. But it isn't until they are at home and have had a chance to talk to their spouse that they actually buy the ticket. Keeping American Airlines in front of the consumer during the daytime planning stage was even more important than maintaining a presence during the evening transaction stage. It all made sense once Yu thought about the complete picture.

Yu can laugh about it now. "The data led me to do the exact wrong thing because I was interpreting it the wrong way. I wasn't looking at the whole picture," Yu tells me over breakfast.

Similar to Yu's mistake, the Rio, MGM, and Tropicana erred by not understanding the behavior of their consumers and having a microview of their business. Actually this was a relatively small mistake compared to the one made by the Marriott Casino in Puerto Rico. And of course when they made their horrific mistake, members of the MIT blackjack team were there to exploit them.

Puerto Rico has never been a common destination for card counters. Its casinos have poor rules intentionally implemented to discourage card counters from making the trek from the mainland.

The Marriott followed this strategy to a tee. They had horrible blackjack rules, only allowing doubling down on hard 9, 10, and 11. They didn't allow you to split your hands if you already had split them once.

But a bit of serendipity would lead Mike Aponte and company down to the island. Mike was one of my early mentors in blackjack. He was one of my best friends at the time and had been playing on the team for a few years before recruiting me to join. Mike was such a proficient blackjack player that after our team dissolved he went on to win the first-ever World Series of Blackjack.

The early part of his career was spent playing at Foxwoods and in Atlantic City casinos, and it was there that he forged a relationship with a casino host named John B. The role of a casino host is exactly what it sounds like—they are there to take care of you within the casino. A high roller is assigned a casino host as soon as he starts playing at a new casino. The host will cater to your every need, booking rooms and limos for you, getting you reservations at all the best restaurants, and even, in some cases, booking flights for you. Anything you want, they will get for you.

John B. was Mike's casino host, and in a short time they became friends. So when John got a job at the Marriot in Puerto Rico, he invited Mike down—all expenses paid, of course—to check out his new digs. Mike, who is half Puerto Rican, leapt at the opportunity and headed there with a couple teammates.

When he got down there, he realized what a great decision it had been.

Since the Marriott had such poor rules for the player, they had succeeded in keeping the card counters away, but that didn't mean their blackjack game wasn't beatable. In fact their game was very beatable.

In a six-deck shoe, after the shuffle, the dealer has one of the players place a "cut card" anywhere into the deck and the cards are "cut" at the location of that card. Normally, the dealer will place a yellow blank card on the back of the shoe so the players cannot see the back card. For some reason, the Marriot didn't do this, so players could see the back card.

When players can see that back card, they have an opportunity to exploit the casino with a strategy called deck cuts. Since most casinos require that you cut at least one deck (place the cut card at least one deck away from either end), the key skill is to be able to reliably put the cut card exactly one deck, 52 cards, away from the back of the shoe. If the player does this and is able to see the back card of the deck, they will know what the fifty-second card of the next shoe will be.

Knowledge of that card can be extremely valuable if it is a 10 or an ace. The expected value of your hand when you know you will have an ace is 1.5 times your bet, meaning if you bet $100 you can expect to win on average $50.

Tens also have significant value to the player. In fact, knowing you will get a 10 in your hand gives you a 14 percent advantage over the casino. Other cards can also be used to alter the expectations of a hand. Mike recalls a time he hit a 19 because he knew from their cuts that the next card was a 2. A play like this can raise your expectation by more than 100 percent.

Obviously there was a lot of strategy necessary to ensure that you received the 10 or ace, and deck cuts were only effective when you controlled all the spots at the table, but perfect execution of deck cuts was a very lucrative skill.

There are a few practical problems, however, with "deck cuts." For one, the opportunity only happens once a shoe. For a six-deck shoe, this means roughly one opportunity every 15 minutes. The second problem is that there is a high chance for error when attempting to cut exactly 52 cards. And the errors in this case can be rather costly.

But the Marriott was kind enough to alleviate both of these problems. Unlike any other casino, the Marriott allowed the players to cut less than a deck. In fact, Mike and his crew were allowed to cut all the way down to 13 cards. Reliably cutting 13 cards is much easier than 52.

Also, since the Marriott was wary of traditional card counters that rely on playing through as many cards as possible, they had their dealers shuffle the cards more often. They thought they were taking away the card counter's advantage but in actuality they were feeding the beast.

A typical casino will play through anywhere from four and a half to five of the decks in a six-deck shoe, leaving one to one and a half decks unplayed. The Marriott was typically playing through fewer than four decks and at times fewer than three. This increased the amount of times they shuffled by almost 50 percent and the amount of opportunities to do cuts by the same amount.

"I think their 'counter measures' actually tripled our expected win," Mike told me.

And to make things even more beneficial, not only did they fail to cover the back card of the shoe, but their dealers were sloppy and often exposed two or three cards at the back of the shoe. So Mike and crew knew exactly what two to three cards in a row would be near the beginning of each shoe.

Mike laughed as he recalled the consequences of the casino's mistakes. "When most people think of card counting they think you are doing something magical where you know exactly what cards are coming," he said, echoing the misconceptions discussed earlier in this book. "But for the most part it's a pretty mundane process."

"In Puerto Rico though, I got to do some crazy stuff that made me look like some kind of magician," Mike continued. "At one point I hit on a 19 because I knew a 2 was coming. Another time I split 3s and stood on the first 3 because we needed to save cards so that we could use a 10 to bust the dealer. I'm not even sure if they should have let me do this.

"The funny thing is that I couldn't lose down there. Not only did we have a great strategy but we were getting so lucky and just kept winning," Mike said.

Eventually, the Marriott grew tired of losing to Mike and company and, like any casino hoping to maximize profits, decided to cut their losses, banning Mike and his team. But the damage had been done.

Casinos, like many other businesses, make mistakes when they fail to consider the full extent of their actions. Often this is due to a failure to understand and consider the whole picture before they make changes, and often this comes from a desire to make change for change's sake.

This blackjack story could be a cautionary tale to financial regulators who constantly try to fix one thing but mistakenly open another door.

In 2008 the Securities Exchange Commission attempted to stabilize the market by banning short selling on 799 financial stocks. Short selling is the act of selling a stock without owning it. The mechanics behind it are that a short seller actually borrows a stock from someone who already owns it and sells it for the market price. Eventually the short seller buys the stock back from the market and returns what it borrowed to the original owner. Short sellers are basically placing a bet that a stock will go down.

Short sellers have always been a controversial part of the market. They are like the guy who plays "Don't Pass" at the craps table. (At the craps table there are two basic bets you can make. The most common bet by far is a pass line bet where you are seemingly betting "with the shooter." The second bet is the "don't pass" bet and is seen as betting "against the shooter." Even though the odds are slightly higher to play the "don't pass" bet, very few people actually play it. There are psychological reasons for this but suffice to say since so many people are betting the "pass" line, betting "don't pass" seems like a bet with the house. Therefore, "don't pass" players are often looked upon negatively at the table.) Because you are betting against the majority, you are seen as a shady, immoral individual. But short sellers are an important part of any market because they help identify the stocks that are overpriced and overvalued,[1] helping to create realistic price discovery.

If the only people who can sell a stock are those who own it, you are severely limiting a market's ability to accurately price an asset based on all available information. In addition, the lesson of loss aversion would tell us that those who own the stock will be reluctant to sell it at a loss, again artificially propping up the value price of the stock.

The 2008 short-selling ban attempted to "combat market manipulation that threatens investors and capital markets."[2] So in order to try and prevent manipulation, the regulators decided to impose a restriction that in essence manipulated the market, removing what many believe to be an essential part of any market.

Three weeks later, the SEC removed the ban because it did not have the desired impact on the market and actually caused many to lose even more money. The Hennessee group, which tracks performance in the $2 trillion hedge fund industry, reported 5 to 9 percent losses in September alone; much of the losses were attributed to the short-selling ban. In addition, experts believe the short-selling ban may have actually depressed prices even further[3] due to a decrease in liquidity by eliminating important market participants.

The SEC erred because there was tremendous pressure on them to "do something." Yet they failed to consider the potential impact of their decision. In addition, the SEC has misaligned incentives. They are a political organization that needs to prove the worth of their existence. Doing nothing isn't really an option.

Philip Maymin, our resident economist, explains that whenever there is regulation, "as long as someone is exempt, and someone always is, the spread will be larger for those that can do the regulatory arbitrage. There will be profit along the way for those who are connected or find the loopholes. Legislation and regulation just eliminates your competition."

Maymin obviously espouses the free market like many other true economists. The notion of a free market in blackjack is obviously one that I dream about, as our demise was ultimately caused by regulations and restrictions placed on us by the casino. Simply put, they eventually figured out who we were and what we were doing and created restrictions to stop us.

It is an interesting question, though, to look holistically at what the casinos did by getting rid of us. I, for one, have always contended that card counters are good for casinos. As mentioned earlier, blackjack only became popular after people realized that it could be beaten. Yet how many people truly have the intellect, discipline, and commitment to beat it?

Let's skip the intellect question for now since I've already said that you don't have to be an autistic savant to do it. But let's recap discipline. Discipline means that you have to get over things like loss aversion and omission bias. You have to divorce yourself from any sort of confirmation bias and truly trust the data. You have to be comfortable with variance and need to have the proper bankroll to manage risk effectively. Beyond that you have to practice. And I don't mean in the plane on your way out to Vegas. I mean for hours each day.

And therein lies the commitment. Counting cards the way we did was hard work. And, as I've mentioned, it took a tremendous commitment to win. Think of your average gambler, he's in the casino to have fun. He wants to capitalize on the free drinks. There is a reason they give you those free drinks. He wants to flirt with the beautiful cocktail waitress. He wants to have fun.

In our day, we never drank alcohol while playing. We made sure we got our sleep before playing. We practiced for hours before, after, and during a trip. We were masters of our trade.

Simply put, there are not many people who can truly beat the casino counting cards. I would guess less than 1 percent of the people who walk into the casino. Does it make sense for casinos to impose restrictions that may only apply to less than 1 percent of the patrons but may actually cause them to lose money on the remaining 99 percent?

Should the casinos that changed their shuffles really have even cared about the few of us who could track the shuffle? If 1 percent was the number of card counters, I would venture to say that the amount of people who could exploit a shuffle would have been more like 0.1 percent. It would have been easy for them to model what the profit/loss was for that decision.

In order to avoid card counters, a casino decides to move from the faster, easier-to-track shuffle back to the longer, more integrated shuffle. Let's say for that 0.1 percent of card counters the casinos are preventing losing, say, 2 percent of their profits. But for the remaining 99.9 percent, the casinos are actually losing because they aren't able to deal as many hands. Seems like a pretty simple answer. But casinos weren't able to look at it objectively because the emotion of trying to stop us, the evil card counters, was too large.

The same analysis can be made about some of their other restrictions. Let's take the no mid-shoe entry rule (a rule that prohibits a player from starting in the middle of a shoe; instead they have to wait to play until after the dealer shuffles). Casinos enacted this rule in direct response to our team play strategy. If you couldn't come in to a table in the middle of a shoe, you couldn't work as a team. But if you are making everyone wait, as the casinos did, you are forcing people who will be losing to you at an average rate of 5 percent per hand to sit at the table and wait, not playing anywhere from ten to twenty hands. At an average bet of $50 a hand (the average table that we'd play at), that is close to a $40 loss for the casino each time a patron tries to sit down. So if we multiply that times 99, we get close to $4,000. At a $1,000 unit, our most common betting amount, we would need to play more than 100 hands to make up that amount.

Add in to this analysis the amount of labor and infrastructure the casinos had to use to stop us, and I'm sure the answer to "Is it worth it to ban card counters?" is a resounding no.

Yet casinos persisted in playing the role of cat to our role of mouse. And a lot lies in the emotion of the dynamic. They did not want to feel like we were getting the better of them, and it made them act irrationally.

Since *Bringing Down the House* and the movie *21* came out, I've had plenty of people come up to me and tell me they were card counters and have been kicked out of casinos. But very few of them upon further inspection were people I would ever feel threatened by if I were a casino employee. Many people think they can count cards, but you can ask them a few simple questions to assess their abilities and often they will fail at this challenge. The fact that casinos ban these people is incredible to me. It's sort of like our credit card companies and their overcautiousness, except banning these people is probably costing the casinos a lot more, relatively speaking, than a few extra phone calls to good cardholders.

Finally, card counters are good for the casino because we are good marketing vehicles. We talk about what casinos we go to. We post on message boards and websites. And when people see us betting big money and winning, they think they can do the same thing. When I walked out of the premiere of the movie *21*, the floor of the Planet Hollywood casino was packed with wannabe card counters. I'm guessing the casino made plenty of money that night.

Within this impassioned plea to let the card counter play is a pretty simple business lesson. Make sure you know what you are doing when you make a policy or rule change of any kind. Simply making a change for its own sake will never improve things. Changes set off chain reactions where the end result may be worse than the initial issue.

The only way to truly avoid this is by having a holistic viewpoint of your situation. And certainly analytics can help predict what will happen when there is a change in policy. If the casinos had looked holistically at their situation, maybe we'd still be playing and maybe they'd actually be making more at their blackjack games.

So the answer to why we quit is simple: because the casinos made us. They made it unprofitable for us to continue playing by telling us that we couldn't play, kicking us out, or simply creating restrictions that took away our advantage.

As to the final question, can people still count cards? Manlio Lopez, the inspiration for the character Martinez in *Bringing Down the House*, once said to me, "As long as blackjack is beatable, there will be people trying to beat it." And I've already explained, blackjack will always be beatable, that's why it's popular. So, yes, you can all go out and try to make your fortunes tomorrow in Vegas, but the better bet is to use the lessons in this book to succeed in the business you are in.

APPENDIX: BASIC STRATEGY CHART

Basic Strategy

4–8 Decks, Dealer stands soft 17, Double after split

Dealer's up-card

Player's hand	2	3	4	5	6	7	8	9	10	A
5–8	H	H	H	H	H	H	H	H	H	H
9	H	D	D	D	D	H	H	H	H	H
10	D	D	D	D	D	D	D	D	H	H
11	D	D	D	D	D	D	D	D	D	H
12	H	H	S	S	S	H	H	H	H	H
13	S	S	S	S	S	H	H	H	H	H
14	S	S	S	S	S	H	H	H	H	H
15	S	S	S	S	S	H	H	H	SR	H
16	S	S	S	S	S	H	H	SR	SR	SR
A2	H	H	H	D	D	H	H	H	H	H
A3	H	H	H	D	D	H	H	H	H	H
A4	H	H	D	D	D	H	H	H	H	H
A5	H	H	D	D	D	H	H	H	H	H
A6	H	D	D	D	D	H	H	H	H	H
A7	S	D/S	D/S	D/S	D/S	S	S	H	H	H
2–2	P	P	P	P	P	P	H	H	H	H
3–3	P	P	P	P	P	P	H	H	H	H
4–4	H	H	H	P	P	H	H	H	H	H
6–6	P	P	P	P	P	H	H	H	H	H
7–7	P	P	P	P	P	P	H	H	H	H
8–8	P	P	P	P	P	P	P	P	P	P
9–9	P	P	P	P	P	S	P	P	S	S

Key:

H	Hit
S	Stand
D	Double down/else Hit
P	Split
SR	Surrender/else Hit
D/S	Double down/else Stand

Additional Basic Strategy:

1) Never take insurance
2) Always stand hard 17 or higher
3) Always stand A8, A9, A10 and 10–10
4) Always play 5–5 as a 10
5) Always split Aces

NOTES

Chapter 1 The Religion of Statistics

1. Roger Baldwin et al., "The Optimum Strategy in Blackjack," *Journal of the American Statistical Association* 51 (1956): 429–439.
2. Ari Weinberg, "The Case for Legal Sports Gambling," Forbes.com, January 27, 2003, http://www.forbes.com/2003/01/27/cx_aw_0127gambling.html.
3. A Fourier series breaks down a periodic function or signal into simpler functions that are easier to solve and utilize. In this case, Bob used the Fourier series to better predict the periodic performance of sports teams.
4. Sam Walker, "The Man Who Shook Up Vegas," WSJ.com, January 5, 2007, http://online.wsj.com/public/article/SB116796079037267731-wjPu4ACcg5J5Qvjh05IYEI_Ooeo_20070112.html.
5. Edward Cone, "Got Risk," Wired.com, December 1999, http://www.wired.com/wired/archive/7.12/struve.html?pg=1&topic=&topic_set=.

Chapter 2 Why the Past Matters

1. Roger Baldwin et al., "The Optimum Strategy in Blackjack," *Journal of the American Statistical Association* 51 (1956): 429-439.
2. Tommy Craggs, "Say-It-Ain't-So Joe," *SF Weekly*, July 6, 2005, news section.
3. Ibid.
4. SAS Institute Inc., Customer Success by Industry, November 10, 2009, http://www.sas.com/success/indexByIndustry.html#2100.
5. Nick Curcuru of SAS, e-mail message to author, November 7, 2009.

Chapter 3 Think Like a Scientist

1. The editors, "Debunking the 9/11 Myths: Special Report," *Popular Mechanics*, March 2005.
2. Peter Cohan, "Confirmation Bias in Politics and Business," The Informed Observer, April 21, 2006, http://petercohan.blogspot.com/2006/04/confirmation-bias-in-politics-and.html.

3. Alexei Barrionuevo, "Which Picture of Skilling Will Enron Jurors Believe," *New York Times*, April 21, 2006, Business section.
4. Ibid.
5. Ibid.
6. Jason Zweig, "How to Ignore the Yes-Man in Your Head," *Wall Street Journal* online, http://online.wsj.com/article/SB100014240527487038116045745336 80037778184.html.
7. Ibid.
8. Ibid.
9. Freek Vermeulen, "Beware the Dangers of Selection Bias," *Harvard Business Review* guest blog, March 17, 2009, http://blogs.harvardbusiness.org/ vermeulen/2009/03/beware-the-danger-of-selection.html.
10. Ibid.
11. Ibid.
12. Ibid.
13. Correlation coefficient is a statistical measure representing the relationship between two variables. A correlation coefficient near 1 means that the two variables are nearly perfectly correlated, meaning as variable *a* increases variable *b* will increase in a nearly perfectly linear relationship. A correlation near zero means little to no relationship between the two variables. A negative correlation coefficient means that when variable *a* increases variable *b* actually decreases.
14. Zach Fein, "How NFL Statistics Lead to Wins, Pt. 1: Looking at Win Correlations," EaglesBlog.net, May 13, 2009, http://thesportingtruth. com/?p=1723.
15. Zachary Levine, "How Important Is Turnover Margin?" The Unofficial Scorer, January 4, 2008, http://blogs.chron.com/unofficialscorer/2008/01/ how_important_is_turnover_marg.html.
16. Antonio Regaldo, "Titan's Millions Stir Up Research Into Autism," *Wall Street Journal*, December 15, 2005.
17. Hoovers.com, Renaissance Technology Corp Company Description, http:// www.hoovers.com/company/Renaissance_Technologies_Corp/rrtrfyi-1.html.
18. Hal Lux, "The Secret World of Jim Simons," *Institutional Investor* 34 (November 2004): 38.
19. Ibid.
20. Ibid.

Chapter 4   The Importance of Asking Questions

1. Conversation with author, November 6, 2009.
2. Nate Silver, "Introducing PECOTA," in Gary Huckabay, Chris Kahrl, Dave Pease, et al., eds., *Baseball Prospectus 2003* (Dulles, VA: Brassey's Publishers, 2003), 507–514.

3. Michael Lewis, *The Blind Side* (New York: W. W. Norton & Company, 2006), 34.

Chapter 5   The Impractical Search
for Perfection

1. Thomas Gilovich, Robert Vallone, and Amos Tversky, "The Hot Hand in Basketball: On the Misperception of Random Sequences," *Cognitive Psychology* 17 (1985): 295–314.
2. John Huizinga and Sandy Weil, "Hot Hand or Hot Head? Overconfidence in Shot Making Ability in the NBA," http://web.me.com/sandy1729/sportsmetricians_consulting/Hot_Hand_files/HH_Draft_v04.pdf.
3. Ibid.
4. Alan Schwarz, "Managing with Markov," *Harvard Magazine* 104, no. 5 (May–June 2002).
5. Malcolm Gladwell, *What the Dog Saw: And Other Adventures* (New York: Little, Brown and Company, 2009), 261.
6. CSC website, http://www.csc.com, November 20, 2009.
7. Thomas H. Davenport and Jeanne G. Harris, *Competing on Analytics: The New Science of Winning* (Boston: Harvard Business School Press, 2007), 108.

Chapter 6   Using Numbers to Tell a Story

1. Decision analysts are experts in the field of decision analysis. Pioneered by Stanford University professor Ronald Howard in the 1960s, decision analysis shares many similarities with card counting as it is an analytical method to make better decisions. By identifying alternatives, establishing preferences, and calculating maximum expected utility, decision analysts use a formal framework to make better decisions in business, as we did at the blackjack tables.
2. Wendell Barnhouse, "Criteria Near for Picking Top Bowl Teams," *Star Telegram* (Fort Worth), April 22, 1998.
3. Richard Rosenblatt, "Bowl Game to Be Chosen by Computers," *Associated Press* online, June 10, 1998.
4. Craig Barnes, "Bowl Coordinator Confident Series Will Work," *Sun Sentinel* (Fort Lauderdale), June 13, 1998.
5. MNF Interview with Barack Obama, ESPN.com, November 2008.
6. "BCS Explained," CollegeFootballPoll.com, http://www.collegefootballpoll.com/bcs_explained.html, November, 12, 2009.
7. Definition of "statistics," http://www.merriam-webster.com/dictionary/STATISTICS.
8. Definition of "data," http://www.merriam-webster.com/dictionary/DATA.

9. Pro Football Hall of Fame History Release, http://www.profootballhof.com/history/release.aspx?release_id=1303, November, 12, 2009.

10. Jerome R. Corsi, "What's America's *Real* Inflation Rate?" WorldNetDaily, March 19, 2008, http://www.wnd.com/index.php?pageId=59409.

11. John Williams, "Government Economic Reports: Things You've Suspected But Were Afraid to Ask!" Shadow Government Statistics, October 1, 2006, http://www.shadowstats.com/article/consumer_price_index.

Chapter 7   Never Fear

1. See *Uston v. Resorts Int'l Hotel*, 445 A.2d 370 (NJ, 1982).

2. Henry Tamburin, "Is Card Counting Legal?" June 1, 2001, http://tamburin.casinocitytimes.com/articles/1295.html.

3. Eric Rosenfeld, 15.437 Presentation, MIT, February 19, 2009, http://techtv.mit.edu/videos/2450-eric-rosenfeld-15437-presentation-21909.

4. Roger Lowenstein, *When Genius Failed: The Rise and Fall of Long-Term Capital Management* (New York: Random House, 2001), 143.

5. Jack Brennan, *Straight Talk on Investing: What You Need to Know* (New York: Wiley, 2002), 198.

6. Hal Lux, "The Secret World of Jim Simons," *Institutional Investor* 34 (November 2004): 38.

7. Lowenstein, *When Genius Failed*, 210.

8. Ibid., 164.

9. For the definitive discussion of the Kelly Criterion, see William Poundstone, *Fortune's Formula: The Untold Story of the Scientific Betting System that Beat the Casinos and Wall Street* (New York: Hill and Wang, 2006).

10. E-mail to author, January 11, 2010.

Chapter 8   Making the Right Decision

1. Michael Holley, *Patriot Reign: Bill Belichick, the Coaches and the Players Who Built a Champion* (New York: William Morrow, 2007), 181.

2. Ibid., 182.

3. Ron Borges, "Bill Belichick Heads Off Victory," November 16, 2009, http://www.bostonherald.com/sports/football/patriots/view.bg?articleid=1212305&position=1.

4. NBC Sunday Night Football Postgame Show, November 15, 2009.

5. Dilfer on Belichick's Costly Decision (video), November 16, 2009, http://sports.espn.go.com/boston/nfl/news/story?id=4659264.

6. Brian Burke, "Belichick's 4th Down Decision vs the Colts," AdvancedNFLStats.com, November 16, 2009, http://www.advancednflstats.com/2009/11/belichicks-4th-down-decision-vs-colts.html.

7. Wayne Winston, "Belichick: The Long and Short of It," November 18, 2009, http://www.huffingtonpost.com/wayne-winston/belichick-the-long-and-sh_b_361864.html.

8. Steven D. Levitt, "Bill Belichick Is Great," Freakonomics Blog, November 16, 2009, http://freakonomics.blogs.nytimes.com/2009/11/16/bill-belichick-is-great/.

9. E-mail message to author.

10. David Romer, "Do Firms Maximize? Evidence from Professional Football," *Journal of Political Economy* 114 (April 2006): 340–365.

11. Bill Simmons, "Belichick's Fourth-and-Reckless," November 23, 2009, http://sports.espn.go.com/espn/page2/story?page=simmonsnflpicks/091120.

12. Appearance on *Cavuto on Business*, Fox News Channel, August 18, 2007.

13. Julie Fishman-Lapin, "Prophet of Doom?" Euro Pacific Capital, August 6, 2006, http://www.europac.net/prophet.asp.

14. Cost of Freedom, Fox News Channel, December 31, 2006.

15. Amos Tversky and Daniel Kahneman, "Prospect Theory: An Analysis of Decision under Risk," *Econometrica* 47, no. 2 (March 1979): 263–292.

16. Bruce I. Carlin and David Robinson, "Fear and Loathing in Las Vegas: Evidence from Blackjack Tables," Society for Judgement and Decision Making, vol. 4, no. 5 (August 2009): 385-396.

17. Peter Bernstein, *Against the Gods* (New York: Wiley, 1998), 286.

Chapter 9   When I Won, We All Won

1. MIT Sloan Sports Analytics Conference, "History & Organizers," http://www.sloansportsconference.com/2010/history-organizers/, January 10, 2010.

2. Timothy Geithner, "Statement by Treasury Secretary Timothy Geithner on Compensation," U.S. Treasury website, June 10, 2009, http://www.treas.gov/press/releases/tg163.htm.

Chapter 10   Why People Hate Math and What to Do with Them

1. Press release, "Most US Companies Say Business Analytics Still Future Goal, Not Present Reality," December 11, 2008, http://newsroom.accenture.com/article_display.cfm?article_id=4777.

2. Ibid.

3. New York Yankees 1973 Yearbook.

4. Michael K. Ozanian and Kurt Badenhausen, "The Business of Baseball," Forbes.com, April 16, 2008, http://www.forbes.com/2008/04/16/baseball-team-values-biz-sports-baseball08-cx_mo_kb_0416baseballintro.html.

5. Erik Brady, "Wizards Show Jordan the Door," USAToday.com, May 7, 2003, http://www.usatoday.com/sports/basketball/nba/wizards/2003-05-07-jordan-out_x.htm.

6. Press release, "Michael Jordan to Become Part Owner of the Charlotte Bobcats," June 15, 2006, http://www.nba.com/bobcats/release_jordan_060615.html.

7. Ibid.

8. Leigh Buchanan, "The Office: Too Smart for Comfort," Inc.com, February 11, 2009, http://www.inc.com/articles/2009/02/the-office-too-smart-for-comfort.html.

9. Stanley Gudder, *A Mathematical Journey* (New York: McGraw-Hill, 1976), ix.

10. Vistaprint Career Fact Sheet, January 15, 2010, http://careers.vistaprint.com/VPRTFactSheet.pdf.

11. Ibid.

Chapter 11   The Brain Cells in Your Stomach

1. Andy Bloch, October, 15, 2009, http://www.andybloch.com.

2. Ibid.

3. Definition of "intuition," October, 20, 2009, http://dictionary.reference.com/browse/intuition.

4. Kevin Lynch, "Who Is Paraag Marathe? Numbers Added Up to Quick Rise," SFGate.com, January 23, 2005, http://articles.sfgate.com/2005-01-23/sports/17357970_1_ucla-head-stanford-business-school.

5. http://dictionary.reference.com/browse/intuition.

6. Interview with the author.

7. The Strike 3 Foundation is a charitable agency that heightens awareness, mobilizes support, and raises funding for childhood cancer research. It was founded in 2008 by MLB pitcher Craig Breslow. http://www.strike3foundation.org/.

8. Velle E. La Neal, III, "Figuring out the R. A. Dickey Signing," *Minneapolis Star Tribune*, December 26, 2008.

9. P. E. Tetlock, *Expert Political Judgment: How Good Is It? How Can We Know?* (Princeton, NJ: Princeton University Press, 2005).

Epilogue

1. Charles M. Jones and Owen A. Lamont, "Short Sale Constraints and Stock Returns," September 20, 2001, http://papers.ssrn.com/sol3/papers.cfm?abstract_id=281514.

2. Press Release, "SEC Halts Short Selling of Financial Stocks to Protect Investors and Markets, September 19, 2008, http://www.sec.gov/news/press/2008/2008-211.htm.

3. Michael Brenner and Marti G. Subrahmanyam, "End the Ban on Short-Selling," October, 1, 2008, http://www.forbes.com/2008/09/30/short-selling-ban-oped-cx_mb_1001brenner.html.

INDEX